ENERGY AND THE ENVIRONMENT: POLICY OVERVIEW

INTERNATIONAL ENERGY AGENCY

INTERNATIONAL ENERGY AGENCY

2, RUE ANDRÉ-PASCAL, 75775 PARIS CEDEX 16, FRANCE

The International Energy Agency (IEA) is an autonomous body which was established in November 1974 within the framework of the Organisation for Economic Co-operation and Development (OECD) to implement an international energy programme.

It carries out a comprehensive programme of energy co-operation among twenty-one* of the OECD's twenty-four Member countries. The basic aims of IEA are:

i) co-operation among IEA participating countries to reduce excessive dependence on oil through energy conservation, development of alternative energy sources and energy research and development;

ii) an information system on the international oil market as well as consultation with oil companies;

iii) co-operation with oil producing and other oil consuming countries with a view to developing a stable international energy trade as well as the rational management and use of world energy resources in the interest of all countries;

iv) a plan to prepare Participating Countries against the risk of a major disruption of oil supplies and to share available oil in the event of an emergency.

IEA Participating Countries are: Australia, Austria, Belgium, Canada, Denmark, Germany, Greece, Ireland, Italy, Japan, Luxembourg, the Netherlands, New Zealand, Norway, Portugal, Spain, Sweden, Switzerland, Turkey, United Kingdom, United States.

Pursuant to article 1 of the Convention signed in Paris on 14th December 1960, and which came into force on 30th September, 1961, the Organisation for Economic Co-operation and Development (OECD) shall promote policies designed:

- to achieve the highest sustainable economic growth and employment and a rising standard of living in Member countries, while maintaining financial stability, and thus to contribute to the development of the world economy;
- to contribute to sound economic expansion in Member as well as non-member countries in the process of economic development; and
- to contribute to the expansion of world trade on a multilateral, non-discriminatory basis in accordance with international obligations.

The original Member countries of the OECD are Austria, Belgium, Canada, Denmark, France, the Federal Republic of Germany, Greece, Iceland, Ireland, Italy, Luxembourg, the Netherlands, Norway, Portugal, Spain, Sweden, Switzerland, Turkey, the United Kingdom and the United States. The following countries became Members subsequently through accession at the dates indicated hereafter: Japan (28th April 1964), Finland (28th January 1969), Australia (7th June 1971) and New Zealand (29th May 1973).

The Socialist Federal Republic of Yugoslavia takes part in some of the work of the OECD (agreement of 28th October 1961).

TABLE OF CONTENTS

List of Figures

List of Tables

FOREWORD

Energy production, transformation, transport and use have important impacts on the earth's environment. Energy policies increasingly play a central role in dealing with a broad range of local, regional and global environmental concerns. Given the complexity of these problems, there is a growing need to understand the link between energy activities and environmental protection and to carefully evaluate the full scope of opportunities presented by preventive or remedial action, taking into account energy security and overall economic considerations. At their most recent meeting in May 1989, IEA Ministers reaffirmed their commitment to finding solutions to environmental problems associated with energy activities because they are fundamental to the maintenance of adequate, diversified, economic and secure energy supplies. Moreover, recognizing the international nature of many of the most important environmental issues, Ministers instructed the IEA Secretariat to participate fully in the international debate to address such issues as acid precipitation and the threat of global climate change.

As a contribution to this process, this study examines the impact on energy security of existing and proposed environmental measures and discusses policy options and instruments that might be selected to achieve the objectives of both energy and environmental policy. It is essentially designed to provide an overview of the often complex issues involved. Though it stops short of recommending particular strategies, the analysis highlights the importance of assessing and comparing different responses and instruments. As such, this study can serve as a reference and be viewed as a stepping-off point from which policy-makers can work to develop specific policy frameworks suitable to conditions in individual Member countries.

This study has been prepared by the IEA Secretariat and is published under my responsibility as Executive Director of the IEA. It does not necessarily reflect the views of the IEA or its Member governments.

Helga Steeg
Executive Director

EXECUTIVE SUMMARY

Introduction, Background and Methodology

There is growing awareness that more must be done to mitigate or avoid the major environmental problems that are facing us today. The environmental impacts that can arise from energy activities are numerous. One element of ensuring and maintaining energy security is adequately assuring environmental protection from degradation that could potentially be associated with the production and use of energy. An underlying assumption of this study is that balancing and integrating energy and environment objectives is desirable. The purpose of this study is to examine the range of policy measures that might be taken before the year 2005 in order to accomplish energy activities in the least environmentally damaging manner and at the least cost.

With this precept in mind, the IEA has completed a major overview of the links between energy and environment in OECD countries in order to clarify the choices available to policy-makers. The study accomplishes this by examining what we know about environmental approaches relevant to energy activities, their impact on the energy sector and possible policy choices to advance both energy security and environmental objectives. The lessons learned can help to structure and guide new and revised policies, approaches and strategies that are needed to handle major environmental problems related to energy activities. For example, there is in many cases a synergism between energy and environment objectives. Some fuel substitutions, virtually all improvements in energy efficiency and the development of new, inherently less polluting and more energy efficient energy technologies are examples. It will be important to continue and amplify such areas of mutual gain. This study stops short of recommending particular strategies. Rather, it notes that, except for actions which clearly make sense in their own right, it is important that all of the possible actions and instruments are assessed and compared before decisions are made on which combination of actions should become part of the response strategy. Part of the problem is that there is an urgency to make decisions, but that such an analysis takes time.

Environmental Impacts and Implications for Energy Security

This study starts by describing major known and suspected energy-related environmental impacts by fuel. These environmental consequences of energy activities are extensive but so, by now, are the systems devised by governments in conjunction with industry to prevent, minimise, control or eliminate such impacts. These actions to protect the environment, which are also described in the study, have, of course, affected energy activities by internalising at least some of the related environmental costs. This in turn has changed patterns of energy supply and demand, although very gradually and rather imperceptibly. The study thus finds that the considerable actions taken to date have achieved substantial progress in environmental protection and yet were able to be developed and implemented in a fashion that has not affected energy security.

Nevertheless, as environmental regulations become more comprehensive and more stringent, environmental aspects of energy activities (e.g., prevention, control, and damage repair) have an increasing share in the overall investment and operational costs. Environmental and safety measures can have weighty implications for total electricity generation costs, particularly in countries in which the generation mix has a high share of coal and/or nuclear energy. Thus, the scope and magnitude of some of the problems still requiring solution leads to the conclusion that careful structuring of future responses will be necessary to achieve energy security in an environmentally sensitive manner. It will be particularly important to examine the full environmental impacts, on a full fuel cycle basis, of all policy options.

Framework for Energy and Environment Decision-Making

In evaluating the status of efforts to take environmental impacts into account, the study concentrates, for illustrative purposes, primarily on ambient air quality, acid deposition, global climate change, land use and siting impacts and focuses most of its analysis on these. In assessing possible actions, this study considers primarily the limited time-frame of actions that can be taken before the year 2005 and uses and advocates a particular methodology which is illustrated graphically in Figure 1 (the Framework for Energy and Environment Decision-Making). The objective of any analysis would be to look for those actions which have the potential to provide the energy needed for an activity with the lowest environmental impact at the least cost and the maximum of energy security possible.

The analyses should consider, for a full range of likely responses, the status, trends, technical and market potential of actions by industry, consumers and governments. Such stock-taking includes assessment of the costs and benefits, the problems and limitations that have been encountered, possible spin-offs, both positive and negative, the trade-offs, if any, and underlying economic factors which might accelerate or slow the desired shifts. Such an assessment of limitations also includes analysis of needs for R&D and demonstration or better dissemination of technologies and of infrastructural needs and institutional problems.

Figure 1
Framework for Energy and Environment Decision-Making

```
┌──────────────────────────────────────────────────────────────┐
│                        STEP ONE:                             │
│         IDENTIFY ENERGY/ENVIRONMENT INTERACTION               │
└──────────────────────────────────────────────────────────────┘

┌──────────────────────────────────────────────────────────────┐
│                        STEP TWO:                             │
│                IDENTIFY POTENTIAL RESPONSES                   │
└──────────────────────────────────────────────────────────────┘
```

Greater Energy Efficiency	Add-on Pollution Control Technologies	Other[1]

Fuel Substitution[2] and Flexibility	"Clean" Energy Technologies[3]

Consider
- Applicability, potential impact, cost, timing
- Barriers (political or institutional), limitations, spin-offs, trade-offs
- Needs for R&D, demonstration, dissemination or infrastructure

```
┌──────────────────────────────────────────────────────────────┐
│                       STEP THREE:                            │
│               IDENTIFY POTENTIAL INSTRUMENTS                  │
└──────────────────────────────────────────────────────────────┘
```

Information	Regulation[4]	Economic Instrument[5]

Consider
- Applicability, effectiveness, consumer behaviour, micro- and macro-economic impact

```
┌──────────────────────────────────────────────────────────────┐
│                        STEP FOUR:                            │
│                 DEVELOP STRATEGY BUNDLE:                      │
│                   policies and instruments                   │
└──────────────────────────────────────────────────────────────┘
```

Consider
- Possible follow-up work to refine strategy
- Areas for improved policy making

1. Other responses would be mostly non-energy-related, such as structural changes in economic systems.
2. Fuel substitution refers to switches in fuel quality or fuel type (e.g., from fossil fuels to renewable energy sources), or temporary fuel switching to minimise seasonal or short-term environmental impacts (e.g., from gasoline to natural gas).
3. "Clean" energy technologies are defined here as those which combine more energy efficient processes or operations and reduced pollutant production without necessarily entailing a change in the form of energy used.
4. Regulation here is meant to include the so-called "command and control" and related measures, which are used in protection of the environment (from emission standards to the requirements of environmental impact assessment procedures) and all of those applied to energy security (from end-use efficiency standards to requiring the use of fuels in certain sectors).
5. Economic instruments include the broad areas of taxes, charges, subsidies, and pricing policies, whether used to reinforce regulations and thus increase the overall effectiveness of their environmental protection actions or to subsidise the support of R&D, development and demonstration of new pollution-control or "cleaner" energy technologies.

The study analyzes the range of policy instruments (e.g., information, regulation and economic instruments) that can possibly be used to change the rate of implementation of a response. Factors to assess include the applicability of the policy instrument, its effectiveness, particular limitations, and micro- and macro-economic effects as well as political barriers and consumer behavioural characteristics.

Possibilities for Action

Emerging or heightened concerns about the environmental impacts of energy activities should not only present a mandate but also an opportunity. There are numerous actions which have demonstrated their ability to meet energy and environment aims. The study finds that, at least when considering actions to be taken between now and the year 2005, it is thus probably not so much a question of entirely new responses but rather are of more directed responses and the better application of measures that are already well known and tested.

The study explores the pros and cons of likely responses and raises diverse questions which still need to be addressed in considering steps which could contribute more to solving such problems. These questions are reflected in the suggestions for further work presented below. The following summarises the findings regarding the major "candidate" responses considered by the study.

Greater Energy Efficiency. An improvement in energy efficiency is regarded here as any action, including energy conservation actions, undertaken by a producer or a consumer of energy products, which reduce energy losses. Energy efficiency improvements can therefore be implemented through hardware improvements, such as technological enhancements, or software actions, such as improved energy management and better operational practices. These actions can contribute in a major way to achieving energy security in an environmentally acceptable way. It reduces environmental impacts through the direct reduction of emissions that might have otherwise occurred. It also reduces the need for new facilities and operations involved with the production, transportation, transformation and distribution of the various energy forms which all in turn carry some environmental impacts. In looking at the need to control environmental pollution from a single facility, energy efficiency actions would often need to be supported by pollution control technologies or fuel substitution. It is mainly in the aggregate, then, rather than on the individual project basis, that improved energy efficiency can have a major impact on environmental protection. Energy efficiency enhancements have occurred mainly in response to drastically and precipitously higher energy prices, perceptions of price rises or scarcity and, in particular, where technological innovations allowed them. Barriers have been and are being addressed by a large number of government actions. Past gains varied for the different end-use sectors but were in the large part offset by increased energy demand resulting from economic growth.

In the *industrial sector,* major increases in energy efficiency were achieved in most countries. Barriers typical to the sector include lack of information and financing, conflicting priorities, risk perception, desire to avoid disruptions, etcetera. The most promising potential lies in the continued "incorporation" of more efficient new equipment where production process changes are being made anyway. Efficiency gains and barriers for the residential/commercial sector roughly parallel those of the industrial sector; the most promising potential lies in incorporation of efficiency into new structures and equipment used in the sector and in changing operational procedures and habits.

Increasing demand for electricity makes the *electricity end-use sector* a high priority, especially as there exists substantial potential for efficiency improvements in this sector. In addition to the savings already achieved, gradual improvement over the next 20 years is envisioned as capital stock is replaced. Barriers to achieving remaining potential are similar to those found in the industrial sector, but perhaps with different weights. Government interventions that have been particularly effective in achieving greater electricity efficiency in end-use include pricing policies (and metering practices), information programmes, incentives and regulations. A priority is the establishment of regulatory frameworks that provide economic incentives for utilities to encourage end-use efficiency improvements when such improvements would benefit the utility system as a whole.

Electricity transformation, which dominates the transformation sector both in size and amount of conversion losses, is undergoing gradual but slow improvement in its conversion efficiency. The commercial advantages arising from even minor refinements in these systems are such that there is usually adequate incentive to operators to pursue best practice at all times and to incorporate the more efficient new plant (where it has been clearly proven) as quickly as possible. The outlook for the sector is that its relative size is likely to increase with the continued increase in electricity intensity in OECD economies but only gradual efficiency gains are likely. Losses might stabilise or decline slowly. The most likely near-term target for policy actions in the transformation sector appears to be the encouragement of technological enhancements, such as repowering generation facilities with more efficient or "clean" energy technologies instead of life extensions which merely extend the use of inefficient older facilities.

Vehicle efficiency is also very important as, unlike in other sectors, the consumption of oil in the transport sector rose dramatically between 1973 and 1987 (in OECD countries). Analysis has found that large increases in fuel efficiency of new cars have been achieved, primarily through technological improvements. However, changing driving habits, a trend towards purchasing larger cars and increased road congestion and other factors, to a large extent influenced by economic growth, have offset the gains, particularly in recent years. Fuel demand for passenger motor travel is expected to continue to increase, although demographic factors and saturation effects in OECD countries could eventually moderate the increases. Numerous small efficiency improvements in vehicle and engine design will probably continue. In assessing the potential environmental benefits to be gained from greater efficiency in the transportation sector and possible actions, one must consider technical potential for efficiency gains, the effectiveness of vehicle efficiency standards and trends in the other offsetting factors mentioned above.

Summarising the possibilities for greater energy efficiency, great technical potential remains in a number of sectors for improvements but the achievable potential could be considerably less because of consumer attitudes and economic factors. In the near-term, the opportunity exists for the accelerated introduction of energy-saving technologies in all sectors. In particular, the electricity end-use sector and vehicles promise substantial potential. However, if demand for services provided by electricity and for transportation continues to increase at current rates, any efficiency gains in these sectors would be offset. National and international collaboration programmes are already in place in the areas of energy technology demonstration and dissemination. These could be extended to place additional emphasis on the environmental benefits of new more energy efficient technology.

Achieving a change in the rate of efficiency improvements depends most critically upon the price incentive to different consumer categories, attitudes and other factors in consumer decision-making, replacement rates of equipment as well as on the pace of technological improvements. Price transparency is essential for influencing consumer decisions on energy efficient actions because such transparency leads to the use of more efficient energy systems. However, analyses of elasticities indicate that the price of energy would have to rise very considerably above present levels, for example, in order to hold aggregate energy consumption constant throughout the rest of the century. Continued economic growth will be the key to maintaining the pace of technological development and the turnover of capital stock.

Recognising the environmental advantages of energy-efficiency investments would in many cases make them a more viable response. A number of countries are in the process of reassessing their efficiency programmes to see whether efforts to increase the visibility of energy efficiency and for emphasizing and explaining the externalities, such as the environmental benefits, might be justified. A few of the actions already taken include information campaigns, tightening vehicle and appliance efficiency standards, taxation, restructuring electricity tariffs, allowing electricity efficiency improvements in competitive bids for new electricity supply and subsidising CHP schemes.

Add-on technologies. Add-on pollution control technologies are in widespread use for stationary combustion sources as well as mobile sources. Except in some cases where they can help recover valuable products that would otherwise be lost, their development and use has been primarily a response to government requirements to limit pollutant emissions. Some government financial aid has at times been provided (in addition to regulation) for their development or introduction. These technologies can be highly effective in reducing the output of emissions, used either separately or in combination, although most of them require small amounts of additional energy for their operation.

The use of add-on technologies will undoubtedly continue and expand as new pollutants and sources are brought under control. There have been, however, a number of cases where add-on technologies in themselves have been insufficient, even with the best available technology applied. Certain add-on technologies are still under development and promise lower control costs or control for previously uncontrolled substances. At present, the development of add-on technologies for control of carbon dioxide (CO_2) emissions from fossil fuel combustion is only in the conceptual stages for utility applications.

Fuel Substitution. Historical fuel shifts were motivated by many different factors; paramount among these were the availability of economic alternatives and the technologies to use them. Substituting fuels has involved permanent movements between energy alternatives (e.g., from fossil fuels to nuclear or renewable energy sources); temporary fuel switching to minimise seasonal or short-term environmental impacts (e.g., from gasoline to natural gas); or the use of higher quality (less polluting) forms of the same fuel (e.g., from high-sulphur to low-sulphur coal). More recently the growing recognition of environmental problems has affected fuel choices. To determine the comparative effects on the environment of different fuel choices, it is imperative to look at the full fuel cycle and the environmental impacts at all stages.

Notable alterations in fuel choice occurred after the mid-1970s, largely as a result of energy security and environmental objectives explicitly supported by government policy-makers and of uncertainty about future fuel costs. The greatest shifts occurred in the utility sector and through changes in residential and commercial building space heating. The observed shifts in the industrial sector were less marked and often were the result of structural changes and not of fuel substitution. Both siting constraints and a variety of fuel use restrictions played some part.

Some substitutions, such as using certain renewable energy sources in place of fossil fuel combustion, will probably continue to have limited market penetration until their development is further advanced and costs are more competitive. Others are possible now. Examples from this latter category examined in this study are: substitutions in electricity generation and for the transport sector, both of which could involve natural gas.

Modest increases in the production of *natural gas* beyond what is currently planned are potentially possible without affecting resource costs. In terms of market penetration, increases in natural gas supplies above those forecasted (perhaps 10% above) could probably be easily substituted in the industrial, residential/commercial and electric generating sectors. Substitution in the transport sector would require major infrastructural changes, some technological development and perhaps economic incentives to accomplish a switch. Existing or planned natural gas pipelines and distribution networks would be able to supply such additional volumes without prohibitively high transportation costs or major delays. Such modest increases in the use of natural gas would probably pose few energy security risks.

Some steps have already been taken to promote natural gas, primarily for energy security reasons. Governments are actively reviewing existing policies or measures which pose impediments to increasing natural gas production or use. The policy changes made have worked to eliminate or modify unwarranted restrictions on gas use, over-regulation of prices or market access and discriminatory tax policies. Questions on the limitations placed in some countries on access to pipeline or distribution networks and on the development of gas supplies or the construction of gas transport or storage systems are also being addressed. Other policies have included: supporting public information campaigns which explain to consumers the benefits of converting to gas or modifying tax or other policies to increase further the financial incentive to convert to natural gas or dual-firing capability.

With respect to fuel substitution in *electricity generation,* before 2005, a significant portion of the increase in electricity demand will be met by nuclear power installations already under construction. The electricity sector offers other opportunities for fuel, although many of these opportunities could not be fully realised until well after 2005. There is near-term potential for increased use of natural gas and for increased power production from renewable energy sources, especially hydropower and biomass in some countries. Continues progress in development and cost-reduction of wind, photovoltaic and other technologies could increase the contribution from these renewable energy sources. But it is nevertheless not likely with present trends that such increases could eliminate continued growth in coal requirements, perhaps increasingly met with low sulphur coal and hard coal.

Electricity generation is strongly influenced by governments, either directly as owners or as regulators. Therefore, there is a wide range of instruments which governments might choose for achieving fuel substitution objectives. But there are also limitations: the longevity of capital investments in generating facilities, mean that many of the existing opportunities can only be realised gradually over a period of several decades or more. Governments also can influence *electricity demand,* primarily via electric utilities and their regulators.

In the *automotive sector,* there are a number of different fuels (natural-gas based, biofuels and electricity) which, if substituted for at least part of the fuels now in use, could produce environmental and energy security. But their contribution to motor-vehicle fuel requirements without large governmental intervention before 2005 is likely to be small. The greatest environmental gains during this period appear likely to be by the accelerated introduction of unleaded or low volatility gasoline. But some contributions might also be made, especially in specific cities or regions, through the introduction of CNG or fuel-flexible vehicles. Aside from availability questions, unresolved issues involve the comparable environmental and economic costs (i.e., ranging from fuel production to motor vehicle manufacturing and use) of the different major options available and the potential to exploit limited motor-vehicle markets (e.g., fleets).

In general, despite the many complementary effects of fuel substitution noted above, there are still areas where there can be conflicting effects, that is, where achieving energy security objectives would be costly in environmental terms or vice versa. It is fair to say, taking an overall view, that the various market factors and government policies that influenced fuel substitution have in some cases had both complementary and conflicting effects. In addition, there are differing national perspectives on the environmental effects of the certain energy sources (e.g., nuclear energy, coal, hydro-electricity, and biomass) which lead to different opinions on which effects are complementary or conflicting. In any case, the potential environmental benefits of each substitution option differ, as do their likely economic costs and energy security implications. Detailed assessments are necessary and should examine the effects and interactions of the alternative fuel substitution possibilities on all stages of the production, transport, conversion and final end-use of the types of energy involved as well as the underlying economic factors which might accelerate or slow down the desired shifts.

"Clean" energy technologies. "Clean" energy technologies combine more energy efficient processes or operations and reduced pollutant production without necessarily entailing a change in the form of energy used. A lot of the efforts to date have aimed at developing inherently "cleaner" technologies for those energy sources. This is the case, for example, for fossil fuels, which are otherwise among the most polluting, because the costs of complying with environmental regulations have been the highest for these sources. Like add-on technologies, "clean" technologies sometimes have good capabilities for reducing pollution levels. Unlike add-on technologies, "clean" energy technologies have been primarily designed for new equipment and facilities. Nevertheless, their application to existing facilities, such as power stations, is possible through repowering. Coal use has been a major focus of the development of "clean" technologies. Most of these technologies are not fully commercial, although a number are in the late demonstration stages.

The full potential of these technologies is still being investigated. The shift of R&D effort and support towards "clean" energy technologies is accelerating their development in member countries. Penetration of "clean" technologies will eventually be limited by the rates of growth of new facilities and by life extension opportunities. Their introduction into the market will broaden the range of options from which companies can choose to comply with often increasingly stringent environmental regulations, if the regulations so allow.

Identification of Areas for Improved Policy Making

Policy Instruments/Interventions and Macro-Economic Effects. Applying policy measures to implement improved environmental protection not only produces the direct influences that were intended upon the producer, consumer and/or the investor, but also involves indirect costs and benefits to the economy as a whole. Such effects could have impacts on the economic growth which is necessary to provide environmental protection on an economically sound and socially acceptable basis. While the macro-economic effects of the use of such interventions to protect the environment have often not been made explicit, it is nevertheless useful to anticipate and, to the extent possible quantify such effects for proposed policy measures.

Need for Integrated Analysis and Responses. None of the possible responses are without their trade-offs, whether it be the social and economic structural adjustments involved, the additional energy required to produce a higher quality fuel or the increase of solid wastes caused by air pollution control using certain add-on technologies. In conditions of uncertainty about environmental impacts, greater integration of environmental and energy decision-making so that all dimensions are represented to decision makers is probably the best way to insure that likely trade-offs are adequately considered in any action. In order to achieve such integration, analyzing and comparing the full selection of possible energy and non-energy actions must be built into the process of development of policies. There needs to be a focus on the procedural aspects of decision making, especially as they relate to balancing energy and environmental goals, to ensure that this integration actually occurs at the earliest possible stage. The development of integrated responses depends as much on the introduction of new policy as on that of new technologies. A number of countries are at present developing methodological tools which can help the decision-maker in performing multi-dimensional analyses. These should provide a better basis for identifying balanced and integrated solutions.

Need for Flexibility and Effectiveness in Environmental Control. While the extensive interventions made to date have in fact achieved some measure of internalisation, the manner in which the internalisation has been achieved has not in all cases been the most efficacious. For this reason, the study concentrates especially upon at the range of instruments that have been applied, specifically in order to identify beneficial or undesirable effects that were unanticipated when the policy was adopted and implemented. The study identifies a number of areas needing new or revised methods in order to allow the flexibility needed for energy security without sacrificing environmental achievements. These include the use of fuel use restrictions, siting difficulties and the formulation of air pollution regulations.

Fuel use restrictions are in use for the purposes of both energy security and environmental protection. They can be applied on all or part of a fuel cycle and can have a direct and immediate impact on energy activities. All types of fuel-uses have been affected by these direct impacts; the most common are in electricity generation and transport. Such restrictions can have high social and economic costs; often they lead to more lasting changes imposed on energy activities, such as changes in fuel choice or technologies or even longer-term structural approaches. In some cases recourse to other solutions has been exhausted and environmental degradation (or the risk of environmental degradation) has continued to be considered unacceptably high. In these cases, further measures are likely to have a very major impact on energy activities, such as the phasing-out of whole fuel cycles. For example, decisions on new facilities using coal, and particularly on further shifts towards these fuels are thus becoming increasingly difficult in many countries, although not reflected in current coal production and use. Decision-making processes should be improved so that fuel use restrictions are avoided as much as possible.

Energy facility siting constraints have had an effect on fuel choice through their impact upon the range of energy supply options that are made available and the quantities of various energy forms actually exploited or produced. The scale of the impact observed varies considerably according to the activity and the country. The balance between fossil fuels and electricity, for uses where these two energy forms are substitutable (e.g., domestic space heating), has probably been modified in some countries by difficulties in developing nuclear, hydroelectric, or even coal-fired generating capacity. In other countries, where electricity generation is almost entirely based on fossil fuels, the balancing occurs amongst the different ways to burn fossil fuels. Siting difficulties, together with an uncertain regulatory situation for many utilities, pose a threat to system reliability in some countries.

Review of decision-making processes is vitally needed to deal with the environmental aspects of siting new energy activities. The cumulative effect of local, relatively isolated siting constraints have produced impacts comparable to a national restriction or freeze. Three fuel cycles may be most affected by this trend: nuclear fuel (because of concerns about safety, decommissioning and waste disposal), coal (because of measures in process or likely at every stage of the fuel cycle, especially if actions begin to mitigate global climate change) and hydroelectricity (because of its impact on environmentally sensitive sites). New or revised approaches may be needed to facilitate siting decisions without sacrificing public involvement; for example, compensation in some form to those likely to be affected may be necessary and could in turn be internalised within the cost of the project and passed on equitably to the benefitting population.

The study finds that the formulation and implementation timing for compliance with regulations affects the feasibility of certain responses. Some regulations have no means to effectively consider energy efficiency improvements as a means to reduce pollutant emissions, for instance. Longer implementation periods provide more scope for developing and implementing better controls. This requires early engagement of likely-to-be-affected industry, consumer and government interests in developing feasible and preferred response strategies.

There is an increasing reliance upon international approaches to global and transboundary environmental problems, using such means as international conventions and protocols. Improving and developing existing and future international co-ordination and harmonization efforts is a growing challenge for national governments and relevant international organisations. The balance that has to be achieved between the performance criteria of environmental acceptability on the one hand (environmental effectiveness, cost-effectiveness, equity and flexibility) and of energy security on the other (reliability, availability, adaptability and diversity) should now be considered at the international level as well as at the national and individual polluter's level. It is imperative that all concerns, including, inter alia, energy interests, are represented in the process of development and implementation. Particularly important is identifying what has worked well in the past in developing and implementing coordinated, flexible and equitable approaches at the international level, especially where targets for emission reductions are considered.

Conclusions

Major outstanding environmental problems relating to energy present a high-priority mandate and an urgent challenge, not only to work to solve the problems but to do it in a way that is best for the economy and energy systems themselves.

Actions can be taken now and indeed are already under way: notably, better communication to energy consumers (as responsible public awareness and pressure requires good information) and enhancing efforts to increase the pace of energy efficiency improvements and conservation. These actions make sense in their own right and will bring mainly benefits without additional costs. Governments, recognising the importance of public institutions setting good examples, are actively developing strategic plans and making some of the institutional changes to accommodate the heightened cooperation in policy-making.

Regardless of the method used to obtain the goals, taking action will result in substantial future internalisation of environmental costs. This will undoubtedly cause significant changes in the relative costs of energy supply and use with corresponding shifts in fuel choice as well as changes in overall demand. Fossil fuels could see resultant major cost increases because of the problems of ambient air quality, acid rain, and global climate change. For nuclear energy too, in some cases, increases can be expected for safety, decommissioning and long term storage of high level wastes.

Some additional actions may be necessary in the future when the global environmental situation is better understood. If it is determined that more aggressive responses are necessary, this may dictate alternate approaches than presently under consideration. In view of the long lead time for R&D, a strong and sustained effort in advanced, energy related research and development for application in the post-2005 period is required.

The more severe the problem, the greater the likely changes. The identification of preferred candidates for actions should look for those which are "robust" with respect to the full spectrum of environmental problems for which action still needs to be taken.

Any strategy developed must account for the dynamic and differing aspects of the energy usage and environmental ramifications. On the one hand, society needs to ensure that environmental damage will be prevented or limited to acceptable levels. Such certainty has been most often obtained through regulation. On the other hand, economic (and energy) systems work best when there is adequate flexibility to make choices. The need for flexibility grows with the magnitude of changes that will be needed. While these differences may never be settled, there are some areas where improvements can be made. Better policy co-ordination at all levels of government, engaging as early as possible a wide range of actors (governments, private industry and individual consumers) is essential. In particular, such co-ordination must be implemented throughout the full cycle of technology development and commercialisation and must extend to the selection of responses and policy instruments. Continuation of the active exchange within and among countries about the lessons learned from using different approaches is needed.

With regard to the specific potential of the various responses, the high technical and economic potential of energy efficiency improvements (especially in electricity, transportation and industrial uses) that could most benefit the environment is notable. The potential of fuel substitution and flexibility is also great. In some sectors, structural and behaviourial changes may be highly effective, for example in the transport sector, traffic management and encouragement of inter-modal shifts. Implementation of responses depending upon the actions of individual consumers remains difficult because of the myriad of decision makers involved and because it can be exceedingly difficult to predict with accuracy just how individual consumers will react. The importance of analyzing and addressing these non-technical factors might well be recognised in national assessments of the potentials that are likely.

Emissions and their effects on the environment occur at all stages of the fuel cycle, contributing to one or more environmental problems. The entire fuel cycle and the full set of environmental problems must be considered in order to capture the full effects of using one type of fuel rather than another, reducing demand in one sector versus another, or of adopting one technology or policy approach rather than another.

Environmental concerns and the resulting governmental actions to ensure environmental protection have been at the root of innovation in environmental technologies as companies have recognised a large and growing market for new products. Both industry and government energy R&D and demonstration programmes in pertinent energy sectors have begun to focus at least part of their efforts on those technologies with multiple energy and environment benefits, most notably those offering greater energy efficiency, using renewable energy sources or "cleaner" energy technologies.

It is vital to maintain national and international energy R&D, demonstration and dissemination efforts. These are required both to provide incremental improvements in the efficiency, economics and environmental performance of energy technologies to be applied before 2005 and to lay the foundation of technologies for environmentally sustainable energy policies and programmes beyond 2005. International collaboration in the field of energy technologies, such as that presently conducted under the auspices of the IEA, is extremely useful in this respect.

Given the complexity and magnitude of current and emerging environmental concerns, expert opinion and analysis (considered alongside reliable information) is increasingly needed in the provision of advice to policy-makers. Therefore, in parallel, it is also important to sustain programmes to improve the scientific understanding of global environmental change. This understanding is critical to define both risks and appropriate response strategies, whether they are strategies of control or adaptation. In many cases governments have felt the need to recommend or take environmental action based only on partial, but convincing, evidence due to the importance of the environmental risks involved. Improved scientific and analytical methods make it easier to base decisions more on scientific evidence and balanced assessments than on political judgement.

International agreements to coordinate environmental approaches are likely to continue to grow in importance as an approach to solving transboundary and global environmental problems. The more stringent the measure, the more urgent is the need to identify the most cost-effective strategies (or at least the relative costs consequences) for achieving the environmental objectives.

Areas for Further Work

Numerous areas of further work for countries and for international organisations are suggested in the Summary and Conclusions based on the findings of the study. In order to support better policy co-ordination and analysis of policy measures and thus to smooth negative implications for energy security, where they occur, the following major work items are included in the IEA 1990 Programme of Work:

- comparative analysis of the full range of responses for all end-use sectors beginning with the transport and electricity end-use sectors with the goal of developing abatement strategies which offer flexibility, certainty and cost effectiveness, to the maximum extent possible;

- consideration of policy instruments in the context of applicability and effectiveness and with respect to specific environmental problems assessment and quantification of the likely impacts of the application of such instruments on energy consumption, energy efficiency and intensity, fuel mix and costs and their combined effect on the energy sector in general;

- consideration of possibilities and effectiveness of encouraging very specifically those energy efficiency actions which are most beneficial for environmental protection;

- consideration of fuel availability and trade-offs and the effects the use of policy instruments for fuel substitution;

- development of a strategy to allow greater penetration of "clean" energy technologies with great potential but which are not fully commercial;

- better understanding of the complexities of the decision-making process as it relates to the energy and environment interface, in particular, questions relating to the ability of industry to take advantage of market-based instruments;

- development of better methodologies for the use of decision-makers to allow consideration and planning of full-fuel cycle, multi-pollutant, multiple response strategies;

- assistance with the effective prioritisation and design of R&D, demonstration and dissemination efforts, including their integration, along with accompanying policy instruments, into energy policies and international collaborative efforts aimed at achieving an environmentally acceptable energy system at an acceptable price; and

- examination of actions that could be taken (before 2005) which have potentially significant impacts beyond the year 2005, for example CO_2 scrubbing, photovoltaics and other renewable energy sources, and fusion.

I. INTRODUCTION

The regional and local effects of human activities on the environment have been the focus of detailed policy attention in Member countries for at least two decades. Certain environmental problems are increasingly recognised as global in scale and, as such, require international co-operation to understand their implications for technical, industrial and economic decision making. This is particularly true for the energy sector. This study is a broad analysis of the policy aspects touching the relationship between energy and the environment.

The energy sector, which spreads a complex web of activities throughout the economy of industrialised countries, is participating in this evolution. Environmental objectives and instruments for environmental control already play a significant role in shaping some of our energy choices. There is growing acceptance by policy makers that environmental issues and the measures designed to alleviate them will gain even more importance in the years ahead. It is, therefore, essential to consider approaches that might meet the objectives of both energy security and environmental protection.

As stated by the IEA Governing Board at Ministerial level in July 1985, May 1987 and more recently and emphatically in May 1989, solutions to the environmental problems associated with energy are fundamental for the maintenance of adequate, diversified, economic and secure energy supply. Ministers, therefore, stressed the importance of reconciliation of energy and environmental objectives and committed themselves to promote actively in their policies those lines of action which advance both objectives. In following up these decisions, the IEA has, as a first step, prepared a study concentrating on emission controls in electricity generation and industry, that was published in 1988 [1][1]. In the discussion on the follow-up of this study, first priority was given to a "broad brush" policy study of long-term impacts on energy security of existing and proposed environmental measures and of policy options and instruments that might be required or appropriate to achieve in the best way the objectives of both energy and environment policy.

---

1. Numbers in brackets designate references and sources listed at the end of the study in Annex 3

Chapter II provides an introductory background on environmental regulatory trends, both national and international. These trends in environmental policy and management usually occur as a response to a rise in public concern and scientific and technical developments, combined with economic considerations. Chapter III reviews major ongoing and emerging areas of environmental concern and the role played by energy-related activities in eleven such areas. Chapter IV provides a typology of environmental approaches and instruments already in use to control many of these concerns. Chapter V examines how these approaches to environmental control are applied to energy activities. A fuel-cycle review, presented in more detail in Annex 1, shows the scope of environmental control approaches currently implemented or considered from energy production through to end-uses.

The study then turns to a detailed identification and assessment of the primary and secondary impacts of ongoing and emerging environmental approaches on energy activities and their implications for energy security. Chapter VI provides, by way of an introduction, a definition of energy security and its interface with environmental protection. Primary and secondary impacts of environmental approaches on energy activities are subsequently identified, along with resultant trends and possible future impacts. Chapter VII assesses implications for energy security in terms of the effects on energy intensity, the supply and demand balance, the fuel mix and oil substitution. It also examines the general issue of diversity and flexibility, as well as effects on indigenous supply options, technology choices and on the dependence on non-IEA supplies and on energy trade.

The study then examines responses and policy choices for the time frame of the year 2005 in terms of possibilities, constraints and areas for further analysis. Chapter VIII provides a conceptual framework for balanced and integrated energy and environment decision-making. Chapter IX examines various available and possible policy responses: pollution control based on the use of add-on technologies, greater energy efficiency, fuel substitution, "clean" energy technologies. Chapter X focuses on policy instruments and their micro-economic and macro-economic effects. Chapter XI considers areas for improved policy-making on three key issues: flexibility and effectiveness, improved decision-making processes, and international harmonization and co-ordination. The last Chapter provides a summary and a set of major conclusions drawn from the study and considers possible follow-on work needed to refine and support the design and implementation of appropriate policy responses and instruments.

The study is essentially designed to provide an overview of the complexities of issues involved in achieving energy and environmental objectives. The analysis presented stops short of recommending particular strategies, but does highlight the importance of assessing and comparing the various responses and policy instruments. As such, it can serve as a reference and be viewed as a stepping-off point from which policy makers can work to develop specific policy frameworks suitable to conditions in individual Member countries.

II. BACKGROUND ON ENVIRONMENTAL TRENDS IN THE ENERGY SECTOR

1. The Development of Policy for Environmental Protection

Environmental policy of today reflects developments of the last 20-30 years. During this time, the appearance of environmental problems, changes in public awareness, economic considerations as well as national and international trends have profoundly affected the directions of environmental policy. A glance at environmental policy developments as they relate to energy over the last two decades reveals the changing balance and influence of isolated decisions and the trends that emerge are indicative of the direction of future developments.

2. Environmental Problems and their Understanding

The risk and reality of environmental degradation have become more apparent. Growing evidence of environmental problems is due to a combination of factors. Over the last 20-30 years, the environmental impact of human activities has grown dramatically due to the sheer increase of world population, consumption and industrial activity. Though some levels of pollution have been reduced, many environmental impacts have grown in scale and crossed a threshold beyond which their effects on human health or ecosystems no longer go unnoticed. In general, the ability of science to identify and measure the production and effects of potentially harmful substances has greatly advanced. Throughout the 1970s most environmental analysis and legal instruments of control focused on conventional pollutants, defined in terms of pollution thresholds (for sulphur oxide (SO_x), nitrogen oxides (NO_x), particulates, and carbon monoxide (CO)). Now concern has extended to the control of micro- or hazardous air pollutants, which are usually toxic chemical substances and harmful in small doses, as well as to that of globally significant pollutants such as CO_2. Aside from advances in environmental science, developments in industrial processes and structures have led to new environmental problems. For instance, in the energy sector, major shifts to the road transport of industrial goods and to individual travel by cars has led to an increase in road traffic and hence a shift in attention paid to the effects and sources of NO_x and VOC emissions.

With increasing evidence and concern came greater policy attention, reflected by the expansion and sophistication of regulatory practices. Generally, there is a political imperative to make policy and regulatory decisions despite some remaining scientific uncertainty. Due to increased ability to identify hazards, the numbers of pollutants and substances on lists of concerns have multiplied several times over. A clear understanding of their effects, interactions and acceptable levels of exposure or concentrations is, however, often much less forthcoming. Science presents evidence upon which policy-makers must make reasonable decisions or, in some cases, decide to wait for more evidence. However, the process of policy-making is inevitably uncertain and interpretative in its use of science. Some hazards are of a nature that does not allow waiting until full scientific evidence can be provided. As a result, pressure resulting from heightened public concern as to a particular hazard may lead to policy actions which are based upon partial scientific evidence.

In addition, policy-makers are increasingly faced with the challenge of anticipating environmental degradation that may occur. This often means that they are expected to take action designed not only to minimize existing environmental impacts, but also to avoid the appearance of new environmental problems, through preventive rather than curative approaches. This requires foresight which sometimes involves considerable scientific and technical uncertainty, as the solution of one environmental problem today can become the problem of tomorrow. It is no longer enough to support the development of a fuel or energy technology for its positive emission performance if the same technology or fuel introduces an intractable waste problem, shifts pollutant balances or poses new environmental hazards.

3. Public and Political Awareness

Though individual countries have for many years been making determined efforts to solve problems, such as air pollution caused by prevailing urban development, public awareness of the environment in the OECD region as a whole grew rapidly in the 1960-1970s. This public awareness is reflected in the expanded role of environmental policy and regulation, which is marked by such developments as: the National Environmental Policy Act (1970) of the United States; the Basic Law for Environmental Pollution Control (1967) in Japan; the EC First Action Programme on the Environment (1973); and the UN Conference on the Human Environment (Stockholm 1972). These are only a few of the developments in OECD countries that characterised the response of the state to public concern [2].

Since this time, the "environmental movement" has become a political force and, as such, effective in influencing general policy directions as well as individual project outcomes. The growth of environmental consumer groups and political parties has served as a means to independently develop data, analysis and positions on key policy areas, thus contributing to the information available on environmental issues. The participation of such groups, in many instances, has been institutionalised into the decision-making process of Member governments and some international organisations.

IEA governments recognise the problems of environmental quality and are taking the issue of the environmental impact of energy activities seriously. The national policies of the 1980s are characterised by tendencies to reinforce existing policies in the direction of preventative rather than curative action. International policy is characterised by greater emphasis on co-ordination and harmonization of environmental control efforts. The definition and practice of development efforts that are "sustainable" has also been the subject of recent discussion, as highlighted in the World Commission on Economic Development report, "Our Common Future" [3]. Growing environmental problems, scientific evidence and public concern have thus turned the attention of policy makers more clearly to defining regional and international long-term levels of environmental quality.

Industry now also provides consistent and constructive participation in the environmental decision-making process. The growing number and complexity of environmental regulations imposed on energy activities in recent decades often met with opposition from industry representatives who were faced with significant investment requirements, increases in operating costs, delays in receiving construction and operating permits and regulatory uncertainty. The outstanding pragmatic question of industry was often whether the environmental control costs were justified by the value of the environmental results. Industry recognizes, however, that it is better to anticipate and to influence than to be caught off-guard or be on the defensive on environmental regulatory matters. A good example is the establishment of CONCAWE as an environmental research extension of major oil companies in Europe. Though there are still conflicting opinions on particular issues, the change to note is the broadened participation and openness of discussions on energy-environmental issues.

4. Economic Considerations

Economic considerations have long been a cornerstone of the determination of acceptable levels of environmental protection. Generally, as the level of environmental protection is increased, the marginal cost of control rises considerably. As a result, though in some cases 90 to 100% reductions of pollutants may be technically possible, it is often unrealistic in economic terms to strive for such a target. The task of the policy-maker is to consider and balance the costs and benefits of protection in the determination of what may be an acceptable level of protection.

Benefit-cost analysis is probably, in theory, the soundest approach to economic evaluation, but its use in practice has been severely limited by the difficulty of quantifying the "benefits" of protecting environmental quality. Wide variation in individual assumptions can result in vastly different benefit-cost ratios for the same level of regulation. Depending on one's perspective, it could be argued that the benefit-cost approach to decision making has resulted in regulation that is either too lenient or too strict. Other approaches have been developed to supplement cost-benefit analysis: one in particular is cost-effectiveness evaluation of alternative strategies for meeting a particular environmental objective. The goal is to use the most cost-effective way to achieve a particular end rather than determining if the result is greater than the cost. The trend in cost-evaluation work is to look beyond simple add-on control options to opportunities for systems management. The tools for this type of systems approach to least-cost analysis are still developing along with the necessary data bases. The emphasis in the economic discussion has clearly shifted away from the quantification of environmental benefits to a more careful definition of the costs and micro- and macro-economic effects of amelioration strategies.

5. International Trends

From an international viewpoint, there has clearly been a spread of environmental concern and a cross-fertilization of ideas regarding strategies for environmental management. Common international thinking is evident in the trend to coordinate national environmental policies among developed countries. Transboundary, and in some cases global, aspects of environmental problems are increasingly being recognised and addressed through international fora, such as, the OECD, the United Nations' Economic Commission for Europe (UN-ECE), the United Nations' Environment Programme (UNEP), the World Meteorological Organisation (WMO), the Intergovernmental Panel on Climate Change (IPCC), and the European Community (EC).

International developments on the environment have to date affected the energy sector primarily on issues of air and water quality, marine pollution control and more recently of hazardous waste disposal. International law or treaties have been developed to guide individual national policy towards an international objective. So far as agreements set out quantified targets of environmental quality, such targets are usually based on what is politically achievable rather than on scientific evidence for environmental control alone. Therefore, nations that are strongly addressing environmental issues sometimes have achieved or even superseded from the outset the targets found in international agreements. It is these same countries that are also often in the forefront of the support for such international agreements.

The nature of the European Community action on environment is different from other international fora in that it can establish legislation for all of its members. It carries out its environmental policy through the adoption of directives which are binding upon member states and outline specific obligations of each state pursuant to EC policy on a certain issue. In most cases these directives have included detailed targets and a timescale for meeting them. Their implementation is left to national governments who in turn select and adopt the necessary actions. The EC has been active in environmental policy since 1973 and has implemented directives on a broad range of topics, notably air pollution, water pollution, noise, waste disposal and recovery and environmental protection mechanisms or procedures (including environmental impact assessment and environmental information systems).

Acid rain is one example of a transboundary issue that stimulated international action on air pollution in Europe [4]. In the late 1960s, evidence of acidification in Scandinavia was revealed, which was followed by stepped-up analysis and research on eco-system effects of acid deposition and air pollution. The Stockholm Conference on the Human Environment, held in 1972, focused on acid rain and more significantly, on the need for international co-operation to resolve environmental problems. Public awareness grew along with news of alleged acid-rain effects, such as lake acidification and the die-back of fish populations and of forests. Therefore a regional solution was sought to respond to the political need to reduce the emissions identified as precursors to the acidification problem.

Set up in 1979 by the UN-ECE, the Convention on Long-Range Transboundary Air Pollution led to the signature in 1985 of the UN-ECE protocol on SO_x which called for an emission reduction of 30% by 1993 from 1980 levels [5]. By 1988, under the same Convention, the UN-ECE succeeded in the development of a protocol for NO_x reduction, which was signed by 24 countries who agreed to limit emissions before 1995 to 1987 levels. Twelve of these countries also declared their commitment to further reducing their national NOx emissions by 30% by the end of 1994 at the latest. The NOx Protocol was unique in its recognition of credit for prior action in the establishment of international limits. A credit was incorporated in the Protocol so as to take into account the increasing marginal cost of control and avoid penalizing countries which had taken early unilateral control actions. Additionally, supporting work has been underway since 1987 to develop proposals for a protocol on volatile organic compounds and to strengthen the original protocol on SO_x. The EC has also recently adopted a Directive on the control of SO_x and NO_x emissions from large combustion plants.

Under the auspices of UNEP and WMO, the Intergovernmental Panel on Climate Change (IPCC) was recently set up to develop collaborative analysis on all aspects of climate change (scientific understanding, socio-economic effects, response strategies, etc.). This effort is a necessary pre-condition to the development of any international agreement on greenhouse gases and climate change.

6. National Policy Trends

National policy developments on environment and energy generally originate from either the need to respond to an identified national or regional problem or from the need to meet a policy objective as set out in an international agreement. As mentioned above, the international dimension has become increasingly important in recent years with the political pressure to build international consensus on transboundary or global environmental concerns.

The structure of national policy in OECD countries generally develops around the different environmental media (e.g., air, water, soil) setting out broad criteria for protection of environmental quality on the basis of the protection of public health and of ecological damage. A secondary policy objective has been the protection of material goods from pollution damage. Recent emphasis has been on the consideration of appropriate policy responses to ameliorate long-term effects on economies, trade and society as a whole of more gradual environmental changes, such as ozone depletion and climate change.

In a national context, the interrelationship of environmental policy to other sectors of the economy is increasingly scrutinized. The macro-economic impact of environmental measures, the Polluter Pays Principle and the broad issue of internalising environmental costs are examples of areas for such analysis. Other policy actions, such as, in the area of economic development and energy, are also assessed in the light of national environmental objectives. Environmental management must compete with other priorities of governments for funding. The resources allocated to environmental programmes generally follow the perception of environmental risks and problems. The increased level of funding for research on environmentally favourable energy technologies in many countries reflects a higher level of political commitment.

Given the local and regional nature of many environmental problems, it is natural that the interpretation and implementation of national policy may be left to subnational levels of government and refined as necessary to fit with specific conditions of the region. For example, in the United States, Australia, Germany and Japan it is possible for regional air pollution regulations to be more stringent than national requirements. National legislation, in these cases, serves as a guideline for development of region-specific regulations. In the United States, not only does state legislation sometimes exceed national requirements, but there is also wide variation in the interpretation found among individual states. As a result, the driving force of environmental controls applied to energy activities in a given region may be environmental, economic or political characteristics that are particular to that region alone.

Even when the broad authority of interpretation is not granted to them, regional or local authorities can directly influence energy projects through their review of environmental impact assessments of the siting of new energy facilities. Further, local authority often extends to transport and land-use planning which can directly or indirectly affect energy decisions.

III. AREAS OF ENVIRONMENTAL CONCERN

Environmental problems span a continuously growing range of pollutants, hazards and eco-system degradation over ever wider areas, for example local, regional and global. Some of these problems may arise from observable, chronic effects, for instance, on human health, while others may stem from the perceived risk of a possible accidental release of hazardous materials. A significant number of these environmental issues relate to energy production, transformation and end use which can be either contributing factors or the main causes. Eleven major areas of environmental concern where energy can play an important role can be identified:

-       major environmental accidents;
-       water pollution;
-       maritime pollution;
-       land use and siting impact;
-       radiation and radioactivity;
-       solid waste disposal;
-       hazardous air pollutants;
-       ambient air quality;
-       acid deposition;
-       stratospheric ozone depletion;
-       global climate change.

The interface between energy and environment is complex and constantly evolving. Increasing awareness of the environmental consequences of economic activities in general and energy activities in particular means that many areas of environmental concern are quite recent. As a result, the knowledge of the mechanisms involved in the impacts of these activities may still be incomplete and in some cases speculative. For each of these broad problem areas for the environment, the following outline presents the pollutants and hazards involved, as well as the cause-and-effect relationships that have been identified between energy activities, pollutants and environmental effects. The importance of energy activities in the generation of major pollutants is summarised in Table 1 below [6, 7, 8, 9, 10, 11].

Table 1

Importance of Energy Activities in the Generation of Air Pollutants

Pollutant	Man-Made as % of total	Energy Activities as % of total	Energy Activities as % of man-made	Contributions as % of energy-related releases
SO_2	45[3]	40[3]	90[3]	. Coal combustion: 80[1] . Oil combustion: 20[1]
NO_x	75[3]	64[3]	85[3]	. Transport: 51[1] . Stationary sources: 49[1]
CO	50[3]	15-25[3]	30-50[3]	. Transport: 75[1] . Stationary sources: 25[1]
Lead	100[3]	90[3]	90[1]	. Transport: 80[2] . Combustion in stationary sources (including incineration): 20[2]
PM	11.4[3]	4.5[3]	40[1]	. Transport: 17[1] . Electric utilities: 5[1] . Wood combustion: 12[1]
VOC	5[1]	2.8[3]	55[1]	. Oil industry: 15[1] . Gas industry: 10[1] . Mobile sources: 75[1]
Radionuclides	10[3]	2.5[3]	25[3]	. Mining, milling of uranium: 25[2] . Nuclear power stations and coal combustion: 75[2]
CO_2	4[4]	2.2-3.2[3]	55-80[3]	. Natural Gas: 15[1] . Oil: 45[1] . Solid Fuels: 40[1]
N_2O	37-58[3]	24-43[3]	65-75[3]	. Fossil fuel combustion: 60-75[3] . Biomass burning: 25-40[3]
CH_4	60[3]	9-24[3]	15-40[3]	. Natural gas losses: 20-40[3] . Biomass burning: 30-50[3]

Notes:
(1) Estimates for OECD countries.
(2) Estimates for United States.
(3) Global estimates.
(4) Global estimates of contribution of anthropogenic CO_2 to **increases** in CO_2 concentrations and to global warming is much larger.

Sources: Environmental Trends Associated with the 5th National Energy Plan, Argonne National Laboratory, 1986 (for the United States Department of Energy).
A Primer on Greenhouse Gases, D.J. Wuebbles -- J. Edmonds, 1988 (for the United States Department of Energy).
The State of the Environment, OECD, 1985.
The Greenhouse Issue, Environmental Resources Ltd., 1988 (for the Commission of the European Communities.)
Carbon Dioxide Emissions and Effects, IEA Coal Research, 1982.
The Greenhouse Effect, Climatic Change, and Ecosystems, B. Bolin -- B. Döös -- J. Jäger -- R. Warrick, 1986 (for SCOPE-ICSU).

1. Major Environmental Accidents

There is widespread and increasing public debate about the risks posed by industrial activities. This concern has concentrated recently on the risk of major environmental accidents. Increased public awareness can be related to the fact that developments in industrial structures have resulted in an increase in the scale of production units as well as an increase in trade flows of hazardous substances. Urbanisation and demographic concentration have also played their part in worsening the gravity of major accidents, in terms of human lives lost, as well as injured or displaced people [5]. Finally, though major industrial accidents do not always result in large-scale environmental damage, awareness of the risk of disaster-scale ecological accidents (affecting eco-systems rather than human health) has become more acute.

An exhaustive inventory of relevant energy-related activities would be meaningless as the distinction between perceived risk and actual accidents varies widely as does the scale at which occurrence or risk is considered significant. Some of the most important energy-related areas of perceived risk and/or actual accidents are listed below:

- on-shore and off-shore blow-outs, explosions and fires due to the production, treatment, transport and use of oil and gas, such as, fires at refineries, oil rigs, gas storage tanks, explosions of pipelines, etc.;

- maritime pollution due to oil tanker accidents, as well as soil and water pollution due to spills from rail and road tankers;

- radioactive releases resulting from nuclear accidents in the course of the production of nuclear energy, or the transport, treatment or storage of radioactive materials (fuel or waste);

- hydroelectric dam failures causing flooding and landslides;

- land subsidence and landslides due to mining activities, as well as explosions in mines;

- spontaneous combustion of stored coal or spoil dumps, as well as explosions due to methane build-up in refuse dumps and coal mines.

This list can be extended to include a variety of accidents involving a broad range of energy activities, ranging from the failure of a wind generator blade to a fire in a photovoltaic power station resulting in the release of toxic aerosols from the combustion of the cell components, or spills of PCB from electrical transformers.

2. Water Pollution

Both the quality and the quantity of water resources are increasingly important issues, especially in the case of groundwater, if only because of its role in the supply of drinking and irrigation water. Aside from non-point sources, such as, agriculture (pesticides), surface water pollution has, on the whole, been substantially reduced in IEA countries. Relative to other economic activities, energy activities may no longer play a major role in surface water quality problems [12]. Efforts have been made and are still being made to control these pollution problems. The following energy-related sources of pollution are identified:

- power plants and refineries produce effluent containing hazardous chemicals, such as chlorine and metals and other various suspended or dissolved solids;

- onshore oil and geothermal energy production pose the problems of brine disposal; although they vary considerably according to the properties of the reservoir, geothermal fluids can contain toxic chemicals, such as benzene, arsenic, mercury and boric acid and can release gases, such as carbon dioxide and methane that come out of solution when the pressure is released;

- acid drainage from existing or abandoned mines and coal preparation wastes from coal washeries and waste from pollution control can all contaminate surface waters;

- thermal pollution from the discharges of cooling systems of power plants, or from geothermal facilities can threaten aquatic life.

At the beginning of the 1970s, thermal pollution was regarded as a major concern, given the number of operating power stations and further projected growth. The subsequent slow-down of construction of new facilities has relegated this concern to a study area rather than one of control.

In the area of groundwater pollution, there is still a considerable and widespread lack of information and associated uncertainty about the level of pollution and the identification of energy-related sources. Most of the energy activities mentioned above in relation to surface water pollution have the potential to contaminate groundwater as well, though often in a more insidious and delayed manner. A severe source of groundwater pollution in many Member countries is oil leaks from underground storage tanks. Waste disposal is a growing source of groundwater pollution. Concern that efforts to control air pollution might result in increased water and soil pollution is emerging as air pollution practices producing wastes, such as FGD sludge, become more widespread.

3. Maritime Pollution

Much concern has centred on maritime pollution resulting from large accidental oil spills. However, the main source of marine-based pollution remains shipping operations. It is estimated that one tonne is discharged for every 1 000 tonnes of oil transported by sea [8]. If so, 1.1 million tonnes per annum are the result of regular discharge of oil by ships at sea. The remainder, about 400 000 tonnes, is due to tanker accidents. Production platforms are not, in world terms, a major source of oil pollution, even though offshore oil production now accounts for one quarter of world production.

Spills can have serious impact in bays, estuaries or land-locked seas, such as the Gulf of Mexico or the North Sea, where coastal waters are important for fishing, tourism or industry. No comprehensive assessment has been made of the damage to marine ecosystems as a whole.

Much work needs to be done before the effects of oil spills on the high seas can be evaluated more accurately.

4. Land Use and Siting Impact

Land use pressure exerted by economic activities gives rise to concerns that land particularly suited for sustaining agriculture, housing or natural ecosystems could be lost. In the energy sector, mining sites (including land over existing underground mines where subsidence can take place) and hydroelectric reservoirs have attracted the most public attention. Concern has also been voiced about the large land surfaces that might be needed for the large-scale exploitation of renewable energy forms, such as, wind power, solar power stations, or biomass production (wood, peat, straw or sugar cane) which would compete with other land uses.

Other energy-related activities, involving large facilities or complex industrial processes, such as, fuel refining or electric power generation, are subject to, inter alia, environmental concerns about siting sometimes in addition to land-use concerns. In many cases, opposition to siting specific projects (the so-called "Not In My Backyard" or "NIMBY" syndrome) stems from a combination of concerns about land use, pollution and accidents, which are not easily separated and evaluated. In addition to energy activities which traditionally have run into siting difficulties, such as, power stations or refineries, growing siting problems are occurring for the disposal of solid wastes ranging from those generated in pollution control operations to high-level radioactive waste containing long-lived radionuclides.

Obviously, all energy-related activities have some sort of siting impact and levels of acceptability are evolving constantly. For instance, there is disagreement about the effects of the electromagnetic fields associated with transmission voltages up to 800 kV on humans and animals. Though evidence of such negative effects is scant, the outlook for utilities (particularly in North America) planning major new transmission projects is not bright. Another emerging concern which is difficult to assess is visual air quality, such as, plume and haze conditions in national parks and other scenic areas. Measuring visibility, identifying contributors to haze visibility and designing remedial measures is proving to be a difficult task [13].

5. Radiation and Radioactivity

Approximately 90% of exposure to radiation is due to natural causes. Nevertheless, supplementary man-made radiation causes considerable concern. Energy activities contribute about 25% to total man-made radioactivity (i.e., about 2% of total exposure to radiation). Though fossil fuel combustion releases radionuclides, ongoing debate about man-made energy-related radiation focuses mainly on the nuclear fuel cycle and its various stages.

Uranium mining and milling releases radon and radon daughters which are potential occupational hazards, as well as process effluent and tailings which may cause groundwater contamination. These activities contribute about one quarter of energy-related radioactivity, though this share represents only about 0.5% of total exposure to radiation. Radon and radon daughters are naturally occurring gases which can be found in concentrations far in excess of those associated with nuclear energy activities, including uranium mining.

Normal reactor operation produces low-level radioactive emissions which are not considered to be harmful. Potential risk of a failure and the environmental effects of an accidental leak remain the major area of concern, though much has been done to demonstrate that safety in operation has been and will in the future be maintained and further improved. This issue has evolved over the last decade and now extends beyond the issue of reactor safety and accident prevention to include problems such as emergency planning and decommissioning. It has also taken on a more explicitly international dimension, with heightened public and political awareness of the transboundary risks of accidents involving nuclear facilities.

Nuclear waste disposal involves varying degrees of hazards depending on the characteristics of the wastes and whether or not they are released into the environment or isolated from the biosphere. There are large differences in the perceived potential for damage and the corresponding level of concern about low-level waste containing short-lived radionuclides and high-level waste containing significant amounts of long-lived radionuclides which need to be isolated for thousands of years.

Decommissioning of nuclear facilities has so far mainly concerned research reactors. According to current forecasts, only 61 commercial nuclear reactors will be decommissioned by the end of the century in Western Europe and North America. By 2030, this number should rise to 404. In the meantime, the environmental problems posed by the decommissioning of nuclear plants are still being identified. There is increasing worry that the risk of exposure to radiation would be high throughout the dismantling of the components, especially the reactor vessel.

6. Solid Waste Disposal

Solid waste disposal can pose environmental problems of two types. First, if the waste is classified as hazardous, that is, considered to be a potential health or environment threat (definitions of the term "hazardous" vary widely), it might release hazardous pollutants and result in air, water and soil pollution, which constitute major issues in themselves. Most of the solid waste considered hazardous is generated by the chemicals and metal industries. Energy-related activities accounted for about 12% of this waste in the United States in 1983 [6]. Secondly, though the waste may not be considered hazardous, it can still pose disposal problems merely for a question of space and appropriate containment. Solid wastes from energy activities include, for instance, bottom ash from power plants, which is usually not hazardous.

A major and growing source of waste has developed along with air pollution control itself. Sludge from FGD devices and collected fly ash from particulate control devices contains trace elements, such as, arsenic, lead, cadmium, selenium as well as radionuclides, though the concentrations are so low that the waste usually is not classified as hazardous. This is the case of a number of energy-related solid waste types, as new techniques, such as FBC, produce waste that has not as yet been studied precisely [14]. Quantities of scrubber sludge and fly ash produced are projected to grow dramatically over the next decades. In the United States, the majority of wet scrubber systems are designed to produce a waste requiring disposal. In Japan and Europe, limestone/gypsum systems are more widely used and are the fastest growing systems. The commercial use of wastes from pollution control as products for the building industry and transportation surfaces is limited by the size of the market. Accumulating over time, they might require large tracts of land for disposal with adequate containment practices to avoid water contamination.

7. Hazardous Air Pollutants

Hazardous air pollutants, are usually emitted in smaller (often locally concentrated) quantities than those that are the focus of ambient air quality concerns, though the definition of hazardous or toxic air pollutants varies. For instance, the long-range transport of certain hazardous air pollutants is a topic of increasing concern particularly in Scandinavian countries. Lead pollution from vehicles has been an ongoing problem for many years, and its health effects are well documented. In fact in some countries, such as the United States, lead is classified as a conventional pollutant rather than a toxic or hazardous pollutant. Organic compounds and among them hydrocarbons, have long been considered traditional air pollutants because of the role they play in photochemical oxidant formation. More recent studies have shown that some organic compounds have adverse effects on human health.

For some hazardous air pollutants, dose-response causes and effects are only now being demonstrated. It is here a matter of health effects, suspected or observed, though complete data is lacking. The number of suspected hazardous pollutants is very large and knowledge of sources, emissions and effects is still developing. The concern is about both localised effects where these micro-pollutants are discharged and regional for the toxic pollutants, such as, cadmium, lead, and possibly PAH and mercury which can be transported over long distances. A major potential difficulty with the control of some trace elements is that no threshold concentration can be clearly agreed as acceptable.

Several energy-related activities emit hazardous air pollutants:

- hydrocarbons, such as benzene, emitted fugitively from oil and gas extraction and processing industries. The contribution of each source category varies considerably from country to country and inventories still need to be completed;

- the use and combustion of petrol and diesel oil for transport causes emissions of hydrocarbons (including polycyclic aromatics or PAH) and dioxin and are a major source of energy-related toxic air pollutants. Mobile sources still accounted for 87% of lead emissions in the United States in 1980, largely due to the use of leaded fuel in older vehicles [6]. This share should fall sharply to a few percent by the early 1990s due to the implementation of regulatory requirements for low lead fuels. Similar control efforts are under way in most Member countries to reduce or remove lead in gasoline;

- small quantities of arsenic, mercury, beryllium and radionuclides can be released during the combustion of coal and heavy fuel oil in power plants and industrial boilers. These substances are trace constituents of coal and heavy fuel oil that become airborne during combustion [15];

- mercury, chlorinated dioxin and furan emissions (to mention a few) from municipal waste incinerators are causing increasing concern. Studies are under way in a number of IEA countries to determine the level of contamination around these facilities. Whether they present a serious risk to public health is proving to be difficult to assess.

8. Ambient Air Quality

Concern about air quality is focused on two categories of pollutants:

- those attributed to discharges emitted directly into the ambient air, the most important ones being SO_x, NO_x, PM, VOC and CO;

- those that are formed in the atmosphere by the photochemical reaction, (i.e., in the presence of sunlight), of other precursor air emissions, the most important ones being VOC and NO_x, leading to the build-up of ozone and peroxyacetyl-nitrate (PAN).

Excessive concentrations of these pollutants and of ozone have demonstrated health, welfare and ecological effects as well as nuisance effects (e.g., odours, decreased visibility) which are usually felt locally and sometimes regionally [16]. VOC and NO_x have been recognised as responsible for photochemical smog, such as that found in the Los Angeles Basin. In some cases local and remote rural situations can also be influenced predominantly by up-wind emission sources and long-range transport of photochemical precursors and products, especially ozone and particles.

Air pollutants, as well as precursors of photochemical oxidants, are emitted from a variety of stationary and mobile fuel combustion sources; energy-related activities contribute significant quantities of all of the pollutants cited. For instance, recent estimates show that stationary combustion facilities are a major source of SO_2 and NO_x emissions. Mobile sources (transport vehicles) account for 75% of CO emissions in OECD countries.

Unlike SO_2 or NO_x, which are mainly related to combustion and comprise only a few compounds, VOC are generated by a variety of sources and comprise a large number of compounds with very different toxicities, reactivities, emission rates, etcetera. In terms of anthropogenic non-methane VOC, the transport sector is, in Europe, the second largest source after the solvent industry (40%), with car exhausts contributing 25% and evaporative emissions amounting to 12% [17]. As inventories of VOC sources develop, it is becoming apparent that policies aimed at reducing ozone levels should take into account the contribution of natural sources (e.g., soil and vegetation) of VOC releases into the atmosphere, because human activities may only be responsible for around 5% of total VOC releases globally. But in some areas, the contribution of man-made VOC may be much higher. For instance, in the Netherlands, the contribution of anthropogenic sources is in excess of 90%. In Western Europe, energy-related activities account for 55% of man-made emissions, equally distributed between mobile sources and stationary sources (oil and gas industries). It is difficult to provide universally applicable evidence on the way VOC and other emissions contribute to ozone formation. This is due to the non-linearity of the relationship between precursors and photochemical production, the lack of data concerning VOC emissions, and their chemical distribution [18].

Transportation causes 13% of man-made PM emissions in the OECD countries; 20% is due to stationary combustion sources [8]. Having been relatively well controlled, especially in large, concentrated stationary combustion sources, PM emissions from these sources seemed, until recently, of less concern. In the United States for instance, emissions of PM declined by 54% between 1970 and 1980 [6]. But emissions from transportation activities are an emerging problem. This is the case in particular for the health threat presented by the respirability of particulates from heavy duty diesel engines and their presence near the ground in heavily populated areas. In addition, it now appears that those particulates not entirely removed by the efficient control technologies used for large combustion facilities are the smallest and are highly respirable as a result. They also offer a large surface area for fixing toxic substances, hence causing renewed concern about all sources of PM emissions.

Indoor air pollution due to energy-related activities includes the following emissions: CO from kerosene heaters, wood stoves, unvented gas stoves; NO_x from kerosene heaters and unvented gas appliances; PM and VOC from wood burning and fossil fuel combustion appliances. Worries about air pollutants found indoors and which may affect human health are growing, particularly in the case of radon, but also of formaldehyde, CO, NO_x, PM and VOC. Both energy use and improved energy efficiency play an important role in indoor air quality. Some building energy efficiency measures tend to reduce the rate of air exchange and have resulted in increased concentrations of the pollutants involved. More sophisticated ventilation processes can remedy these problems. Knowledge of indoor pollutant dose-response relationships is still incomplete, but it seems likely that, as research progresses, the need for additional indoor pollution control strategies will develop.

9. Acid Deposition

Acid deposition has been found to be mainly related to emissions of SO_2 and NO_x. These pollutants have caused only local concern in the past, largely for health reasons. However, as awareness of their contribution to the regional and transboundary problem of acid rain has grown, concern is now also focusing on other substances, such as, VOC, chlorides, ozone and trace metals which probably participate in the complex set of chemical transformations in the atmosphere that result in acid deposition and the formation of other regional air pollutants. There are still uncertainties about the precise relationship between emissions and observed damage as well as levels of damage, though acid deposition is considered to have a wide range of environmental effects. Further effects can be spread over large areas due to the long distance transport of the pollutants involved. The most commonly cited effects include:

-       acidification of lakes, streams and groundwaters, resulting in damage to fish and other aquatic life [19];

-       damage to forests and sometimes to agricultural crops. This is generally stated as general air pollution damage to which acid rain may contribute;

-       deterioration of man-made materials, such as, buildings, metal structures and fabrics.

Energy-related activities are major sources of the main identified precursors of acid deposition:

- electric power stations, residential heating and industrial energy use account for 80% of SO_2 emissions, with coal alone producing about 70%. Other sources include sour gas treatment which produces H_2S which then reacts to form SO_2 when exposed to air;

- road transport is an important source of NO_x emissions: 48% of total emissions in OECD countries [20]. Most of the remainder is due to fossil fuel combustion in stationary sources;

- as mentioned in the context of the ambient air quality discussion, VOC are generated by a variety of sources and comprise a large number of very diverse compounds.

10. Stratospheric Ozone Depletion

A global environmental problem is the distortion and regional depletion of the stratospheric ozone layer which was shown to be caused by chlorofluorocarbons (CFC), halons and N_2O emissions. Ozone depletion can lead to increased levels of damaging ultraviolet radiation which could cause a rise in skin cancer, eye damage and be harmful to many biological species.

Energy activities are only partially (directly or indirectly) responsible for these emissions. Though energy activities (fossil fuel and biomass combustion) are responsible for 65 to 75 % of anthropogenic nitrous oxide (N_2O) emissions, CFC play by far the most important role in ozone depletion. The main energy-related sources are CFC used as refrigerants in transport and building air conditioning and refrigeration equipment, or as blowing agents in foam insulation. These applications account for about 60% of CFC uses.

11. Global Climate Change

The concern about global climatic change resulting from the effect of excessive concentrations of greenhouse gases is potentially the most important emerging environmental problem relating to energy. Greenhouse gases are presently classified to include carbon dioxide, methane, water vapour, nitrous oxide, ozone, CFC, halons and PAN. These gases are transparent to incoming short wave radiation but relatively opaque to outgoing long wave radiation. Population growth and mankind's activities are increasing atmospheric concentrations of CO_2 and other trace gases. Major scientific uncertainties surround their climatic impact as well as the time frame of these changes. Climate scientists point out that increasing concentrations of these gases could lead to a global warming of the earth's lower atmosphere, resulting in higher global temperatures, changing precipitation and seasonal patterns and causing rises in sea level. Such changes would have wide-ranging effects on human activities all over the world. At present, it is estimated that CO_2 contributes about 50% to the anthropogenic greenhouse effect. Current knowledge of the role of various greenhouse gases is summarized on Table 2 [21].

Energy activities play an important role in the release of anthropogenic greenhouse gases:

-   fossil fuel burning accounts for about 75% of total anthropogenic CO_2 released, the remainder coming mainly from deforestation and oxidation of exposed soil;

-   combustion of fossil fuels and biomass together account for about 65 to 75% of anthropogenic emissions of N_2O;

-   ozone is the product of reactions involving pollutants from fossil fuel use (essentially NO_x and VOC). The same is true for emissions of aldehyde (itself a greenhouse gas) that leads to the formation of PAN, also a greenhouse gas. Some alternative fuels, such as methanol, reduce carbon monoxide pollution but produce increased aldehyde emissions;

-   in the case of methane, most releases are due to the fermentation of organic matter. The distribution and use of fuels, principally natural gas, may account for 10 to 30% of total emissions. There is little precise data on gas losses between the point of production and the point of use. IEA Energy Balances give an average figure of 2.1% for losses in the IEA as a whole in 1987, but venting is not included. Actual losses in gas distribution systems vary greatly according to their age and condition. In addition, methane is also released during the mining of coal.

A number of other pollutants may be contributing indirectly to global warming. For instance, the main sink for methane is the hydroxyl radical whose concentration in the atmosphere decreases as that of CO increases. There is growing evidence that atmospheric CO has increased significantly over the last few decades and modelling studies indicate that much of the observed methane (CH_4) increase can be explained by a concurrent CO increase. The transportation sector is the single largest anthropogenic source of CO.

Table 2
Roles of the Different Gases in the Greenhouse Effect

GAS	A	B	C	D	E	F
CO_2	1	275	346	0.4%	71%	50±5%
Methane	25	0.75	1.65	1%	8%	15±5%
Fluorocarbon 12	20 000	0	0.0004	5%	2%	} 13±3%
Fluorocarbon 11	17 500	0	0.00023	5%	1%	}
N_2O	250	0.25	0.35	0.2%	18%	9±2%

Key: A. Ability to retain infra-red radiations compared to CO_2.
      B. Pre-industrial concentration (in ppm).
      C. Present concentration (in ppm).
      D. Annual growth rate.
      E. Share in the greenhouse effect due to human activities.
      F. Share in the greenhouse effect increase due to human activities.

Source: *Scientific and Technical Arguments for the Optimal Use of Energy*, B. Aebischer, B. Giovannini and D. Pain, Geneva, October 1989.

IV. TYPOLOGY OF ENVIRONMENTAL CONTROL

Environmental control approaches include actions to protect or manage the environment using policy instruments, such as regulations, or economic instruments. They are generally not specific to the environmental control of energy-related activities. They come in many different forms, although there are some conventional forms that are found in most OECD countries. Direct regulatory instruments, also known as "command and control" mechanisms, are mandatory controls or regulations on activities affecting the environment. Included in these approaches are environmental (air, water and soil) quality regulations, fuel quality regulations, fuel use regulations, emission standards, national emission targets (with negotiated responses), prescriptive technology standards, licensing and zoning procedures and various enforcement mechanisms. Another type of approach is embodied in economic instruments. Some of the economic instruments most relevant to energy activities are: charges, subsidies and market creation (emission trading, liability insurance and liability transfer). Environmental control approaches may also use information and consultation as instruments supporting environmental measures.

Protection of the environment is an evolving task in a dynamic situation. In many places where environmental approaches are already in place, and especially where the results of previous actions have not been considered sufficient, stricter approaches or limits are being adopted. Regulations are also being extended to the sources previously unregulated because of the regulatory difficulties involved (e.g., smaller sources). Specific environmental requirements have been overridden, supplemented or replaced when found to be insufficient to deal with the effects of pollution (e.g., stack height requirements) and as scientific understanding and techniques have evolved, making it easier to tailor the approach to the problem. There can be no universal approach or instrument to ensure environmental protection. Instead, tailoring to the source of the problem is needed. Often, therefore, several complementary and mutually supporting instruments are combined to ensure increased efficiency. On the whole, the instruments used, the limits imposed and the coverage still vary tremendously among countries or even within countries. Finally, the realisation of the interactive nature of many of the pollutants and their contribution to more than one environmental effect is leading to the development of integrated (rather than piecemeal) pollution control approaches.

For regional or global pollution problems, regional and international solutions and co-ordination of approaches are also being sought, leading to much more reliance on the development and implementation of protective action via international bilateral or multilateral agreements. Re-examination of policy instruments with regard to their use in international settings is also under way. In addition, new instruments are being proposed or being applied to facilitate the financing of regional pollution abatement, clean-up and prevention, especially those with transboundary effects.

For the purposes of the development of the factual discussion on the specific effects of environmental developments on energy security, it is useful to have an understanding of the various types of environmental approaches which affect the energy sector. Brief descriptions of these approaches and examples of their application to particular energy-related environmental concerns in Member countries are provided below. More detailed discussion of the effectiveness of these policy instruments can be found in Chapter X.

1.   Direct Regulatory Instruments

(a) Environmental Quality Standards

Environmental quality standards are aimed at the protection of human health or of eco-systems. Indicators of "quality" are precisely defined as allowable average concentrations over a specific time period for a given pollutant in a particular region. The standards are usually based on scientific dose-response relationships, that is, the expected health response resulting from a given dose of pollutant. Critical loads are used in some countries as a basis for the definition of environmental quality standards. Environmental quality standards cover the combined effect from all sources at the point where it matters, that is, at the receptor to be protected. Some form of monitoring of pollutant concentration of the receptor is necessary. But the breaching of environmental quality standards does not provide an immediate indication of the action to be taken, but serves only as a signal that the pathway to the receptor contains too much of the pollutant.

Environmental quality standards include ambient air or water quality standards, as well as biological or exposure standards. In the case of some pollutants, there is a full range of environmental quality standards [22]. For instance, EC Directives for the control of lead pollution set biological standards in terms of lead levels not be exceeded in the human bloodstream and exposure standards in terms of the maximum concentration of lead permitted in drinking water. In addition, an ambient water quality standard defines the maximum concentration of a number of pollutants, including lead, for the surface water from which drinking water is to be abstracted. But the most common form of environmental quality regulation is the ambient air or water quality standards. Nearly all OECD countries employ ambient air quality standards to control major air pollutants (most commonly, SO_2, NO_x, CO, lead, PM), and increasingly they are being used to control hazardous air pollutants and VOC. Some OECD countries have ambient air quality objectives that are not enforceable but represent desired goals. The majority of Member countries also use ambient water quality standards as a centrepiece of their water pollution control strategies. For air and water pollution alike, these standards are defined on a national, regional and sometimes local basis. In the case of surface water pollution, standards may vary according to the river, estuary or bay/coastal water considered.

(b) Fuel Quality Regulations (Product Standards)

As a comprehensive regulatory approach, many countries that adopt air quality standards at the same time set emission limits (described below) and product standards. In the case of fuels, these latter standards are structured around the types of fuels in use (e.g., coal, various types of refined oil products, motor fuels), and are limited by the technical possibilities and the costs of cleaning processes for the different fuels.

At present, varying types of fuel-quality standards are in use in nearly all OECD countries. The range and stringency of standards varies; some of the tightest limits on sulphur content are placed on light and medium fuel oil (e.g., no more than 0.2% in several Member countries) and on heavy fuel oil (usually a 1% limit). The scope of the standards is also broad, extending to the household level in the regulation of coal for heating in Germany (maximum sulphur content 1%) and the United Kingdom (1.3%). Fuel quality regulations for transport fuels include limitations set on benzene, lead content or volatility. Standards concerning lead content in motor fuels are converging towards the lowest level compatible with existing engines not designed to run on unleaded gasoline and requiring new engines to burn lead-free gasoline. Many countries have already decided to phase out lead and others are now scheduled to phase it out. In addition to these regulations, the nature of pollution problems, such as ozone levels, have led to the appearance of seasonal regulations, such as requirements to use gasoline with lower volatility levels in summer in the United States.

(c) Fuel Use Regulation

Control of fuel use has been used as a strategy for air pollution reduction or to satisfy general environmental and health concerns, on a permanent or, in the case of seasonal pollution problems, temporary basis. In some heavily polluted areas, such as Ankara, coal use is restricted, particularly in winter. A fuel use policy is proposed in California's South Coast Air Quality Management District, in an effort to meet strict ambient ozone air quality standards. The usage of certain refined oil products and household use of charcoal may be restricted. Fuel use regulations have led in some cases to outright bans, though usually on a temporary basis during periods of high pollution levels in specific areas.

(d) Emission Standards

Emission standards are widely used in air, water and waste management strategies, usually in combination with other regulatory instruments, such as ambient air and water quality standards. They set a maximum allowable rate of pollution output for each generic type of source (transport, power plants, industry) by type of pollutant. A further distinction between types of point sources is made by fuel and often by technology. Allowance for ability and cost to control is common, which is evident in the application of less stringent standards to older and smaller facilities (e.g., for stationary sources). The most widespread use of uniform technology standards is for new facilities; for example, the United States has had such standards for power plants since 1972.

In many countries, emission standards are being extended from new to existing facilities. The EC also recently passed a Directive on emission limits for SO_2, NO_x, and PM from large stationary sources, which will have the effect of bringing standards for new facilities among its member states to a minimum level of uniformity; emissions limit values for SO_2, NO_x and PM are set for all new plants throughout EC Member countries. For existing plants, overall objectives for a gradual and staged reduction of total annual emissions of SO_2 and NO_x are set (target percentage reductions are country-specific). Similarly, transport-source emission limits are widely used in OECD countries.

Emission standards are most often based on the availability of control and new "cleaner" process technologies and their cost-effectiveness. These standards are closely linked to technology and so are often referred to as technology standards even though they do not actually prescribe the use of a particular technology.

"Best Available Technology" (BAT) or "Best Practicable Means" (BPM) control requirements represent a variation on emission limits/technology standards. Usually legislated for particular groups of polluting facilities or hazards, (e.g., large combustion facilities), BAT or BPM standards can be more, or less strict than emission standards, depending upon the interpretation of the legislative language. In the United Kingdom, for example, until recently there have been no specific air emission standards but rather a requirement for the use of BPM control techniques, which do not establish a firm rate of emissions but rather are based on an administrative definition of the term under the guiding environmental legislation.

Similarly, the term BAT is used in United States air and water emission regulations, with the administrative definition including criteria for cost-effectiveness. However, these BAT standards must be at least as stringent as the uniform national technology standard. The Environmental Protection Agency is required to set emission limits but only on the basis of the available technology. At present, all OECD countries have established, or will have established by 1990 at the latest, emission limits for new large combustion facilities for the major air pollutants (i.e., SO_2, NO_x, PM). While some countries have used the BAT or BPM concept (e.g., United Kingdom, New Zealand and Norway), this effectively acts as a surrogate type of emission standard regulation or, in the case of the United States, as a supplementary, more stringent regulation.

(e) Prescriptive Technology Standards

The most rigid form of environmental regulation is the prescriptive technology standard, that is, a precise definition of which type of control technology or method should be applied in a particular instance. Such standards are rarely used because of their inherent lack of flexibility. These standards are nevertheless implicit in a number of air- and water-quality regulations even though they are expressed as emission limits. For instance, stringent limits for NO_x emissions from vehicles mean that three-way catalysts are needed to meet them.

(f) Licensing

There are two types of licences: first, to construct and/or operate facilities or secondly, to sell. Licensing is a key component in the siting of new facilities, along with environmental impact assessments. For stationary sources, licenses are usually required to begin initial operation of a facility. A pre-condition for the license can be the completion of an environmental impact assessment, which may require considerable study time and effort. A license can be revoked should performance fall below a certain level. Thus, the mechanism serves not only as an initial point of control but also as a means of ensuring on-going compliance with other types of environmental measures, such as emission limits or safety regulations.

In theory, licensing the right to sell the products could be extended to all types of energy consuming products, from vehicles to refrigerators. In reality, this type of licensing is mainly used for motor vehicles, requiring minimum levels of environmental performance for these products. The licensing of the right to sell a particular model of motor vehicle is based upon demonstrated technical performance, usually in laboratory conditions. Licenses are also used to control emission performance of in-service vehicles by required annual or bi-annual testing, to enforce vehicle and technology efficiency requirements. The United States is using licensing procedures for tradeable production and consumption rights of CFC in its implementation of the Montreal Protocol.

(g) Zoning

Zoning applies mainly to the siting of stationary facilities by geographically restricting the location of industrial facilities. Often zoning requires that the facilities in question obtain a license for operation, thus showing an ability to meet selected criteria of environmental performance. Both tools in this way can be used together. Industrial development is guided through zoning to less sensitive geographic locations and, through licensing, it is ensured that certain levels of pollution control are achieved. Zoning or land use planning has long been a way to control impacts in the development of large energy-related facilities. Zoning also allows for the use of differentiated environmental standards that are tailored to the characteristics of different regions.

(h) Safety Regulation

Safety regulation is designed to minimise hazards associated with energy (or other) activities, both in terms of occupational risks and in terms of risks incurred by the public. Measures specifically designed to limit occupational risks are not considered in this study. But in many cases broad safety regulations will tend to concern both those working inside a plant and third parties. In the same way, health and safety regulation aimed at consumer protection, though not defined as environmental control instruments, can overlap with more specific environmental regulation.

Most energy-related activities, and particularly energy production and transformation activities, are controlled by safety regulations designed to prevent major environmental accidents. The nuclear industry is an example of an energy activity where safety and environmental protection concerns have combined to give rise to a comprehensive set of regulatory controls. The risks of fire and explosion in the oil and gas industry have also led to the development of strict safety regulations. Safety regulations are involved in most types of direct regulatory instruments, such as, licensing for new facilities or monitoring and maintenance procedure requirements for existing facilities.

(i) Enforcement Mechanisms

Enforcement mechanisms are fundamental to the viability and effectiveness of environmental regulation. Enforcement policies rely on a variety of legal instruments, ranging from licence withdrawal to criminal prosecution. These enforcement measures often involve an economic component as well as the regulatory aspect. In the case of "non-attainment" areas in the United States, such as areas where ozone levels are consistantly well above the federally set limits, the sanctions that are planned include withdrawal of federal financial support for some types of state projects. Non-compliance fees, for example, are imposed when polluters do not comply with certain regulations. The amount charged usually depends upon the benefits obtained from non-compliance. Non-compliance fees and financial penalties are commonly part of environmental management schemes in OECD countries. Examples of these types of fees are found in Australia, Finland, Norway, Sweden and the United States. The United States has recently applied a more stringent type of compliance fee to hazardous waste. The fee level is intended to cover all the costs and damages resulting from "the prohibited release of hazardous wastes in to the environment."

2. Economic Instruments

Economic instruments have commonly been used by countries to reinforce regulations under the broad mandate of environmental protection [23]. The range of instruments varies from effluent charges and tax differentiation to requirements for liability insurance. The oldest and still most commonly found applications are in water pollution management. While economic instruments are also used in noise and waste management, they are less commonly used for air problems due to measurement and implementation difficulties. Often the instrument is intended to provide incentives to control or reduce polluting activities. Rather than being used in isolation from other regulatory tools, economic instruments are usually used in parallel to enhance the overall effectiveness of environmental control. As such, they form an important link between the market-place and regulatory policy.

(a) Charges (taxes)

Charges include a variety of economic instruments commonly used for the purpose of controlling environmental degradation: effluent or emission charges, user charges, product charges and taxes. These different categories of charges and examples of their use are briefly described below.

Effluent or emission charges are based on the quantity and/or quality of discharged pollutants into the environment. *User charges* are a similar concept except that they are direct payments for the costs of collective or public treatment of pollution. Tariffs can be uniform or may differ according to the amount of effluent treated. Although widely used for water pollution management, effluent, emission and user charges are of less importance to energy production and use. France and Japan have an effluent charge for air pollution.

Product charges are charges imposed upon the price of products which are polluting in the manufacturing or consumption phase or for which a disposal system has been organised. Product charges can be based on some product characteristic (e.g., a charge on sulphur content in mineral oil) or on the product itself (e.g., a mineral oil charge). Product charges are well known in the energy industry. For example, lubricant oils have long been the subject of an EC Directive (1975) on the recycling of waste oils. All European Community Member countries, except Denmark, as well as other countries (e.g., Finland) apply product charges on lubricant oils.

Taxes and tax differentials have been most commonly used as incentives in the area of transport, with the application of higher taxes to more polluting vehicles. In 1985 and 1986 a car tax was implemented in Germany, the Netherlands, Norway and Sweden to encourage the purchase of "cleaner cars". Japan is also expected to introduce a tax differential that favours the purchase of vehicles that meet new NO_x standards. Taxes are also used in many OECD countries to differentiate among gasoline prices, applying a higher rate to the leaded variety. Along with a wider availability of unleaded gasoline, these taxes have been effective in boosting the sales of unleaded fuels.

(b) Subsidies

"Subsidies" is used here to describe financial assistance that is intended to act as an incentive for polluters to alter their behaviour or is given to firms facing problems complying with imposed standards.

Investment assistance to industry is usually intended to aid in the transitional period when new, stricter emission standards are being implemented. Subsidies or financial assistance programmes are used in most OECD countries, mainly for equipment purchases, though some countries also subsidise personnel training or audits. Most commonly, applications are found in water and waste management, although they are also used in air pollution management. The main types of subsidies are grants, soft loans (i.e., below market interest rate) and tax allowances.

Most Member countries provide *financial support for R,D&D* for the development of pollution abatement technologies through a variety of schemes. For instance, Sweden provides prominent support for the development of new "clean" energy technologies; the support is funded by revenues earned from pollution charges. The Netherlands and the United States also provide direct assistance to demonstrate "clean" energy technologies. The United States sponsors the "Clean" Coal Technology Programme in which government funding is equally matched by industry for combustion control technology projects that have potentially high environmental performance. Canada also provides financial assistance on a cost-sharing basis to private-sector technology development efforts.

(c) Market Creation

Markets can be created where actors might buy "rights" for actual or potential pollution or where they can sell their "pollution rights" of their process residuals (recycled materials). Several forms exist.

Emission trading is an alternative to, and in many ways a substitute for, the use of pollution charges. Under this approach, the same type of emission limits exist as under normal pollution control programmes, but a net accounting of performance is kept. If a polluter emits less pollution than the limit allows, the firm can sell or trade the differences between its actual emissions and allowable emissions to another firm which then has the right to release more than its initial limit allows. Under different approaches, these trades can take place within a plant, within a firm or among different firms.

The United States is so far the only country fully allowing for emissions trading as part of its air pollution control strategy. As its air pollution control policy is based on the achievement of ambient air quality standards through the application of emission standards that vary by type of industry or source, emissions trading has been used to provide some flexibility in an otherwise rigid system. Emission trading has also been applied in a more limited fashion in Germany for renovated facilities, or to allow for the licensing of a new facility in a non-attainment area, if reductions are made elsewhere in the same area.

Four different forms of such trading are used in the United States: bubbles, netting, offsets and banking. Bubbles allow a relocation of emission limits between sources, keeping equal total emissions under the bubble. Netting is conceptually similar to bubbles but is applied to modified or renovated point sources that normally must meet more stringent standards. Offsets allow the installation of new point sources in areas which have not met ambient air quality limits, called non-attainment areas, if the additional emissions are offset by reductions elsewhere. Banking allows the storage of excess (above the required) emission reductions through Emission Reduction Credits (ERC). ERC can be used in bubbles, netting and offsets or can be sold or banked for sale to other firms.

Liability insurance creates a market in which risks for damage penalties are transferred away from individual industrial companies or public agencies to insurance companies. Insurance premiums are designed to reflect the probable magnitude of the damage (penalty) and the likelihood that damage will occur. An incentive is created by the possibility of lower premiums, when industrial processes are more secure or result in less damage in the case of accidents. The main example of the use of liability insurance in the field of energy is found in the United States where there are extensive requirements for nuclear power facilities, as well as all other major combustion facilities. In addition, Germany is considering the compulsory use of environmental insurance for all industrial operations likely to pose pollution problems. The instrument is also under discussion or development in Finland and the Netherlands.

Environmental *liability transfer* with the transfer of assets is well established in the United States and appears to be emerging in some European countries (e.g., Germany and the Netherlands). The most dramatic examples of this principle exist in property transfers. In this situation the environmental clean-up for a contaminated site will attach to the new owner of the site, even if the contaminated waste was generated by a previous owner. Likewise the liability for wastes sent away for disposal attach to the original generator of waste. In this way the liability can follow the generator over time; should regulation be implemented at a later date, the generator can retroactively become liable. Concerns over such liability have led to regulation of the transfer of industrial land in several states of the United States, where proof is required that property to be sold is not contaminated.

3. Information and Consultative Approaches

(a) Information Programmes

Information programmes directed at the general public or more specific groups (certain types of consumers or industries) are used to support a broad range of environmental measures and to disseminate technical information. They are most useful when pollution control is related to behaviour (waste disposal, housekeeping and maintenance practices). Information campaigns, such as the European Environmental Year, are also used to heighten public awareness of certain environmental problems and their broad consequences.

(b) Negotiated Responses

Environmental targets, such as total national or local emission targets, are sometimes set on a yearly basis and the means to achieve such targets are then negotiated between polluters and government authorities and may then be translated into legislation. In Japan, agreements are reached between local authorities and industries to ensure that environmental hazards that may result from industrial activities are minimised. Agreed emission limits are often considerably below legal standards. In Canada, multi-stakeholder consultations involve different levels and sectors of government and industry as well as national and local interest groups. The process has been applied to decisions concerning a variety of energy projects, including the exploitation of new oil and gas fields.

Broader consultative procedures set up in Member countries reflect a definite trend towards increased public and non-expert participation in the administrative and regulatory process of the siting, construction and operation of energy facilities, particularly for safety and environmental aspects. The aims and procedures of public inquiries or hearings vary considerably among Member countries. The inquiry usually develops on the basis of environmental impact review or assessment of the development under consideration. Its purpose may be limited to public information, or it can extend to providing a forum for a diverse range of arguments to be expressed and possibly resolved. In some cases, mandatory public inquiries are actually a decisive factor in the decision-making process.

V. FUEL CYCLE REVIEW OF ENVIRONMENTAL CONTROL

In order to understand the full effect of environmental approaches on energy activities and security, it is important to place the major environmental concerns in the context of the fuel cycles, from production to end-use. This viewpoint is useful because, as is apparent from the description of energy-related environmental concerns presented earlier in this study, many of these issues are inter-related. Global climate change, acid deposition and photochemical smog are problems which have some common trigger pollutants, as well as some of their identified sources (notably, fossil fuel combustion) [24]. As a result, their environmental control ultimately poses similar scientific, technical and economic problems, though they may be found on different scales (global, regional, or local) and in different media (soil, water, or air). Rather than compile a list of the environmental impacts of every stage of each fuel cycle which, unless it was possible to quantify the magnitude of these impacts, could be misleading, the review conducted here focuses on which environmental effects are, or are likely to be, the subject of control and how the instruments for environmental control have been applied or are being considered.

The environmental control of energy activities is constantly evolving and as a result, it is necessary to distinguish, as far as possible, between:

- ongoing areas of environmental control, where the sources and effects of pollutants are known and certain environmental approaches have been found to be relatively effective in controlling the problem even though it may not yet be under control in all Member countries; and

- emerging areas of control, where the sources or effects are being assessed and environmental approaches are being tried or considered, but are not widely accepted and implemented.

This latter category would include areas of control for which there is a major trend towards reinforcing the stringency of existing controls or extending them to new pollutant sources as new or improved scientific information is provided and as public or political awareness grows.

It also extends to emerging environmental concerns, for which the effects of certain pollutants are suspected and where there is general uncertainty about control strategies.

The review of environmental control approaches presented in Annex 1 aims at underlining where and how they are, or will be, affecting energy activities, which have been categorised in the following way:

- the oil, gas, coal and nuclear fuel cycles;

- renewable energy sources;

- electricity generation;

- transport, residential and commercial, and industrial end-uses.

A summary of this review is presented in Table 3.

The production and transport of oil is carried out within the framework of a relatively comprehensive set of controls, aimed essentially at preventing and handling accidental occurrences ranging from explosions at oil rigs to ecological disasters due to tanker spills. A major effort is still under way to control less spectacular forms of environmental degradation, such as smaller spills due to shipping operations, in particular through a system of fines and compensation. Oil refining operators face increasingly stringent air and water quality regulations. While some Member countries are approaching the stage where their regulations for SO_2 and NO_x are "technology forcing" standards, others have yet to see their refining industry go through this major technical and financial process. In the case of VOC control, efforts are still limited but will no doubt have to be reinforced in the near future, particularly for the transport and distribution of oil.

Gas production and transport are relatively less affected by environmental control. Problems that might occur during production, treatment and storage, relating both to safety and pollution, have been regulated in Member countries. Recent concern about the contribution of methane emissions (leaks and venting) to the greenhouse effect has not as yet led to any environmental control approaches. This concern also extends to methane releases related to venting in the petroleum production industry and from coal mining.

Coal mining is subjected to a number of controls on siting, management and design aimed at alleviating safety and pollution risks. Despite these efforts, it is apparent that the siting and development of new coal mines does and will encounter severe constraints, particularly in areas with a high density of population. Control measures on acid mine drainage are likely to be tightened, especially as there is substantial scope for development and as stringent measures are not uniformly applied throughout Member countries. The same is true of precautions taken for the transport and storage of coal. Treatment and beneficiation processes are controlled in terms of air emissions and liquid effluents. But the development of more recent operations, such as gasification is likely to exacerbate waste disposal problems, which will lead eventually to more stringent regulations on landfilling and ponding practices [25].

Table 3

Ongoing and Emerging Areas of Environmental Control

Fuel Cycle	Exploration Production	Transport- Storage and distribution	Treatment	Electricity Generation	Transport end- uses	Industrial end- uses	Residential and commercial end- uses
Coal	*Ongoing:* . Siting subsidence, land use and reclamation. . Water quality and acid mine drainage. . Safety. . Waste disposal. . Methane emissions.	*Ongoing:* . Siting, dust control. *Emerging:* . Waste water from coal slurry pipelines.	*Ongoing:* . Waste water and air pollutants (SO_x, NO_x, PM). *Emerging:* . Methanol production. . SO_x, NO_x, PM emissions. . CO_2 from gasification. . Waste disposal from gasification.	*Ongoing:* . Siting. . PM, SO_x, NO_x emissions for new and existing plants. . Thermal pollution. *Emerging:* . Stricter air pollution controls. . FGD and FBC waste disposal. . CO_2 emissions. . Visual air quality. . Radionuclides and heavy metals emissions.		*Ongoing:* . PM, SO_x, NO_x emissions for new, and existing large facilities. *Emerging:* . CO, SO_x, NO_x controls for existing, smaller plants. . FGD and FBC waste disposal. . CO_2 emissions. . Visual air quality.	*Ongoing:* . Fuel quality standards. *Emerging:* . Indoor air pollution. . SO_x, NO_x, PM emissions from smaller combustion units.

Table 3 (continued)

Fuel Cycle	Exploration Production	Transport-Storage and distribution	Treatment	Electricity Generation	Transport end-uses	Industrial end-uses	Residential and commercial end-uses
Oil	*Ongoing:* . Oil spills. . Safety. . Brine disposal. . H_2S releases. . Siting. *Emerging:* . methane releases from venting.	*Ongoing:* . Maritime oil pollution. *Emerging:* . VOC emissions from storage facilities and distribution outlets. . Leaks from underground storage tanks.	*Ongoing:* . Liquid effluents. . SO_x, NO_x, PM, CO emissions at refineries. *Emerging:* . Stricter effluent controls.	*Ongoing:* . SO_x, NO_x emissions. . Siting. . Thermal pollution. *Emerging:* . Waste from pollution control. FGD sludge, de-NO_x catalysts disposal. . CO_2 emissions.	*Ongoing:* . CO, NO_x, HC emissions. . Lead content. *Emerging:* . PM emissions. . Stricter NO_x/VOC controls to limit O_3. . Aldehyde emissions. . CO_2 emissions.	*Ongoing:* . SO_x, NO_x, PM emissions for new, large facilities. *Emerging:* . SO_x, NO_x emissions from existing, smaller facilities. . CO controls facilities. . Waste from pollution control. . CO_2 emissions.	*Ongoing:* . Fuel quality standards. *Emerging:* . Indoor air pollution. . NO_x, SO_x emissions from smaller combustion facilities.

Table 3 (continued)

Fuel Cycle	Exploration Production	Transport-Storage and distribution	Treatment	Electricity Generation	Transport end-uses	Industrial end-uses	Residential and commercial end-uses
Gas	*Ongoing:* . Blow-outs. . Safety. . Siting.	*Ongoing:* . Pipeline siting. . Methane emissions from leaks. . Safety. *Emerging:* . Low level methane emissions.	*Ongoing:* . SO_2 emissions from sour gas. . NO_x, PM emissions. . LNG facilities safety. *Emerging:* . VOC emissions control.	*Ongoing:* . Siting. . NO_x emissions. . Thermal pollution. *Emerging:* . CO_2 and methane emissions.	*Emerging:* . Aldehyde and methane emissions from CNG, LNG and gas based methanol.	*Ongoing:* . NO_x emissions from large plants.	*Ongoing:* . Methane leaks. . Safety.
Renewable energy sources	*Ongoing:* . Siting. . Geothermal air and water quality regulation. . Thermal pollution.	*Ongoing:* . Transmission lines and siting.		*Ongoing:* . Biomass: PM, CO and NO_x emissions for new, large facilties. . RDF: toxic air pollutants.	*Emerging:* . VOC emissions from biomass based alcohol fuels.	*Ongoing:* . Biomass: PM, CO and NO_x emissions for new, large combustion facilities.	*Ongoing:* . PM controls for woodheaters.

Table 3 (continued)

Fuel Cycle	Exploration Production	Transport- Storage and distribution	Treatment	Electricity Generation	Transport end-uses	Industrial end-uses	Residential and commercial end-uses
Nuclear	*Ongoing:* . Siting. . Radon emissions. . Process effluents, tailings releasing radio-nuclides.	*Ongoing:* . Contamination, radiation.	*Ongoing:* . Siting. . Gaseous or liquid fluoride effluents. . Radio-nuclide releases.	*Ongoing:* . Siting, operational radioactive releases. . Low to medium level wastes, disposal and storage. . Thermal pollution. *Emerging:* . Radiation due to decommiss-ioning. . Long term storage of high level wastes.			

Note: The "ongoing" and "emerging" categories for areas of environmental control refer to the situation in most locations in the OECD region.
Source: IEA Secretariat.

The nuclear fuel cycle has long been strictly regulated for safety reasons. Siting, licensing and monitoring procedures remain the basis of environmental approaches to control uranium mining through to nuclear waste disposal, with a complex set of international and national procedures [26]. Though institutional arrangements vary from country to country, they have usually lengthened the licensing process and increased lead times quite significantly and in some cases have not been sufficient to overcome opposition and siting problems. Two other factors are likely to exacerbate these problems, as they will be increasingly involved in the licensing of new plants: decommissioning and waste disposal. Concern may grow as the need of decommissioning increases over the next decades, as will the volume of nuclear waste containing long-lived radionuclides, for which very specific disposal sites will need to be found and controlled.

Renewable energy sources have not been the main focus of environmental control so far in the energy sector, with the exception of hydropower which is subjected to major siting constraints and geothermal production, which is regulated through air and water quality standards. Biomass, solar and wind energy production have space and location requirements that can be specific and compete with other land uses. As recourse to these resources increases, enhancing the scale of possible environmental impacts, more stringent controls could intervene. Overall, there is insufficient data on their wide-scale effects (including for end-uses) and no control approaches have been designed. As in the case of more recently developed techniques, such as coal gasification, there is some reluctance to apply strict regulations that might unnecessarily hinder their development.

New electricity generation from most thermal power stations is subjected to siting constraints. While some problems, such as thermal pollution, are now regulated, others remain unresolved. This is the case of the effects of high-voltage transmission lines, which are still speculative, or of worries about visibility and visual air quality which, though not restricted to electricity generation, does carry the potential of prompting further emission controls. The control of CO_2 releases from power plants remains a major unknown factor in the development of the fuel mix for electricity generation in Member countries.

Stationary end-uses of fossil fuels (in power plants and industry) entail combustion in a broad size-range of facilities. SO_2 is the most controlled pollutant, particularly for new, large facilities. Standards are constantly being extended and upgraded for smaller and existing combustion plants. They include, especially for smaller facilities, the use of low-sulphur oil or coal which will be constrained ultimately by its availability and the cost of desulphurisation. Despite international harmonization (through the EC for instance), environmental control is uneven, especially for industrial facilities. The trend towards stricter standards can lead to the installation of FGD units, the use of new technologies, such as FBC and IGCC, or conversion to natural gas. The situation is even more varied in the case of NO_x controls which are usually more recent. Regulations for more traditional pollutants, such as PM and CO, for smaller facilities are also still limited. Even gas-fired facilities which are as yet relatively unaffected by air pollution control may ultimately need to install SCR or low-NO_x burners if NO_x emission limits were set at below 200 mg/Nm^3, as is planned in Germany. Finally, high-volume solid waste from pollution control is just beginning to attract more attention.

Many Member countries are planning stricter emission standards for SO_2, NO_x and PM for new, large combustion facilities while some countries have already introduced standards for existing facilities. The question of whether or not to apply stricter standards for existing and smaller plants is still being debated in some Member countries. Considerations about the costs and feasibility of extensive retrofit programmes are increasingly conditioned by approaches aimed at achieving overall emission reduction targets. There is a growing realisation that the greatest potential for improving air quality can be found in the existing stock of combustion facilities, including the smaller-scale plants in industry and in the residential and commercial sector.

Both ongoing areas of environmental control (emissions of SO_2, NO_x, PM, CO and surface water pollution) and emerging areas (waste disposal, groundwater pollution and greenhouse gas emissions) pose more difficult problems for coal than for oil and gas. But even fuel oil may no longer be sheltered from drastic control measures, such as fuel bans, as air pollution problems (particularly ozone levels) appear more untractable and natural gas itself is likely to be subjected to increased environmental control, albeit in the longer term.

In the case of transport end-uses of oil products, the drive to get lead out of petrol is progressing. This success should be seen in the light of the fact that the harmful effects of lead were recognised almost as soon as it was introduced into gasoline over 50 years ago. As for other major pollutants in vehicle exhaust, it is clear that in most IEA Member countries, vehicle emission standards for NO_x, CO, PM and lead are and will be further tightened, at a national level and/or through international legislation, such as the new EC Directive ("Luxembourg standards"). This means that the use, mandatory or not, of technologies, such as three-way catalytic converters and oxidation catalysts, will become more widespread and will apply to all categories of gasoline-fuelled vehicles. Particulate emissions standards will be increasingly applied to diesel-fuelled vehicles, the first target sources being light-duty vehicles. Concern about ozone exposure has the potential for further strengthening controls on NO_x emissions and VOC emissions both nationally and internationally. Even so, emission levels remain high because of the sheer number of miles driven (for example, the number of passenger cars sold in Member countries increased by 71% between 1970 and 1986). Fuel or traffic bans (at least for more polluting vehicles in urban areas) are becoming a reality. Recourse to alternative fuels or electric vehicles needs to be considered with a fuel cycle perspective to avoid further environmental degradation, for instance in terms of contribution to global warming.

VI. IDENTIFICATION AND ASSESSMENT OF IMPACTS OF ENVIRONMENTAL MEASURES ON ENERGY ACTIVITIES

1. Energy Security and Environmental Protection

While energy security is and will remain a central element of the energy policies of Member countries, the political, economic and social framework in which energy activities are conducted is constantly evolving. Not all of these changes have implications (either beneficial or detrimental) for energy security in the short term. Rather, only those impacts which significantly affect the diversity of energy sources available and the reliability and flexibility of the energy system in a lasting way should be of concern for energy security. If a longer-term perspective is taken, some of these changes have a significant influence on energy security and broader economic factors. This Chapter of the study first provides the necessary perspective for the analysis by defining the concept of energy security, with particular reference to environmental protection considerations. This preliminary discussion is followed by a review of the observed and possible impacts on energy activities of environmental control measures, leading to an analysis of the implications that some impacts have for the energy security of Member countries.

Energy security requires a reliable availability of energy in physical quantities and at market related price levels which allow sustainable economic development. The main elements for achieving energy security include:

- the existence of physical resources of raw materials and production, transportation, processing and distribution facilities sufficient to meet demand during the foreseeable period;

- the ability to respond to specific short or medium-term energy supply disruptions;

- the ability to reduce the vulnerability of energy systems in a cost-effective manner over the long term, through:

    increased energy efficiency and effective conservation;

.   diversity of energy supply, including fuel type and geographical source;

.   active exploration and development of economic mineral energy resources;

.   timely provision of facilities for producing non-mineral resources and facilities for transportation, processing and distribution;

.   development of new energy technologies;

.   energy and other market structures including pricing mechanisms which facilitate these strategies.

Non-energy factors which can have positive or negative impacts on energy supply and demand patterns and thus on the availability and price of energy supplies include:

-       foreign policy developments;

-       macro and micro-economic developments in non-energy sectors, particularly economic growth in general, industry structures, fiscal policies, international financial and monetary market developments, and economic developments for non-Member countries;

-       international trade;

-       general technological progress;

-       demographic developments and individual lifestyles;

-       general political and social concerns, in particular for environmental and safety reasons.

While their relative importance can change over time, environmental and safety concerns are having a growing impact on energy developments. Both the physical availability of sufficient energy and the ability to use it increasingly depends on whether it can be provided and consumed in an environmentally acceptable way. Therefore, policies which respond both to energy and environmental issues are important for achieving and maintaining energy security. Environmental control measures can have positive and negative impacts on energy activities. On the one hand, they can stimulate the diversification of energy supply, the development of new technologies and improvements in energy efficiency. On the other hand, especially if inadequately conceived, they can adversely affect energy developments, increase costs and financial risks or even exclude certain options.

Because of the great variety of possible causes, the nature and duration of market disturbances, and because of the highly complex and frequently changing set of inter-relationships which determine both demand and supply in the long term, it would be meaningless to attempt to quantify levels of either short-term or long-term energy security. Decisions on how best to ensure energy security have elements that are specific to individual countries and will therefore be made in the context of particular national circumstances. But an individual country's energy security is inevitably linked to global energy market developments. Therefore, effective multilateral co-operation and co-ordination, primarily in the IEA, is an essential element for Member countries' energy security. Recognition of the implications of supply and demand developments and non-energy factors in non-Member countries should also contribute to overall energy security.

2. Scope of Environmental Impacts on Energy Activities

Energy activities are primarily determined by physical and technical possibilities on the one hand and economic and financial realities on the other. As a result, there are two broad *primary impacts* which environmental measures may have on energy activities:

- physical restrictions placed on the development or operation of energy activities, such as fuel restrictions or siting constraints;

- changes in the costs of energy supply and use.

Any change in physical supply of energy, or changes in demand, will be translated into changes in costs and prices. This applies to the affected form of energy and its close substitutes, as well as to competing energy forms and uses. It is ultimately this cost/price effect which will trigger producer and consumer responses to the changed market conditions. In addition, environmental measures and changes in energy activities both have macro-economic impacts, which may, in turn, produce feedback effects. For instance, environmental regulation and expenditure affect income distribution, economic performance and industrial activity, all of which influence energy demand, energy intensity, technological development, expenditure on energy research amongst others. While it is necessary to be aware that energy and environmental considerations should not be considered in isolation but rather as factors influencing and influenced by a broader economic system, the detailed review of such inter-relationships is beyond the scope of this study.

These primary impacts can induce a variety of *secondary impacts* on the many factors shaping energy activities. Possible secondary impacts include:

- changes in supply;

- changes in demand;

- effects on fuel choice and the competitive position of fuels;

- effects on technology choice and R&D priorities.

Obviously these impacts do not form mutually exclusive categories, but rather are inter-related with common feedback effects. However, the distinction between primary and secondary impacts is useful for approaching energy security issues.

Because environmental measures are only one of many factors affecting the pattern of energy supply and use, cause and effect relationships are often blurred by the combination of several factors acting together. In addition, environmental measures are in some cases only modifying the scale or pace of changes in energy activities. The variety of energy situations and environmental approaches in Member countries means that any one impact will very rarely be significant in all countries simultaneously. However, the occurrence of an isolated change in energy activities induced by environmental measures is noteworthy for its implications for energy security if it points to broader effects in the future.

3. Identification of Primary Impacts on Energy Activities

(a) Physical Restrictions on the Development and Operation of Energy Activities

Current Impacts of Environmental Measures. Environmental control approaches have the most direct, immediate and apparent impact on energy activities when such measures are aimed specifically at restricting or preventing the development and/or operation of all or part of a fuel cycle. In the short term, the impact can be more far-reaching if the measure is applied at the beginning of the fuel cycle. Restrictions on production (such as on oil exploration and drilling) have an immediate effect on all other stages of the fuel cycle and are therefore perceived as the most constraining. In the longer term, more limited end-use restrictions (for instance, bans on lignite for domestic heating uses) may also be felt throughout the fuel cycle, with indirect impacts rippling outwards and affecting all related energy activities.

The control instruments which may cause primary impacts on energy activities include fuel-use regulations (fuel requirements, restrictions or bans), licensing and zoning (siting constraints) as well as broad policy measures aimed at stopping, phasing out or delaying energy activities in the course of national energy planning and at the project planning stage. Fuel use restrictions are usually applied in two cases:

-   in a short-term or localised way, during periods when pollution is high, or in areas that are particularly sensitive, often in emergency situations;

-   on a durable basis, when the requirement and use of even the best available technology is not sufficient to achieve environmental quality objectives or when the costs of applying more flexible regulatory or economic control measures is too high or their implementation is impracticable.

Such instruments are being used as a response in a growing number of cases where the scale and untractable nature of temporary or continuing environmental problems are becoming more apparent.

The siting of a broad range of large-scale energy-related activities has been and is being more vigorously contested, though environmental measures themselves may be only one aspect of the reason for the constraint. Within the limits imposed by licensing requirements and zoning, procedures, such as public enquiries or environmental impact assessments, are in fact designed to ensure appropriate siting decicions. Nevertheless, these might not be sufficient to resolve conflicting interests and overcome public opposition. The addition of more and more environmental criteria to those that are characteristic of a particular activity (e.g., availability of water, geology and accessibility) can lead to two possible situations:

- the development of the energy activity becomes impossible due to siting constraints, in which case projects are abandoned or frozen indefinitely;

- the energy activity can still be developed, but only after considerable delay and substantial modifications to the initial project, in which case the impacts are reflected in the costs of the project.

The range of energy-related activities that have been curtailed, delayed and/or modified substantially for environmental reasons at the siting stage is very broad: coal and uranium mining, hydroelectric developments, on-shore and off-shore oil and gas drilling, LNG facilities, synfuel plants, oil refineries, nuclear and coal-fired power stations, a number of energy-intensive end-use facilities, as well as waste disposal and storage. The scale of the impact observed varies considerably according to the activity and the country. For instance, electricity transmission corridors and gas pipeline projects have been vigorously contested in North America, but in the end they have generally been able to proceed, though often with cost impacts from, amongst others, delays, relocation and legal battles. As siting almost always has the potential for causing major, local impacts, the population in the immediate vicinity of a particular energy development often objects to the local inconvenience caused by a project that benefits a much broader population. This sort of opposition causes the most difficulties, particularly when the activity is strictly site-specific and large-scale, as is often the case for the early stages of fuel cycles. For instance, Canada and the United States have announced moratoria on several offshore oil drilling projects. Because of siting difficulties, many proposed hydroelectric projects have been abandoned in the planning stage, as have been some large windmill parks. Though less site-specific activities, such as nuclear or coal-fired power production, can be considered for a broader range of sites, in practice difficulties in siting (even at a local level, such as those due to the NIMBY syndrome) have resulted in cut-backs in planned installed capacity on a national scale in some countries.

The operation of new or existing energy-related activities can be restricted by environmental control measures resulting in temporary or definitive closures. Two situations can arise:

- closures can be mandated when existing environmental requirements (such as those laid out at the licensing stage for instance) are not fulfilled by the operator. The closure is then a sanction for non-compliance, which may be lifted if appropriate measures are implemented;

- new scientific evidence of environmental risk or degradation, or more stringent regulation can make the continued operation of the facility unacceptable. Unless new technical, financially bearable solutions are implemented, the facility may be forced to close down.

The impact of fuel use restrictions and bans is being felt on a broader scale than ever before. All types of end-uses have been affected by these direct impacts. Restriction of transport end-uses are becoming more common, although recourse to fuel restrictions or fuel bans is still usually limited to specific areas during periods of high pollution levels, as an emergency measure. This has occurred in a number of cities where high ambient concentrations of CO, NO_x or photochemical smog are recurring with increasing regularity, particularly in summer or during temperature inversions. The list of cities affected by such restrictions is getting longer, as traffic is growing steadily in most urban areas. Pre-eminent examples include Los Angeles, Milan, and Athens due to their local geography. Temporary control measures result in varying degrees of restriction, ranging from selective technological bans (as in the case of the anti-smog laws in several German Länder where only "clean" cars can be driven) to partial traffic bans for private vehicles (curbs on rush-hour traffic in Los Angeles). Stationary combustion facilities may also be required to reduce their activity considerably during these pollution episodes.

Restrictions on the use of bituminous coal or lignite for residential space heating have been introduced recently in cities, such as Dublin or Ankara which have experienced severe smoke pollution in winter. These restrictions are less extensive than those applied in some cases in the transport sector. Smoke control areas have been designated where only authorised fuels (such as smokeless coal or gas) can be burnt. The United Kingdom has for many years instituted restrictions on the use of coal in designated urban areas to limit air pollution.

Resultant Trends in Energy Activities. Restrictions imposed on energy production and use can have high social and economic costs; recourse to such action is in some cases a symptom of the failure of other regulatory measures to prevent or mitigate environmental damage. Restrictive measures are temporary, stop-gap measures which, when possible, lead to more lasting changes imposed on energy activities, such as changes in fuel choice or technologies which may require longer-term structural approaches. For instance, in Ankara it has been recognised that the situation requires structural changes in a system geared to burning lignite. The necessary effort to change the fuel base of domestic heating is already underway. A gradual phasing out of the use of lignite in boilers and its replacement by low sulphur coal will take place while the expansion of the gas grid proceeds over the next decade (see the upcoming section on secondary impacts).

Such alternatives are nevertheless limited by the availability of reliable and economic alternative energy sources and of proven control technologies. When recourse to both these solutions has been exhausted and environmental degradation (or the risk of environmental degradation) is still considered unacceptably high, any further measures are likely to have a very major impact on energy activities, such as the phasing-out of whole fuel cycles. Public concern about the safety of the nuclear fuel cycle provides instances of broad policy decisions resulting in the gradual phasing-out of nuclear power (as in the case of Sweden, with a national deadline set for 2010) or in nuclear power plants never being completed or even, in some cases, being dismantled before they go into service.

The cumulative effect of local, relatively isolated siting constraints have produced impacts comparable to a national restriction or freeze. This trend is likely to amplify as concerns about other parts of the fuel cycle (e.g., decommissioning and waste disposal) are increasingly involved at the power plant licensing stage. The operation of the coal fuel cycle might be increasingly constrained by the impacts of environmental measures taken at every stage of the fuel cycle especially if actions begin to be taken to limit global climate change. In countries that do not possess indigenous coal resources, such as Sweden, the siting of even "clean-coal" facilities has become increasingly difficult and in cases such as the power station of Oxelösund, impossible.

Future Impacts of Environmental Measures. A number of areas of environmental concern have the potential for producing major, primary impacts on energy activities and whole fuel cycles, well beyond local siting constraints and temporary use restrictions. This is the case of ozone control, for which research indicates that even the application of the best available control technologies for NO_x and VOC emissions might not, in many cases, ensure that acceptable levels are reached. All activities producing, transporting and using fossil fuels would be concerned by measures designed to control ozone levels and especially industries such as refineries, which emit VOC and NO_x. The transport sector, as a major source of both VOC and NO_x, is the focus of much attention and any action being considered is made more drastic by the fact that fuel substitution is difficult and traffic volumes are increasing. In the Netherlands and in some parts of the United States, national or local authorities are considering implementing plans that would substantially modify fuel use and traffic levels. Two recent examples of this trend are provided below, for the states of Texas and California.

In Texas, the State Legislature has enacted a State Land Office proposal requiring state agency vehicle fleets, school district bus fleets and urban transit bus fleets to convert to alternative fuels with comparably lower emissions than gasoline or diesel fuel on a phased-in schedule from 1989 to 1998. Compressed natural gas (CNG), propane and methanol, respectively, are expected to be the most likely fuels adopted in response to the legislation. The State Air Control Board is authorized to broaden the alternative fuel conversion requirement to cover local government and large private sector fleets in urban areas which do not otherwise attain national ambient air quality standards. The full implementation of the legislation could affect over 600 000 vehicles in Texas by 1998.

In California, local authorities in the Los Angeles Basin have recently adopted a plan proposing to gradually phase out traditional transport fuels in favour of "clean" fuels, methanol or electricity for commercial fleet vehicles. The plan also calls for banning the use of fuel oil and coal in most industrial and utility applications by the mid-1990s so that the only authorised fuels would be natural gas or methanol.

Although some limited technological solutions to reduce CO_2 emissions from fossil fuel combustion are available in the near term, energy conservation and improved energy efficiency on the one hand, and fuel use restrictions or bans on the other, are high on the list of possible strategies for limiting global climate change. The potential impact of such measures is many orders of magnitude larger than in any of the cases mentioned above, possibly requiring a major structural adaptation of energy systems as we know them. Coal and to a lesser extent, oil would be affected. While natural gas would be less affected by measures designed to reduce CO_2 emissions, the problem posed by methane leaks from certain natural gas distribution systems is receiving increasing attention. This concern also extends to methane releases relating to venting in the petroleum production industry and from coal mining. Nuclear power and hydro-electricity and, in the longer term, renewable energy sources could appear to be preferred options in strategies designed to limit global warming. Massive substitution of fossil fuel end-uses towards non-carbonaceous fuels and electricity might be necessary. While the analysis of policy options develops and solutions, such as increased energy efficiency, or others, such as reforestation, are being weighed, it is clear that concern over climate change will make it more difficult to decide on the prospects for coal. For other energy sources, it will be more a matter of trade-offs among concerns about greenhouse gas emissions, ground-level ozone pollution, acid deposition or radioactivity, all of which have in the past been strong enough to have direct impacts on their development and use.

(b) Changes in the Costs of Energy Supply and Uses

Current Impacts of Environmental Measures. The broad range of environmental control measures are modifying cost elements at all stages of every fuel cycle. The list below, which is not meant to be exhaustive, provides examples of how environmental measures in the past have acted on the cost equation of new or existing energy activities, as environmental costs have become an integral part of the costs of energy projects. In many cases, the effects examined here reflect the increasing internalization of environmental costs discussed in more detail in Chapter X of the study.

Licensing requirements and more generally, siting constraints, can affect investment and operating costs in a number of ways. The licensing procedure usually entails providing evidence that any environmental degradation caused by the project can be controlled in an appropriate fashion. The applicant must bear the cost of carrying out the necessary research and putting together the scientific, technical, social or economic arguments that are needed. The sophistication of the evidence required can range from a limited environmental impact statement to a comprehensive assessment of the environmental aspects of the projects, including a thorough presentation of remedial measures proposed. A key point in environmental impact assessments is the time needed for and the cost of monitoring the existing state of the environment. In addition, siting constraints may cause substantial modifications to be made on the initial project. These modifications may result in extra costs not only at the design stage, but also for the operation of the plant. For example, it took several years and the successive rejection of three locations before a site was found for the Pego coal power station in Portugal. The site that was approved was not optimal in terms of either proximity to electricity load centres, or accessibility to coal supply from the coastal terminal facilities.

Further cost increases may occur through the lengthening of the licensing procedure. For instance, in Canada environmental factors now account for one year, out of a total lead time of seven to ten years, for major hydroelectric projects. In some cases, such as the James' Bay project, longer delays may occur (an extra five years in this case). These delays unavoidably have a cost that is compounded in some cases by the uncertainty of the outcome of the licence application and a corresponding increase in the financial risk of launching a project.

The installation of environmental control equipment can be made necessary by environmental measures, such as ambient air and water quality standards, point source emission limits, specific control technology requirements or the use of best-available-technology. Both existing facilities (retrofitting) and new facilities are affected. In fact, regulations are usually more stringent for new facilities and for larger ones. Investments in environmental control equipment include:

- add-on pollution control technologies, such as FGD or SCR units for stationary combustion sources, catalytic converters for transport vehicles, and waste water treatment systems;

- equipment or process changes which modify or replace existing systems, such as low NO_x burners for coal- or oil-fired boilers, or conversions to less polluting fuels that require changes in energy-using equipment (gas boilers, engines that can run on lead-free petrol, etc.);

- "clean" technologies, such as IGCC, with inherently lower emissions and improved efficiency which can be applied to new equipment and facilities or, in some cases, retrofitted to existing ones (repowering).

Some of the costs incurred can sometimes be recovered, for example, when pollution control reduces loss of raw materials or with the installation of new, more efficient technologies. This is the case for the refining industry, where gravity-separation, waste-water treatment systems added to meet water quality standards are cost effective due to the value of the oil recovered. But the use of certain control technologies can result in a 1% to 6% reduction in the efficiency of energy use and a corresponding increase in energy costs.

Site rehabilitation and clean-up requirements aimed at limiting environmental impact at the end of the life time of an energy-related facility and in the course of its dismantling are now frequently laid out at the licensing stage. Their cost can then be taken into account at the time of the investment. For many energy activities, site rehabilitation and clean-up operations are relatively recent obligations: for existing facilities, the environmental measures that the operator will have to implement, and their costs, will often only be identified when the problem actually arises. Experience with coal mines points to continued high costs for site rehabilitation due to a general trend towards more stringent requirements, particularly in two areas: visual impact and soil and groundwater contamination. Experience with decommissioning of nuclear power plants or offshore oil platforms is still limited and the corresponding costs can be difficult to estimate.

Environmental controls over waste disposal have increased in scope and complexity over the last few years. As a result, waste disposal can now be considered as a substantial cost item in a variety of energy production and use activities. Waste disposal costs occur when wastes from energy activities or from pollution control in energy activities are either recycled, dumped or destroyed with or without prior treatment, either by the waste producer or by an independent waste disposal company (particularly in the case of hazardous waste). Where the waste can be recycled, its commercial value may offset disposal costs. This is the case of elemental sulphur from sour gas treatment, oil recovered from wastes produced by the oil industry and gypsum from FGD units, though the markets for these products is limited. In the case of destruction (e.g., incineration) or dumping (e.g., landfilling or ponding) more stringent environmental controls and siting constraints are reflected in increased disposal costs.

Environmental measures can also involve increases in costs relating to insurance and liability in the case of an accident affecting human health, economic activity, or eco-systems. Operators of energy activities are increasingly likely to have to pay financial compensation and/or cover the costs of the clean-up. Liability insurance is now commonly used to replace the financial risk of having to bear these costs, for instance, for nuclear power facilities and large combustion plants in the United States. Third party insurance up to limits specified by the state is required for all nuclear plants in OECD countries. The plant owners are required to pay compensation regardless of whether they have been negligent. In recognition that the amounts the plants can be expected to provide may be exceeded in the case of very severe though very infrequent accidents, most OECD states have agreed to be responsible for further compensation up to agreed limits. Countries, such as Germany, Finland and the Netherlands, are considering making insurance liability compulsory. To offset some of these costs, a system of state compensation may exist to provide for cases when the damage would exceed the maximum amount of the operator's liability. This is the case for nuclear operators in countries that have signed either the Paris Convention or the Vienna Convention on civil liability for nuclear damage.

A variety of other economic instruments that are used for environmental control have a direct impact on the costs of energy production and use. Examples include energy product charges or taxes (including tax differentials), such as those applied on coal and oil according to their sulphur content and to gasoline according to its lead content.

The quantification of the exact cost of any of these environmental measures is complicated by a number of factors, such as:

- joint component costs -- it is often very difficult to separate out the costs of pollution control equipment from total production costs, or to assign to pollution control the costs of investments that would have been made anyway for other reasons, e.g., energy conservation, design changes on automobiles, etc. The costs of "clean-coal" technologies which may provide both lower emissions and improved power efficiencies, are difficult to compare with those of add-on control technologies because costs cannot be clearly related only to emission control;

- baseline for incremental control costs -- it is important to establish the baseline from which emission control costs are measured, because different starting points (e.g., current situation versus uncontrolled situation) could give significantly different impressions of cost;

- system-wide effects -- control costs are often only measured within the boundary limits of a plant. However, it is also important to take into account costs of waste disposal or savings from by-product sales. Similarly, in addition to the incremental pollution control equipment costs for a single new car, there are costs associated with fuel and maintenance for the whole population of cars and with changes in the environmental quality of feedstocks and the product mix required at the refinery level;

- retrofits -- control measures applied to existing plants are often significantly more expensive than those at greenfield sites due to built-in plant or site-specific factors;

- cost changes with time -- there is evidence that the costs of individual control technologies, such as limestone-gypsum FGD, have declined over time as technological advances have been incorporated into operating plants and process requirements have become better understood. It is therefore important to use the latest available data to make cost estimates;

- international comparisons of costs -- it has often been noted that cost estimates for the same technology at similar plants differ among countries. As much of this difference is due to differing economic and technical situations and assumptions used, care should be taken in reporting and using costs. However, some differences will still exist among countries due to differences in relative costs of input materials and labour, labour productivity and discount rates.

Resultant Trends in Energy Costs and Prices. Despite these difficulties in quantification, recent sectoral studies show that, as environmental regulations become more comprehensive and more stringent, environmental costs (e.g., for prevention, control, and damage repair) have an increasingly significant share in the overall investment and operational costs of energy activities. The cost of environmental and safety measures can have considerable implications for electricity generation costs, particularly in countries in which the generation mix has a high share of coal and/or nuclear energy. For large combustion facilities in the electricity generation and industrial sectors, a recent IEA study [1] found that estimates assume that costs of environmental control for a broad range of pollutants (e.g., SO_2, NO_x, PM, liquid effluents) amount to 30-35% of the capital cost of new coal-fired plants. FGD and SCR equipment together represent 21% of the capital cost. Experience with the additional costs of retrofit for existing facilities is still limited, but FGD is normally assumed to impose a capital-cost penalty of 10-40%, which could reach 50% for SCR. The debate around retrofit costs is still underway and is in fact central to discussions on the extension of emission standards for SO_2 and NO_x to existing (and smaller) plants. Average resultant price increases will then depend essentially on rate-structure and tax policies. For instance, in the United Kingdom, the government has recommended that the electricity industry should not entirely pass on to consumers the £1.6 billion cost of bringing SO_2 emissions from coal-fired power stations into line with European standards after privatisation. But in the case of the Water Boards (also to be privatised), it was decided that the cost of purifying water supplies should be borne by the consumer.

In the case of transport end-uses, cost increases arise from several factors simultaneously: transport fuels, vehicles (add-on equipment and less polluting engines) and loss of energy efficiency. In the case of gasoline-powered vehicles, while more work is needed to clarify costing methods and assumptions, most estimates report costs of about $800 ($\pm$ $200) for vehicles meeting current United States' standards [27]. Average cost for vehicles meeting proposed European Community standards are generally several hundred dollars lower, although the data are far more variable: for instance, British estimates of costs of meeting EC standards range from £300 to £800[1] when account is taken of the engine modifications necessary to enable a catalytic converter to be fitted. A contributing factor here is that the proposed European standards vary with automobile engine size. It appears also, that all incremental costs are ascribed to emission control and no portion to increased fuel consumption or other performance changes.

The refinery industry provides an important example of an energy activity where environmental measures can substantially affect costs. Environmental controls on the refining industry are becoming stricter in all countries. However, there are still large differences among national environmental legislation resulting in considerable refining cost differences among countries. There is little widely accepted data on the impact on operating costs of environmental laws instituted or planned by national governments and the EC for European refineries in order to comply with fuel quality standards for residual fuel oil, gasoline, gas

---

1.   i.e. U.S.$570 to $1 500 (1989 exchange rate)

oil and effluent standards for air and liquid effluent.

The impact of insurance costs related to environmental regulations on the costs of energy production and use is extremely variable as are the occurrence and magnitude of environmental degradation. Drastic increases in insurance costs are likely after insurance companies have had to face large claims following a disaster. The impact of accidents, such as the Exxon Valdez oil spill in Alaska, on insurance premiums will depend on what decisions on financial compensation are made. This might take some time, as demonstrated by the lengthy settlement for the Amoco Cadiz spill of 1978. In the United States the number of leaking underground storage tanks is estimated at 400 000 by the Environmental Protection Agency, threatening the 80% of the American population that relies on groundwater for their household water supplies. Gasoline marketers in the United States are facing large costs due to new environmental regulations which define financial responsibility requirements. Any tank owner should have a minimum level of $1 million in tank leak liability insurance. Resulting premiums represent such a financial burden that gasoline stations in rural areas which are low-volume outlets, would find so difficult to sustain as to force their closure. By contrast, in the nuclear industry, the number of incidents is small. For the Three Mile Island incident, a negotiated settlement of claims led to the total payment of just over $26 million. In the case of the Chernobyl accident, the offsite costs are estimated by the Soviet Government to be some $8 billion out of the total cost of $14 billion. Even this high level of cost would appear, on a theoretical actuarial basis, to require an annual premium of the order of only $15 000 for a 1 000 MW reactor, as compared to annual fuelling and operations costs of $100 million [28].

A final example of interest is that of the effect of decommissioning costs on the costs of nuclear generation and on the price of electricity. Many utilities are now obliged at the licensing stage to make financial provisions for decommissioning. As with the economics of most long-term environmental issues, the present economic prospects are influenced by discounting procedures. Even considerable variations in discount rates, because of the long period of time over which they are applied, have minimal impact on estimates of the effect of decommissioning costs on the cost of electricity. In the United Kingdom, CEGB policy on decommissioning costs has been to make a charge against the electricity generated by each nuclear power station according to estimates of decommissioning costs, which is then set aside in the expectation that the sum will cover the necessary costs at the date of closure of the station. So far, the total amount accumulated by the CEGB for this purpose is £568 million[1]. In the United States, a Nuclear Regulatory Commission rule adopted in 1988 requires utilities with nuclear facilities to establish decommissioning trusts. It is expected that these trusts will grow to over $60 billion at maturity.

Future Impacts of Environmental Measures. Future changes in costs of energy supply and use due to environmental measures can result either from more stringent measures applied to existing areas of environmental concern, or from new measures still being considered for emerging areas of environmental control. In the case of ongoing regulation, two major cost categories are growing. On the one hand, waste disposal practices and costs could be

---

1.   i.e. about U.S.$1 080 (1989 exchange rate)

substantially modified by the following factors:

-   the volume of waste to be disposed of or by-product to be sold is increasing, which builds up pressure on available dumping sites (the number of which are constrained by siting concerns) while saturating markets available for commercial use of the by-products;

-   the trend towards attaching liability for wastes sent away for disposal to the original generator of waste and towards imposing restrictions on the trade (particularly international trade) of waste;

-   more stringent air, water and soil pollution regulations applied to waste disposal.

On the other hand, investment in some form of environmental control equipment and technologies is rapidly becoming a feature of most areas of environmental control, for both new and existing facilities, as well as smaller plants. Plans exist in most Member countries for more stringent control requirements for SO_2, NO_x, CO, PM and VOC emissions and many micro-pollutants or hazardous pollutants (e.g., lead, radon and dioxin). Such plans are being bolstered by international agreements covering almost all of these pollutants.

In the case of areas of emerging concern, it is becoming apparent that the issue of ozone levels presents a problem of a different sort. The combined control of NO_x and VOC emissions would involve the implementation of control measures in a very broad range of energy activities. Though the corresponding costs would be spread over a variety of energy producers and users, the overall expenditure required for a 1% reduction of photochemical precursors is estimated at 200 million ECU[1] for EC Member countries. Achieving levels compatible with World Health Organisation Guidelines would entail a cost equivalent to 0.2 to 0.4% of total GNP within the EC [29].

Strategies for limiting greenhouse gas emissions are still being discussed, but it seems that in the absence of readily available control technologies, energy costs could be significantly increased, for example, by the burden of equipment and infrastructure expenditure for fuel switching or by the use of economic instruments aimed at reducing the use of fuels and/or technologies which emit high levels of greenhouse gases.

4. Identification of Secondary Impacts on Energy Activities

Physical restrictions placed on energy activities and cost changes may in turn induce changes in energy supply, demand, fuel choice, or technologies and ultimately affect the general economy. The nature and magnitude of these secondary impacts are determined, among

---

1.   i.e. approximately U.S.$200 million.

others, by the following factors:

- whether changes in supply and user costs are significant, compared with, for instance, the total cost of supply or use, or whether they are sufficient to cause secondary impacts, such as changes in demand, technology or fuel choices;

- who bears all or part of the costs or savings resulting from the actions taken to meet environmental requirements (e.g., energy producers, energy users and/or tax-payers). In a market economy, the price of a product reflects the competitive situation and consumers' willingness to pay, as well as the costs passed on by the producer. Therefore, the ultimate price paid by the average consumer might not exactly reflect the cost change experienced by a particular producer;

- whether restrictions placed on siting or fuel use are sufficiently significant, individually or cumulatively, to produce measurable effects, such as the migration or relocation of energy activities, or major shifts in the fuel mix.

(a) Changes in Energy Supply

Energy supply activities are the focus of a broad range of environmental concerns. As such, requirements for them to account for environmental factors have intensified, with notable, though variable effects, on siting possibilities and, to a lesser extent, on production costs.

Changes in production costs relate to the broad issues of industrial relocation and trade. A common concern in both industrial and developing countries has been that, if vigorous national environmental protection measures are established, production costs will increase and the country will be at a competitive disadvantage vis-à-vis nations with lower standards. As a result, relocation of the activity could take place towards countries with less stringent environmental regulation. There could be a trend towards geographical specialisations based on the levels of pollution produced by energy supply industries.

As described in Chapters IV and V of this study, environmental standards vary considerably within the OECD region, with a strong tendency towards increasing stringency. While efforts are made at national and international levels to avoid large differences in environmental standards, the economic costs of achieving a particular environmental quality standard depend, among other things, on the level of industrial activity, its composition and spatial dispersion, as well as a variety of physical and climatic conditions. In terms of energy supply activities, these costs would depend, for instance, on the physical characteristics of the resources exploited. Hence, differences in environmental control costs are unavoidable. In some cases, these costs can be significant, especially if there is an accumulation of environmental constraints. But these costs are often only a small share of total production costs whereas a large number of other factors define the viability of a project and determine its ultimate location.

Siting difficulties, such as those experienced by most large-scale energy supply activities, have had a major impact on the development of the supply infrastructure of many Member countries and have contributed to relocation or migration. For instance, it is widely recognised that siting difficulties have considerably restricted the development of nuclear power generation in many Member countries. France is a notable exception: due to easier siting and a variety of other factors, the nuclear power programme has gone ahead largely as planned. Surplus French electricity is now sold to a number of neighbouring countries. This type of "specialisation" or concentration can occur for any supply activity for which siting opportunities are few and which is not strictly site-specific (e.g., oil refining rather than coal mining).

(b)   Changes in Energy Demand

Effect on Demand of Cost Changes. While environmental costs affect the cost functions of energy producers, they may or may not add to production costs. They may, in fact, also result in profitable process change or more efficient recovery or energy use. Understanding how environmental measures may significantly influence the *level* of energy demand is complicated by the lack of clear instances of major impacts to date. As explained above, this is essentially due to the fact that quantifying precise cost changes due to environmental measures is a difficult process [30]. While the impact on *average* energy costs for energy users appears to be still limited, environmental measures nevertheless hold the potential for further and more significant cost changes. Depending on the price elasticity of demand, if the cost increase is notable, the resulting higher energy prices can ultimately dampen energy demand. Analysis is needed on a sector by sector basis to understand the extent of any such impacts.

The same is true for certain economic instruments used for environmental control. So far, charges and taxes on energy products have been mostly limited to tax differentials on competing fuels, such as gasoline and diesel, or diesel and LPG, as well on the sulphur or lead content of fuels. They have been aimed at directing fuel choice rather than modifying overall consumption levels. Usually fuel charges, surtaxes and levies in existence in Member countries have been implemented in order to increase state revenue. In some Member countries, they are, in addition, specifically used to finance all or parts of policies developed to deal with the negative environmental effects of the fuels used. Though these charges have a stated environmental regulatory function, they are not designed to control overall levels of energy demand. This would only happen if charge levels were raised considerably. Heavier taxes, based, for instance, on emissions of pollutants, such as SO_2, NO_x or CO_2 or other greenhouse gases, would have more far-ranging effects on use patterns and overall demand levels, especially as they would affect a broader range of energy products.

Increased Energy Consumption Due to the Use of Pollution Control Equipment. The use of conventional "add-on" pollution control equipment usually entails a loss of energy efficiency (i.e., the so-called "fuel economy penalty"). FGD systems use energy (for pumping, spraying, conveyors, reheat, etcetera). This is mainly electrical energy which effectively decreases the technical efficiency of the plant. In addition there may be some external energy use, for example gas for the reheating of flue gases. The amount of energy used depends on the type of FGD. The United States Environment Protection Agency has estimated the energy consumption of different FGD systems between 0.75% and 2.7% of gross power generation. For the German industry it is calculated that energy use of the wet scrubbers operating in the country represents 1-1.5% of gross production. This range appears to be representative of recent reports on FGD performance. The energy use of SCR however, is minimal, as the process is based on a chemical reaction with the use of a stationary catalyst and there is no need for flue-gas reheat. In the case of advanced technologies (fluidised bed combustion, integrated gasification combined cycle) any additional energy consumption may be more than offset by increased energy efficiency.

In the case of vehicles, the fuel economy penalty depends on the technologies used to comply with prevailing standards. The fuel consumption of a car equipped with an added-on three-way catalytic converter is 5-10% higher than for a non-catalyst car, but improved design for new models can more than offset this fuel penalty. In the case of lean-burn engine technology, the fuel consumption decreases as do emissions, though this emission reduction may not be sufficient to comply with standards, such as those set recently by the EC for small cars.

Changes Due to Industrial Relocation. It has been argued that Developing countries are at lower levels of industrialisation and have not exhausted the "assimilative capacity" of their environment (i.e., the natural capacity to absorb wastes and render them harmless). It has been argued that they could, therefore, be viewed as attractive locations for polluting activities and in fact could choose low environmental protection standards. Environmental control costs may still be a minor fraction of production costs in many industries, including energy-intensive activities, such as smelting or oil refining. There is, as yet, no evidence of widespread migration of capacity to areas outside the OECD region. There has been some migration of hazardous industries (such as asbestos textiles and building supplies from the United States to Mexico); factors unrelated to workplace health and safety and to pollution control costs are largely responsible for this relocation [31].

(c) Changes in Fuel Choice and the Competitive Position of Fuels

Fuel choices are governed by a number of factors, including price, availability, technology, convenience, cost of use, governmental policy and individual preferences. Measures imposed to protect the environment can affect all of these factors. Changes in conditions of fuel supply and use are reflected more readily in changes in the relative competitive position of fuels than in changes in overall levels of energy demand. Where fuel choice is technically and economically possible, environmental measures have already in some cases contributed to significant shifts at the end-use level and further shifts are apparent in a number of energy activities.

Effect of Cost Changes on Fuel Choice. Different fuels have different environmental impacts and therefore environmental measures will affect their costs differentially. Ultimately, these changes will be reflected in consumer prices and demand. At first, as the cost of environmental impacts are being internalised through environmental measures, it is the price of fuels with the more significant environmental impact which is likely to rise (when and if the costs are effectively passed on to the consumer). As a result, the price of clean, easy to burn fuels over time can be bid up by demand until its price reaches the level of that of a less desirable fuel plus the cost of technology to make it environmentally acceptable. In both cases, as the cost of using a given fuel goes up, consumers will tend to use less of it, or, if they have a choice of alternative fuels, will use another less costly fuel.

The power generation industry is an example of the way changes in conditions of use, including costs, are being reflected by shifts in fuel choice. Electric utilities in Member countries are in the process of evaluating the cost implications of recent environmental standards applicable to new and existing coal and oil-fired plants. In many cases, utilities are still weighing options for providing future capacity. For instance, in the United Kingdom, options considered by the CEGB include the use of (imported) low-sulphur coal, a massive FGD retrofitting programme for existing coal-fired stations and increased reliance on natural gas. In Belgium, industry as a whole must cut its SO_2 emissions by 50% from 1980 levels by 1995. It is expected that this target will require the shut-down of oil-fired power plants, though existing coal-fired facilities will not be affected. In Canada, Ontario Hydro has to meet a 1994 limit of 215 000 tonnes of annual SO_2 and NO_x emissions. Options considered to meet this target include the use of FGD, low-NO_x burners, low-sulphur coal and a greater reliance on nuclear power in the generation mix.

Though economic circumstances have not changed as dramatically as the recent rise in attention to natural gas might suggest, observers point to the changing attitudes of electric utilities towards natural gas. The debate over whether the EC Directive channelling natural gas consumption to privileged uses should be further relaxed to permit and encourage the burning of natural gas to make electricity is a case in point. The emergence of natural gas as an environmentally favoured fuel is a contributing factor in this re-assessment, along with the present surplus of natural gas in Europe. While conversions to natural gas of existing facilities or the planning of new capacity using natural gas require forward planning and do not have an immediate effect on demand and supply patterns, in the case of dual-fuel plants changes in fuel choice are more readily apparent. For instance, in the United States, 10% of the gas burned in 1988 can be readily substituted by residual fuel oil. But some utilities do not switch from gas to oil when it is economical to do so because of local air quality standards. Thus through their effect on fuel choice, environmental regulations are contributing to supporting the relative price of natural gas compared to those of oil products.

Changes in Fuel Choice Due to Restrictions on Energy Production and Use. An immediately observable shift in fuel choice is demonstrated by changes in the balance between low-sulphur and high-sulphur fuels. In the case of residual fuel oil, there is strong evidence that demand has shifted to low-sulphur varieties as a result of recent, more stringent fuel quality regulations. Whereas low-sulphur residual fuel oil use progressed in 1988, international stocks of high-sulphur residual fuel grew excessive and price differentials between sweet and sour residual widened during the year. In the same way, shifts to low-sulphur coal have taken place largely because reducing the sulphur content of the coal burnt is in many cases the most readily available SO_2 control option for plant operators needing to comply with some types of emission regulations.

Those fuel restrictions which have, to date, been essentially temporary measures, have not significantly affected the fuel mix as such, though the trend towards seasonal restrictions in urban areas favours the development of flexible energy systems able to use alternative fuels, such as methanol, as well as fuel oil or gasoline. But a significant potential for change in fuel choice (though not necessarily demand levels) may be the more widespread use of restrictions, such as those imposed in the Los Angeles Basin. This would result in a phasing out of certain fuels on a local basis.

Siting constraints have had an important effect on fuel choice through their impact on the range of energy supply options that are made available and the quantities of various energy forms actually exploited or produced. The balance between fossil fuels and electricity, for uses where these two energy forms are substitutable (e.g., domestic space heating), has probably been modified by difficulties in developing nuclear, hydro, or even coal-fired generating capacity.

Other Effects on Fuel Choice. There are factors affecting fuel choice which are not directly related to price differentials or physical availability and which can also be influenced by environmental considerations. Uncertainty about future costs and availability has in the past proved to be an important factor in fuel preference. The rapid emergence of new environmental concerns and risks, such as climate change, as well as the unpredictability of corresponding environmental control measures, are undoubtedly already affecting fuel choice in favour of environmentally "safe" options. Concern about environmental degradation may also prompt individual consumers to switch to such fuels. Though consumer preference cannot be quantified or isolated from other factors affecting fuel choice, it should not be under-estimated, at least in terms of their potential for tipping the balance when fuel choice is difficult for economic or technical reasons. In the same way, in the case of companies, concern about their public image can also result in choices in favour of "cleaner" fuels.

(d) Effects on Technology Choice and R&D Priorities

The measures taken to ensure environmental protection have been at the root of innovation in environmental technologies, as companies have recognised a large and growing market for new products. Such innovation has occurred both in the private sector, sometimes with government financial assistance, and in the public sector. The recent emphasis on environmental technologies could reduce the level of funds available for other technological developments, such as those in the energy sector. However, it should be noted that both environmental and energy-related funds for R&D grew during the 1970s. The total effort made to develop environment control technologies is greater than is indicated by the proportion of OECD government expenditure for environmental R&D (ranging from 0.6 to 2.9% of total OECD public sector R&D funding, versus a range of 1.0 to 23% for energy R&D in 1980) [32]. This is because there has been significant redirection of energy R&D programmes toward environmentally favourable or "clean" energy technologies, such as "clean" coal technologies. Improving the breakdown and updating of these figures would be useful.

Most effort has been directed towards the installation of "add-on" control technologies. For these, there is almost invariably a net operational or capital cost or both, thus reducing profits and resources for other innovations, such as energy efficiency or improved processes. However, some of the activity -- essentially where changes in equipment design or production processes are made -- has resulted in technologies with lower overall pollution control costs than the add-on type, and with spin-off benefits, such as energy savings. Examples of energy savings are mentioned above in the section on demand. Both private-sector and government energy R&D programmes in pertinent energy sectors have begun to focus at least part of their efforts on these "clean" energy technologies with combined energy and environmental benefits.

The type and form of environmental requirements affect the development and rate of commercialisation of environmentally related technology. For example, so-called technology-forcing regulations, though rarely used, can stimulate technological innovation. In Germany, NO_x regulations were set so stringently that only a technology available from Japan could meet them. Industry in effect had the choice of licensing the Japanese technology or developing its own, which it eventually did. Best-available-control-technology standards can have a similar but less drastic effect or can actually discourage further technological development, depending on how they are interpreted and implemented.

VII. ASSESSMENT OF IMPLICATIONS FOR ENERGY SECURITY

1. Effects on Energy Intensity and the Balance between Supply and Demand

Add-on pollution control equipment generally requires additional amounts of energy to operate and therefore decreases energy efficiency. As discussed above in the section on changes in energy demand, the fuel penalty involved in the use of pollution control equipment is variable but is generally relatively small. Despite the considerable pollution control activity to date, there has not been a perceptible impact on energy intensity in IEA Member countries. Several effects have probably offset any increases that might have been expected. The greatest of these has been the increased energy efficiency and structural changes which have occurred over the same time period for other than environmental reasons and which together have produced the strong downward trend in energy intensity observed during the 1970s and 1980s (which might have been somewhat stronger without the fuel economy penalty of pollution control equipment).

However, effects on energy demand from pollution control equipment might be expected to become discernable in the longer term after decisions to comply with recent national legislation and international agreements to limit emissions of SO_2 and NO_x are implemented. The introduction and further commercialisation of several promising "clean" energy technologies may have an offsetting effect. However, the more recent environmental initiatives to control or abate VOC, respirable particulate matter, and hazardous air pollution have the potential to further add to the energy demand (and cost) for pollution control. Much more analysis on the extent of these initiatives and of the likely commercialisation of "clean" technologies would be needed to determine the magnitude of the increase in energy demand to expect.

Increased energy production costs may result from the installation and operation of control equipment, more difficult siting and licensing procedures and fuel use restrictions. These might in the future become more generally discernable elements in energy pricing. For example, pollution control requirements can be expected to further affect refinery costs, coal processing costs and the cost of using oil, natural gas and coal as boiler fuels. Such requirements will tend to make fossil fuels less convenient and more costly to use. Ultimately, there will be a normal market adjustment and all of these factors -- cost, availability, convenience and preference -- will be reflected in consumer prices and demand.

This might then lead to a shift in demand away from fuels which need costly environmental controls, possibly causing supply difficulties for environmentally preferred fuels. As the internalization of environmental costs continues, environmental concerns have the potential to cause major changes in the relative costs of energy supply and use with corresponding shifts in fuel choice as well as overall demand levelling or reduction.

The factors mentioned above could cause imbalances between supply and demand if energy and environmental objectives were not taken into account together. Further analysis is needed of policy measures that could be considered in order to smooth the implications for energy security of possible sudden or extreme imbalances. For instance, the viability of environmentally favourable energy options, such as shifts to "cleaner" fuels, depends upon adequate provisions being made for the development and long-term availability of alternatives, such as natural gas or methanol produced from natural gas, low-sulphur oil, more efficient or renewable energy technologies and electricity produced from non-fossil fuel generating plants. Because of the possible need to reduce ultimately the use of fossil fuels, environmental approaches designed to reduce the size and likelihood of major accidents are also worthy of detailed study. As such, they could help to decrease opposition to supply options perceived to have high risks, thus allowing for renewed growth of these options. These issues are discussed in more detail in Chapters IX and X of the study which are concerned with responses and policy instruments.

Environmental concern and measures taken to reduce the environmental impact of energy activities are, in some respects, providing major incentives for the implementation of policies supporting energy security. Improved energy efficiency and conservation as well as the promotion of renewable energy and other non-fossil resources are priority options for environmental control that have strong positive implications for the energy security of Member countries.

2. Effects on Diversity and Flexibility of Supply and Demand

The effort that Member countries have made to reduce their reliance on insecure sources of imported oil over the last 15 years is supported by fuel-switching efforts carried out for environmental purposes (from oil to natural gas in vehicles for instance). In the transport sector, more attention is focusing on R&D efforts to promote a higher degree of diversification in transport fuels which would in turn improve the environmental performance of vehicles. Options that could make a contribution probably by the turn of the century include compressed natural gas, methanol and ethanol, especially if the transition can be facilitated by flexible-fuelled vehicles currently under development. Dual-fuel and multi-fuel electricity generation, where economic, can likewise contribute to energy security through the added flexibility provided by fuel-switching possibilities. Increased interest in, and development of, environmentally beneficial multi-fuel systems (used to comply with seasonal environmental requirements, for instance), could augment such flexibility and therefore improve energy security.

By contrast, resistance to the siting of coal, nuclear and hydro-electricity generation facilities and waste disposal facilities, has been a major problem in many countries. This has added to the uncertainties about future electricity planning. Given such siting difficulties, together with an uncertain regulatory situation for many utilities, there is a threat to system reliability in some countries. As available lead times are shortened, this may result in shifts to generating fuels which might then pose energy security problems in the medium to longer term.

Like energy decisions, decisions on environmental protection are often necessarily made under conditions of uncertainty. Resulting actions may subsequently be revealed to have responded to threats to the environment which were not as severe as originally thought. In this case, environmental protection decisions will have costs which may exceed the actual damage. Alternatively, delay of decisions until the precise extent of the threat is revealed can result in more rapid action than would have been the case had precautionary action been taken at an earlier date. For example, if the environmental threat is subsequently determined to be very severe, rapid re-orientation of the energy sector may be required. When such dramatic changes are required, the net effect on the energy sector and energy security may be larger than if precautionary action had been taken earlier (before science had established the true extent of the threat).

Coal is considered to be an important factor in achieving secure energy systems. There has been considerable success in OECD countries in switching from oil to coal. However, the operation of the coal fuel cycle is increasingly constrained by the emergence of a variety of environmental concerns (e.g., acid deposition, respirable particulate matter, photochemical oxidant pollution and, more recently, global climate change), especially until debate about how best to approach controlling these problems is settled (particularly in the case of those which do not seem to have economically and technically feasible solutions). At present, fuel use restrictions are used as a last resort in specific areas where application of the best technologies available and other environmental approaches have been insufficient. These restrictions, therefore, are only very locally and often only seasonally felt and technological developments may further soften their impacts on energy diversity. Nevertheless, as efforts increase to establish an energy system that will supply and use a diverse range of energy forms that are also environmentally favourable, environmentally based preferences for certain energy sources, at least in the short term, might lead to a narrowing of fuel choices, thus reducing flexibility and diversity and posing energy security problems in the medium to longer term.

To the extent that environmental concerns restrict the siting of mining and drilling operations, the development of indigenous energy supplies may be restricted. The use of any economically attractive and available indigenous energy source has considerable energy security benefits for the IEA as a whole and thus has inspired the development of technological solutions for any environmental problems posed by the development of indigenous fuels. These efforts could be expected to continue although, as already stated, acceptable solutions to all of the emerging environmental problems may be costly and long in coming.

3. Implications for Energy Trade and Investment and Dependence on Insecure Sources of Supply

The trend towards the international harmonization of environmental approaches along with other related efforts should help to reduce competitive inequities where they exist. While lack of harmonization was not a major factor in causing the structural changes observed over the last decade, divergence in stringency of environmental requirements among countries, combined with continuing or increasing siting difficulties, could eventually lead to migration of energy-intensive industries such as refineries out of OECD countries. The availability of reliable refining capacity within the OECD region has a significant bearing on the energy security of Member countries.

Given the wide diversity of energy structures among Member countries, energy trade has a significant and growing importance for the energy security of individual countries as well as the IEA as a whole. At the same time, as trade between IEA countries has increased, dependence on potentially insecure sources from other regions has declined. Where international markets exist, as for oil, coal, and -- more regionally -- natural gas and electricity, free energy trade is essential to let these markets perform well. However, a wide range of barriers to energy trade still exist, although they have been reduced in recent years. Environmental measures have the potential to modify significantly patterns of energy trade and investment although to date there is no clear trend indicating this. With the accumulation of environmental measures imposed, particularly on fossil fuels, preferences for environmentally favourable fuels could create additional motivation to relax trade restrictions on these fuels. For instance, increased demand for natural gas would increase exploration and development activity. It could also create pressure to further open up markets and to develop the necessary infrastructure for previously less accessible gas supplies, in lieu of indigenous or imported coal, thus leading to more trade between IEA and non-IEA countries and possible increased dependency on potentially insecure sources. Decreased demand for some less environmentally attractive fuels could force marginally economic production operations out of business.

The economy has flourished for most of the period in which environmental protection measures have been implemented. Energy security, which became a high priority concern after 1973, has also been largely improved over this period. To date, most environmental protection policies have been developed and implemented in a fashion which balanced both energy security and environmental protection goals. Technologies and techniques have been developed which met both requirements without much sacrifice to either goal. The key to avoiding incursions on energy security because of environmental factors may well be careful "implementation timing", in conjunction with full and early co-ordination of energy and environmental concerns. This is the focus of the last four chapters of the study.

VIII. A FRAMEWORK FOR ENERGY AND ENVIRONMENT DECISION-MAKING

The subsequent chapters of the study examines the range of policy measures that might be taken in order to further both the objectives of environmental protection and of energy security. This chapter specifically illustrates a conceptual framework with which policy choices might be made in the interface between energy and environment. An underlying assumption is that balancing and integrating energy and environment objectives is desirable and is a matter of choosing responses which accomplish energy activities in the least environmentally damaging manner and at the least cost. The chapters that follow draw mainly on the findings of the previous chapter of the study: the impacts of energy activities on the environment presented in Chapter VI and the implications of environmental measures for energy security examined in Chapter VII.

The "response framework" proposed is presented in Figure 1. It represents the decision-making process which might be undertaken in considering responses to one or more interactions between energy and the environment, such as acid deposition, urban air quality or global climate change. While highly simplified and mixing decisions taken by the private sector with those taken by governments, the framework helps to illustrate first that there are a range of actions that might be taken (e.g., improving fuel efficiency, substituting fuels, adding control technologies, using "clean" energy technologies, etc.) which can be more or less effective in fulfilling concurrently the particular energy and environment objectives under consideration. This step thus involves determining the effectiveness of the various responses and considers the applicability and potential of the possible policy responses as well as their cost, timing, barriers, limitations, spin-offs, trade-offs and needs for further R&D and demonstration of technology or infrastructure development. It should be underscored that, for purposes of the description and discussion of the various responses, technologies (i.e., both those available today and those under development) are treated as integral to the response or action taken. One result of any assessment of action for the future should include the potential for technology and the need for further development now.

Secondly, the response framework shows that, once an appropriate consumer or producer response has been identified, there is a range of government policy instruments (e.g., information, regulation and economic "market" instruments) which might be used and whose applicability and effectiveness will vary according to the particular response under consideration. As is the case with most major issues, it is unlikely that a single "least-cost" solution can be found to a given energy-related environmental problem. A combination of responses and of corresponding instruments is usually more effective in tackling such complex issues. Finally, as a bundle of responses and policy instruments is selected as an appropriate strategy for dealing with the problem(s) at hand, the framework suggests that there may well be areas where existing policies could be improved or new policies developed in order to enhance the effectiveness of the bundle selected. Indeed, consideration of what has gone before must be the first step in any such analysis, as a myriad of responses and policy instruments have already been applied in the past to meet numerous objectives. In practice, any analysis must include not only how to respond better in the future but also how to improve any existing responses that may no longer be appropriate. In addition, numerous iterations through the response framework at ever increasing level of detail and analysis are necessary before a strategy can be adopted and implemented.

The chapters that follow on responses (IX) and policy instruments (X) attempt to develop in a preliminary way the rationale for the use of the possible responses and policy instruments to formulate balanced and integrated energy and environment strategies and to take stock of what is known about their potential. It must be recognised at the outset that this part is not meant to provide recommendations as to which responses should be chosen to deal with any particular combination of energy and environment interactions. Rather, it is intended to illustrate the state of knowledge on the potential of known responses and policy instruments and the broad range of considerations that must be included in any analysis being undertaken in order to make policy choices. Chapter XI then focuses on some specific areas where policy making might be improved and outlines major areas where further work by the IEA might be undertaken.

Figure 1
Framework for Energy and Environment Decision-Making

┌───┐
│ **STEP ONE:** │
│ IDENTIFY ENERGY/ENVIRONMENT INTERACTION │
└───┘

┌───┐
│ **STEP TWO:** │
│ IDENTIFY POTENTIAL RESPONSES │
└───┘

┌──────────────────┐ ┌──────────────────┐ ┌──────────────────┐
│ Greater │ │ Add-on Pollution │ │ Other[1] │
│ Energy Efficiency │ │ Control Technologies │ │ │
└──────────────────┘ └──────────────────┘ └──────────────────┘

┌──────────────────┐ ┌──────────────────┐
│ Fuel Substitution[2] │ │ "Clean" Energy │
│ and Flexibility │ │ Technologies[3] │
└──────────────────┘ └──────────────────┘

Consider
- Applicability, potential impact, cost, timing
- Barriers (political or institutional), limitations, spin-offs, trade-offs
- Needs for R&D, demonstration, dissemination or infrastructure

┌───┐
│ **STEP THREE:** │
│ IDENTIFY POTENTIAL INSTRUMENTS │
└───┘

┌──────────────────┐ ┌──────────────────┐ ┌──────────────────┐
│ Information │ │ Regulation[4] │ │ Economic Instrument[5] │
└──────────────────┘ └──────────────────┘ └──────────────────┘

Consider
- Applicability, effectiveness, consumer behaviour, micro- and macro-economic impact

┌───┐
│ **STEP FOUR:** │
│ DEVELOP STRATEGY BUNDLE: │
│ policies and instruments │
└───┘

Consider
- Possible follow-up work to refine strategy
- Areas for improved policy making

1. Other responses would be mostly non-energy-related, such as structural changes in economic systems.
2. Fuel substitution refers to switches in fuel quality or fuel type (e.g., from fossil fuels to renewable energy sources), or temporary fuel switching to minimise seasonal or short-term environmental impacts (e.g., from gasoline to natural gas).
3. "Clean" energy technologies are defined here as those which combine more energy efficient processes or operations and reduced pollutant production without necessarily entailing a change in the form of energy used.
4. Regulation here is meant to include the so-called "command and control" and related measures, which are used in protection of the environment (from emission standards to the requirements of environmental impact assessment procedures) and all of those applied to energy security (from end-use efficiency standards to requiring the use of fuels in certain sectors).
5. Economic instruments include the broad areas of taxes, charges, subsidies, and pricing policies, whether used to reinforce regulations and thus increase the overall effectiveness of their environmental protection actions or to subsidise the support of R&D, development and demonstration of new pollution-control or "cleaner" energy technologies.

The framework for decision-making presented here for discussion and instructive purposes is highly simplified and fails to communicate the need for balance and integration in energy and environment responses. In practice, there are often several or many decision-makers. Government goals get carried out in the dynamics of the market place, primarily by the private sector and individual consumers. There are almost always numerous goals (regarding energy, environment, economic development, safety, etc.) sometimes conflicting and other times complementary, simultaneously acting on the decision-makers. The different possible responses illustrated in Table 4 are not really separate and discrete; often they interact. Certain combinations of responses may present the least cost (while still achieving the environmental objective) and yet they may in fact be constrained by other requirements put in place to achieve some of the other goals. Thus, it is rarely an easy process to make decisions regarding the efficacy and comparative costs and benefits of the options available. Simplified examples are used here to illustrate some of the complexities surrounding decision-making in this arena.

For example, the operator of an industrial coal-fired electricity generation facility who must meet new requirements related to the control of traditional pollutants, such as SO_2 and NO_x, will consider possibilities within the context of a great many factors, for example, the purpose and nature of the operations, the specific characteristics of the facility, budget, availability of financing for any changes in operation needed and even overall financial viability at that site. The operator may find that a great variety of steps are technically possible, either separately or in combination. Emissions-control equipment can be added to the combustion plant (e.g., FGD or dry injection of sorbents). Fuel substitution could include switching to low-sulphur coal or to other low or no-sulphur fuels (e.g., oil or natural gas). Reducing emissions by reducing fuel use might be accomplished by more vigorous energy management, process control, process changes, waste heat recovery or the co-generation of heat and power. "Clean-coal" combustion technologies with inherently lower SO_2 emissions could be used, simultaneously achieving reductions of emissions of other atmospheric pollutants and higher energy efficiencies. It is even possible that the decision maker could arrange to finance similar actions by other facilities elsewhere which would have the desired emission-reduction effect for less cost[1] or could shut down the facility in lieu of making the necessary changes.

Individuals, purchasing products or commodities or deciding on a certain course, can have significant impact on the achievement of environmental and energy objectives. Taking the problem of ozone pollution in major urban areas, the same set of generic responses are applicable (i.e., greater energy efficiency, etc.) but the specific actions will be entirely different. Attempts to reduce emissions from vehicles could include increased fuel efficiency of vehicles, substitution of natural-gas based fuels for gasoline in road transport, the use of three-way catalytic converters, inter-modal shifts to mass transit or bicycles, improved traffic management and computerised systems to reduce road congestion. All of these depend to some degree on individual choice while some of them require government or industry actions as well, for example, in the setting up of necessary infrastructures or requiring catalytic converters.

---

1. If allowed by the structure of regulations.

As will be amplified for specific responses in up-coming chapters, it is the economics, the availability of technology, the knowledge of what is available and having sufficient flexibility, motivation and capability to act that will ultimately determine the combination chosen by the individual or facility decision-maker. Any of these factors can become a barrier to achieving the lowest cost combination of actions. Some choices will be eliminated where the limitations are too great. Where they result from prior regulations and other government policies already affecting the facility, it will be important to review whether these are compatible with the new requirements of environmental origin.

Governments consider the magnitude of the environmental and energy problems before them and judge the ability of the different actors and adequacy of the different responses to produce the best possible result under the circumstances. They sometimes then intervene to influence a desired outcome. For governments, the selections actually made by individuals or businesses should not matter as long as there is reasonable certainty that their major relevant objectives, in this case environmental and energy-related, are being met. Limitations on choice could result in higher costs without corresponding benefits. In an effort to increase productivity, governments may try to reduce, wherever possible, limitations which increase costs unnecessarily.

For example, in the case of acid rain and the coal-fired facility, the regulations and standards already applying to the facility might effectively eliminate the possible use of more energy-efficient processes or CHP. Some countries subsidise or otherwise favour CHP plants and the use of their heat in DH systems as strategies for achieving both energy and environmental benefits in industrial and building energy use. However, the cost penalty imposed by the (de facto) requirement of add-on technologies can retard the commercialisation of this less established though environmentally more favourable technology. Strict standards for smaller CHP plants that require the use of FGD and/or SCR are an additional burden to CHP/DH introduction. In taking a balanced and integrated view, a government might decide that some intervention would be warranted if it felt that CHP/DH development was important, but impeded because of environmental regulations. The exact form of such an intervention is also a matter of choice: for example, the reformulation of emission standards, support for R&D of particular technologies or assistance with investment costs. Specific constraints on the employment of the optimum responses and the need for incorporating adequate but reasonable flexibility in meeting environmental requirements are discussed further in Chapter XI.

However, there are further complications which often restrict the effectiveness of a government's decision-making process. A fragmented structure of responsibilities and authorities is found in many countries. For example, responsibilities for traffic signal management, setting emission standards for vehicles, protecting urban air quality and developing mass transit systems may lie with totally different government entities, some local and others national. Sometimes no organisation exists to carry out new responsibilities or for coordinating a diverse set of agencies with partial jurisdiction for a problem. This fragmentation may pose significant difficulties for carrying out certain strategies, such as those involving urban traffic. Consumer decisions and pressures from environmental citizens groups can be equally important. Chapter XI covers the importance of consumer information and of understanding the causes and effects of consumer decisions on energy and environment objectives, the integration of decision-making and need for co-ordination of R&D. The number of complications generally increases with the increasing number of policy goals under consideration at any one time, as is the case with the energy and environment link.

Assurance that environmental goals will be met is important but complicated, however, when there is a multiplicity of environmental problems which must be controlled or prevented. Multi-pollutant analyses are complex and time-consuming but necessary to identify the candidates which appear to offer the best solutions. Otherwise, a method promoted for handling one environmental problem may exacerbate another or solutions to two environmental problems taken in isolation might cost far more than if the two problems were solved concurrently.

Likewise, solving trans-boundary environmental problems often involves bi or multi-lateral governmental efforts in wholly new areas of co-operation. It is increasingly clear that some environmental problems transcend the conventional governmental intervention mechanisms that have been developed for dealing with localised pollution problems. The recognition began with having to cope with acid rain but is even more obvious when considering the risk of global climate change. The adequacy of present international mechanisms to aid the search for solutions to global environmental problems is further discussed in Chapter XI.

The size and extent of an environmental problem causes additional complexities in strategy analysis and development. The major reductions in emissions of greenhouse gases that may be necessary illustrates the need to consider strategies which involve the full range of responses available regardless of the source of the problem. The absence of CO_2-control technologies reduces the possible energy-related contribution to improving energy efficiency and fuel substitution which together may not be enough to achieve the desired result. There may thus be scope and need for resorting to non-energy actions, such as volume-oriented measures, and for using the concept of "emission compensation", similar to that of emission trading, but on a global scale or "global bubble". The analysis of possible responses to climate change would then systematically assess whether somewhat less reliance on the energy sector over others to deal with global climate change might actually result in significantly lower costs in some instances to achieve the same effect.

Achieving multiple goals most often requires a good combination of responses. Yet, none of the possible responses are without their trade-offs, whether it is the additional energy required to produce a higher quality fuel or the increase of solid wastes caused by air pollution control by particular add-on technologies. Thus, the quality of the result will always be difficult to predict because of the complications mentioned above. In conditions of uncertainty about environmental impacts, integration of environmental and energy decision making so that differing points of view are represented to decision makers is probably the best way to insure that likely trade-offs are adequately considered in any action. The approach to energy and environmental objectives should start with agreement on the multiple criteria which will serve as a basis for decision-making. And, as the factors which will determine the optimum combination themselves vary over time, any analysis must reflect the dynamic aspects of the energy system itself.

In recognition of the complexity of the range of possible responses to many different environmental requirements, it is becoming obvious that balanced and integrated responses, incorporating to the maximum extent possible both energy and environment goals, are essential. In order to achieve such integration, analyzing and comparing the full selection of possible energy and non-energy actions must be built into the process of development of policies. It is hoped that in this way that most balanced and integrated, (i.e., least-cost, least-emissions and maximum energy-security) solutions can be achieved. A number of countries and the IEA are at present developing methodological tools which can help the decision-maker in performing full-fuel-cycle, multi-pollutant and multi-objective analyses, for both national and international analyses. The objective of their analyses is identification of "robust" energy and environment systems and technologies which have the greatest leverage for achieving the combined goals. These new and revised approaches, which may allow for more built-in flexibility without sacrificing environmental goals, are being developed and should be encouraged.

There also needs to be a focus on the procedural aspects of decision making, especially as it relates to balancing and achieving energy and environmental goals, to ensure that this integration actually occurs. The development of good strategies depends as much on the introduction and revision of policies as on new technologies. This could push back these limits and make it possible to exploit the full potential of available options to achieve the best possible solutions. Uncertain consumer reactions and choices should also be considered as they are likely to have a strong and sometimes unpredictable influence on energy and environment options. This is one reason why fully integrated approaches to energy and environment policy-making have not generally been achieved. While it might be assumed that individuals and institutions make decisions based on rational, economic or technical reasons, in reality, human and institutional behavioural responses to risk and uncertainty can hinder the implementation of strategies that are based on rational behaviour alone. Any analytical framework used for decision-making should acknowledge and incorporate human behaviour, especially for those responses, such as energy efficiency and fuel switching, which are highly dependent on individual consumer decisions.

Table 4
Illustrative Response Strategy Impact Matrix
(in period before the year 2005)

Environmental Problem	Efficiency[1]	Add-on Pollution Control	Substitution[2]	Clean Energy Technology	Other (Non-Energy)
Siting	+	+	0	+	
Solid Waste	+	-	+	-	useable byproducts
Greenhouse Gas	+	?	+	+	reforestation
Radionuclides	+	?	+	+	
Acid Rain	+	+	+	+	liming lakes and streams
VOCs/Ozone	+	+	+	0	"control" of natural sources
Hazardous Air Pollutants	+	+	+	0	new materials

Key: 0 = no impact, + = some potential impact, - = negative impact (i.e., "bad" for environment), ? = unknown, e.g., technology not yet commercially available.

Notes: (1) Impact of energy efficiency could be significantly higher if targeted.
        (2) Impact of fuel substitution can only be this high if the substitution is targeted but is limited to no higher for retrofit by rate of replacement of existing facilities.

Source: IEA Secretariat.

IX. POLICY RESPONSES

Choices of responses in the area of energy and the environment are largely determined by the technical options that are available or are likely to contribute to reducing the environmental impact of energy activities, while meeting energy needs. These technical options can be broadly categorized as follows:

-        pollution control based on the use of add-on technologies;

-        greater energy efficiency;

-        fuel substitution;

-        "clean" energy technologies;

-        other responses, such as structural changes in economic systems.

It is clear from this list of options that the choice of categories was largely suggested by the purposes of this study and that these policy options are not new.   They involve familiar concepts, even if there are differing definitions and usages of terms, such as   "clean" technologies.   In addition a certain overlap is unavoidable, as "cleaner" technologies often involve some energy efficiency improvement or even partial substitution and that several of these options are often considered simultaneously. For any given energy-related environmental concern, the range of feasible options that can be developed for an existing or new facility may be more limited than the options described here. Further discussion of all but the last of these possible responses is provided below, along with an assessment of their achievements and likely potential, as well as what barriers to their further development and implementation remain. The focus is largely on actions which can be taken over the near-term period (i.e., before the year 2005). The category of "other" responses may be highly significant in changing either environmental conditions or energy security or both. While the discussion of such responses is beyond the scope of this study, they should be included in all actual policy analyses and decision-making.

1. Pollution Control Based on the Use of Add-On Technologies

(a) The development and use of add-on pollution control technologies

Add-on pollution control technologies involve the use of treatment systems with little change in operating or production processes, in order to reduce the environmental impact (emissions to air or water for instance) of an energy activity. Most, though not all, add-on technologies involve end-of-line treatment. A broad range of add-on technologies have been and are still being developed to remedy environmental impacts. Major examples of such technologies used for the control of emissions from mobile and stationary sources can be found in Table 5. As shown in this Table, though add-on technologies are usually originally designed for new equipment and facilities, they can also almost always be retrofitted onto existing installations, albeit perhaps more expensively, where a large potential for emission reduction lies.

Add-on technologies have been extensively used for pollution control throughout Member countries. In the United States, over the period 1973-1980, 80% of all pollution abatement investment consisted of end-of-line treatment. In Denmark between 1975 and 1980, about 70% of industrial pollution abatement expenditures concerned the use of add-on technologies rather than the use of new production processes [32]. Unfortunately, more recent or comparable statistics for other countries or other sectors are not available, but it is reasonable to assume that it is still more common to resort to add-on control technologies rather other responses for air pollution abatement. In the case of most existing facilities, add-on control technologies are in fact the main option for reducing pollution.

The widespread use of add-on control technologies is relatively recent. Taking the example of SO_2 control for stationary sources, techniques for removing SO_2 from flue gases have been available for some time and indeed were used in some power stations from the 1930s. But a major expansion in such control equipment has taken place only since 1971. According to the IEA Coal Research database on world SO_2 control systems, control equipment is currently in place in 434 coal-fired units with a total capacity of over 400 GWt [33]. The use of three-way catalytic devices (TWC) on vehicles started in the seventies in the United States and Japan, following the introduction of pollution regulation. Today, virtually all the passenger cars sold in North America and Japan are equipped with TWC. EC standards have recently been amended requiring larger cars to be equipped by 1992 with TWC and medium and small cars to use such technologies as oxidation catalysts by the same date. This means that at present over 40% of all new cars sold in OECD countries are equipped with catalytic converters and that the percentage will begin to rise dramatically in the near future [34].

The use of add-on technologies has been essentially induced by regulations based on emission standards. Most legislation makes some sort of reference to technology, sometimes implicitly or by using complicated and not always unambiguous terms: "the present state of technology", "the best practicable means", for example [32]. Though the meaning of these terms and the way emission standards are expressed vary according to the country and from one case to another, the massive recourse to add-on technologies for pollution control has been encouraged by the manner in which environmental legislation has been framed. For instance, point-source emission standards, when expressed as an energy-input related standard or as a concentration of pollutant in flue gases, do not encourage recourse to options involving improved energy efficiency.

Considering economic instruments used for environmental control, subsidy schemes have played in some cases an important part in the development and use of add-on technologies. A survey conducted in OECD countries [23] shows that a broad range of grant, soft loan and tax allowance schemes have been specifically designed and implemented to promote traditional add-on technologies, particularly in the areas of air and water pollution control. In a number of member countries, such assistance schemes have been implemented for limited durations to expedite solutions to specific environmental problems, as a complement to regulatory measures. The study notes that there is evidence of a partial shift from supporting end-of-line technologies to more emphasis on the development and use of new, "cleaner" technologies. In fact, some indications exist that financial assistance for traditional add-on technologies used to comply with regulations will be considerably diminished, if not terminated, in the medium term.

(b) The limitations of add-on pollution control technologies

Add-on technologies suffer from a variety of technical and economic limitations. Installing add-on technologies represents, for the operator, a non-productive investment and often increases operating costs. One of the most obvious constraints is that of costs, particularly in the case of smaller applications. For air pollution control, this limitation has become apparent for both stationary and mobile sources. Technical limitations have also been reached as regulations have been upgraded and extended to a broader range of pollutants and sources. Available add-on technologies are not necessarily capable of keeping up with this trend, in terms of both reliability and effectiveness, due to a variety of inherent constraints.

The cost of add-on technologies often does not change proportionally to the size of the facility which they must control and can prove to be a large burden for smaller facilities. While add-on control technologies used for large plants can in principle be scaled down for use in small plants, high costs limit their use in smaller facilities. In the transport sector, the recent debate around the upgrading of EC emission standards for vehicles has highlighted the cost penalty of TWC applied to smaller cars. The cost per car of such devices ranges from 4% for larger cars to 20% for small, less expensive cars [27].

The continued, demonstrated reliability of certain add-on technologies has yet to be established in all locations and applications. In the meantime, the upgrading of environmental standards has accelerated the mandatory use of such technologies. The implementation period, that is the time allowed between the adoption of a standard and its enforcement, plays an important role in the choice of control technology. In the Federal Republic of Germany, for instance, the short time-scale of the FGD retrofit programme contributed to accelerating the widespread introduction of FGD systems. A balance should be sought to ensure that pollution control opportunities offered by the development of better add-on technologies are realized without exposing users to technical risks.

Beyond limitations related to the reliability of recently developed add-on technologies, which are likely to be resolved ultimately, there lies the problem of the effectiveness of these technologies in terms of pollution control. In the case of reductions in the exhaust emissions of gasoline, the limit is already in sight. The newest car models produced in the United States remove up to 96% of the pollutants emitted by engines as compared with those produced before federal controls were first imposed in 1972. The cost and technical sophistication of removing the remaining traces of HC, CO and NO_x would be prohibitively high. In certain areas where the use of TWC and other control technologies is already required, it is insufficient to stem the build-up of overall pollution levels which is primarily related to the increase in the number of vehicles and miles driven. This is particularly evident in the Los Angeles area, which has the world's most stringent emission standards for vehicles.

At a time when a broader range of pollutants are being included in control plans and increasing attention is being paid to the interactions between pollutants, the fact that most add-on control technologies usually only control a single pollutant or category of pollutants is a disadvantage. Taking a cross-media view of pollution, it was noted in Chapter V that many add-on technologies produce waste that may cause disposal problems. While some of these problems (for instance, the disposal of de-NO_x catalysts) still seem remote, others, such as the disposal of sludge from lime/limestone-type FGD, are already real in areas with limited disposal facilities. As the use of calcium carbonate as a sorbent for SO_2 releases CO_2, scrubbers may add another 4% to a power plant's CO_2 emissions. The use of certain add-on control technologies may thus conflict with a policy of minimizing CO_2 emissions. It should be noted that the use of limestone sorbents in advanced technologies, described in the "clean" technology section below, may also increase CO_2 emissions.

Finally there is the question of the fuel economy penalty attached to the use of most add-on technologies. This is largely a matter of scale and may not in many cases be a major consideration at present. But the increased use of fossil fuels and the resultant CO_2 emissions that any fuel economy penalty implies, must be taken into account when alternative pollution abatement strategies are considered.

(c) Future development of add-on pollution control technologies

Add-on technologies, both existing and under development, are likely to continue to make a significant contribution to air and water pollution control. The OECD-wide trend towards the adoption of state-of the-art pollution controls to reduce emissions from a broad range of stationary and mobile sources is still under way. A number of countries have only recently introduced or upgraded emission standards. Others have set more stringent standards for implementation at a future date or will need to introduce controls to meet international agreements (e.g., for the EC Large Combustion Plants Directive, compliance deadlines in 1990, 1993, 1998 or 2003). Though some energy users can use other means, such as energy substitution, to satisfy some environmental regulations, there is a large and sometimes captive market for add-on technologies in a variety of industrial, electricity generation and transport applications. Not only is the retrofit market largely the domain of add-on technologies, but also for some uses, such as vehicles, add-on control technologies are often still the only means of meeting the needed emission reductions without structural or lifestyle changes. In addition, a large number of new facilities will also be using add-on technologies. Though standards for new equipment and facilities are usually more stringent than those for existing ones, they can usually still be met by adding traditional end-of-line technologies rather than through major design changes or new processes.

Beyond those markets for existing technologies, such as FGD or TWC, there are at least two other reasons why the use of add-on technologies is likely to expand further. With the increasing stringency of regulation, particularly for air pollution, even the so-called "clean" energy technologies or select-use technologies [discussed in the corresponding section below] may require the addition of control technology. Until recently, it was believed that advances in combustion technology might actually allow the use of catalysts on vehicles to be eliminated. However, recent experience indicates that low HC and NOx levels are not possible across the range of normal driving conditions through the use of lean-burn technology alone. Lean-burn engines are no longer sufficient to comply with the new EC regulations on air pollutant emissions from vehicles. Research has now turned to the possibilities offered by combining lean burn engines with add-on technologies, such as catalytic converters. Furthermore, the extent to which alternative motor fuels, such as methanol, will need add-on pollution controls has yet to be established.

The other expansion area lies in the growing body of add-on technologies currently in the research and development stages. Table 5 provides examples of promising technologies which are for the most part well-established or have reached the demonstration stage. Research is also under way to reduce further emissions, to control new pollutants or new sources and to increase the efficiency of add-on technologies to reduce their cost. Processes for capturing CO_2 from gases (and liquids) are currently available, such as aqueous potassium carbonate scrubbing, alkanalamine-based solvent and cryogenic separation. The energy and capital investment requirements are high and alternatives for the eventual storage and disposal of CO_2 appear extremely limited. Optimistically, there is hope that technological breakthroughs would diminish the overall cost, if R&D were initiated in a determined way.

Table 5
Examples of Add-on Air Pollution Emission Control Technologies

	Pollutant Controlled[1]	Impact on Energy Efficiency[2]	Status[3]
1. STATIONARY SOURCES			
Fossil Fuel Combustion Facilities			
. Low-NO$_x$ burners	NO$_x$	Variable	Commercial
. Catalytic combustion	NO$_x$, CO	+	R&D
. Furnace sorbent injection	SO$_2$	Variable	Demonstrated
. Off-stoichiometric control	NO$_x$	Variable	Commercial
. FGD (wet or spray-dryer)	SO$_2$	-	Commercial
. Combined de-SO$_2$,/-NO$_x$ FGD	SO$_2$, NO$_x$	-	Commercial
. SCR	NO$_x$	-	Commercial
. Electrostatic precipitators	PM	-	Commercial
. Baghouse fabric filters	PM	-	Commercial
Other Stationary Facilities			
. Floating covers or roofs for storage tanks and waste water separator bays	VOC	+	Commercial
. Vapor recovery in petroleum distribution activities	VOC	+	Commercial
2. MOBILE SOURCES			
Gasoline-Fuelled Vehicles			
. Reduction catalyst	NO$_x$	-	Commercial
. Oxidation catalyst	HC, CO	-	Commercial
. Three-way catalyst	NO$_x$, HC, CO	-	Commercial
. Thermal reactor	HC, CO	-	Commercial
. Engine tuning (ignition timing, air/fuel ratio and mixture preparation)	HC, NO$_x$, CO	-	Commercial
. Exhaust gas recirculation	NO$_x$	-	Commercial
Diesel-Fuelled Vehicles			
. Trap systems	PM/PAH	Variable	Commercial
. Trap oxidizer systems	PM/PAH	Variable	Demonstrated

Notes:
(1) *pollutant controlled*: main target pollutants
(2) *impact on energy efficiency*: positive (+) or negative (-)
(3) *status*: technologies are classified here as still requiring research and development (R&D), demonstrated in some locations (demons.), or available in the market in some locations (commercial).

Source: IEA Secretariat.

2. Greater Energy Efficiency

(a) Contribution to Environmental Protection

The concept of energy efficiency is broadly defined to capture actions applied across all fuel cycles. An improvement in energy efficiency is regarded here as any action, including energy conservation, undertaken by a producer or a consumer of energy products which reduces losses of energy. That is, it may occur not only in the conversion to final energy forms but also in the production of primary energy resources or the transformation to intermediate or final energy forms. Energy efficiency improvements can therefore be implemented at all stages of the various fuel cycles. Greater energy efficiency can be implemented through hardware improvements, such as technological enhancements, or software actions, such as improved energy management and better operational practices, or by a combination of both approaches.

Most energy-efficiency improvements can produce direct environmental benefits in two ways. First, benefits can be related to the reduction in energy input requirements per unit of output, which in turn generally reduces the quantity of pollutants generated per unit of useful work. The absolute environmental benefits derived in this manner from greater energy efficiency will vary with the type of energy being saved (as pollutants vary by energy source), the extent of the efficiency gain and the nature of the energy process. Most importantly, the improvement in pollution levels will vary according to the pollutant considered: some pollutants are fuel dependent (i.e., their emission levels vary with the amount of energy used). This the case for instance, of pollutants, such as CO_2 and SO_2. Other pollutants, such as NO_x, CO or VOC, are technology dependent. The relationship between their emission levels and the amount of energy used is not linear and depends essentially on the technology applied. In some cases, though less energy may be used (for instance, to travel a certain distance in a smaller vehicle), the production of pollutants may be higher.

Secondly, improvements in energy efficiency usually generate secondary environmental benefits through the effect that reduced energy use has on the environmental impact of the whole fuel cycle and ultimately, on the energy system as a whole. The fuel cycle review presented in Annex I shows that the end-use of energy is only one aspect of the environmental impact of energy activities. By reducing the need to carry out a number of related activities, improved energy efficiency can have a strong cumulative effect on the overall volume of energy activities and therefore on any environmental degradation they might entail. For instance, energy-efficient measures can delay the need to develop new energy resources and sites for facilities for their transportation and conversion, which in turn would avoid added environmental stresses. A large number of energy efficiency measures produce both types of environmental benefits. The generation of pollution is often due to some form of waste of raw materials, such as energy. For instance, improved heat recovery and use, not only reduces the requirement for energy input (which reduces pollutant output), but can also reduce thermal pollution problems.

Table 1 in Chapter III specifies the energy-related sources of major pollutants. This table could be used to identify the energy areas where actions to increase energy efficiency would have the greatest effects on particular environmental problems at various stages of the fuel cycles. For example, enhancing the efficiency of natural gas combustion is less significant in environmental terms than enhancing the efficiency of coal combustion processes because the first would only have direct beneficial effects on one major air pollution problem, whereas the latter could directly help to ameliorate four or five major air pollution problems. Similar reviews of the transportation and industrial sectors show that improvements in energy efficiency in these sectors have equally strong and direct environmental linkages. In fact, in the case of CO_2 emissions, increasing the efficiency of the use of carbon-based fuels is considered an essential element in strategies to reduce levels of greenhouse gases. Preliminary studies on the reduction of emissions of CO_2 using the MARKAL model show that greater energy efficiency is in fact a prerequisite to significant reductions.

More detailed analysis is needed of the contribution of various end-uses to emissions of major pollutants, in order to identify areas where energy efficiency improvements would have a significant impact on specific environmental problems. For instance, the large share of coal in electricity generation in the United Kingdom (compared to countries such as Norway) would imply that specific uses of electricity (such as lighting or electric appliances) account for a significant part of national CO_2 emissions. As this example shows, analysis of greater energy efficiency needs to be country and sector-specific; it is indeed under way in a number of member countries. But in many cases it remains to be completed, especially for more recent concerns, such as greenhouse gases and photochemical oxidants and precursors. In addition, the new perspective that environmental objectives are providing energy-efficiency efforts calls for in-depth methodological work in order to ensure that such efforts rest on reliable and coherent assessments and to maximize the contribution that improved energy efficiency can make to environmental protection.

Unlike most add-on technologies developed for environmental control, improvements in energy efficiency can considerably reduce the cost of pollution abatement. Benefits derived from energy savings mean that energy efficiency expenditure can provide investment returns. As a result, pollution abatement strategies based on energy efficiency actions might be more cost effective, especially if the emission reduction due to energy efficiency improvements can be fully credited. This may depend on the framing of pollution legislation (for further discussion of this issue, see Chapter XI, on flexibility and effectiveness in environmental control).

It should be noted that in some circumstances energy efficiency improvements have not been completely environmentally benign. Certain efficiency measures can produce negative side-effects, for example, ventilation problems and radon build-up in insulated buildings, noxious fumes from urea-formaldehyde-foam type insulation, localised noise problems from heat pump compressors in individual homes, increased pollution from the development and manufacture of energy efficient products and the utilisation of pollutants, such as CFC in refrigerators for added insulation. In almost every case, corrective actions are possible and better planning, design, material selection and siting can reduce or eliminate such negative effects in new efforts of future actions.

(b) Limitations and potential of greater energy efficiency

The substantial gains in energy efficiency stimulated by market forces and energy policies since the early 1970s have either had very beneficial effects on the environment or have offset at least significant degradation that would have occurred from growth in energy demand. The potential contribution of efficiency gains to environmental goals depends not only on the actual environmental benefits resulting from improved efficiency but also on the extent of future efficiency improvements. This analysis concentrates, therefore, on examining historical market penetration rates of energy-efficient measures and what motivated their introduction as a useful indicator of the possible magnitude of the introduction rate of future energy efficiency measures with and without application of policy instruments.

It appears that efficiency enhancements historically were undertaken largely in response to higher energy prices or related competitive pressures, in particular where technological innovations allowed such enhancements to be made. That is, the basic motivation for most observed improvements in energy-efficiency was that of costs or of perceptions of future price rises or fuel scarcity. For example, the energy intensity of industry in the OECD decreased between 1979 and 1985 at 3.9% annually, whereas in the period 1986-1988 the rate slowed to 1.6% a year. The former period was characterised in most IEA countries by relatively high energy prices, while the latter period saw prices fall significantly. This in turn appears to have reduced motivations for implementing new energy-management techniques and investments in more costly but more efficient technologies. Likewise, while sunk capital investments are rarely reversed in response to lowered operating costs, some savings already achieved might also have been reversed to a limited extent where the lower cost of energy may have reduced the incentive to continue behaviourial (e.g., housekeeping) actions. In addition, it should be noted that, at constant technological levels, energy efficiency efforts follow the law of decreasing marginal returns, which is independent from price developments and tends to cause an increase in the cost of further investments in improved energy-efficiency. The development of new technology supported, for instance, by standards and regulations or government-funded R&D has an essential role to play in the continued growth of opportunities for greater energy efficiency.

Unfortunately, for the purposes of determining cause and effect relationships, many actions were taken simultaneously in response to higher energy prices and other developments and had little or nothing to do with saving energy. Some energy-intensive industries closed down while less energy-consuming industries opened. These structural changes, as well as production level and fuel substitution changes in the industrial sector, occurred at the same time as enhancements in the efficiency of production, transportation and utilisation of energy. All of these can provide offsetting and sometimes countervailing effects which are different in scale in different countries. (See the example of Japan in the following discussion of the industrial sector.) Thus, such convenient energy indicators as the changes in industrial energy intensity over time referred to above are really too aggregated to isolate the effects of one factor, such as energy-efficient actions taken in the past.

The impact of government intervention on past achievements in the implementation of more efficient technology and energy management techniques is not known with precision. As indicated by Tables 6, 7, and 8 [36], there are very large numbers and types of interventions that have been made by governments in their programmes to encourage energy efficiency. The ideal analysis would isolate the effects of these government interventions from other motivating factors, for instance price. This, however, would be exceedingly difficult to achieve, especially with hindsight when means have not been incorporated to do the necessary evaluation. As these factors will inevitably be quite different for the energy-production and energy-using sectors, the first step is to take a sectoral view to estimate the relative magnitude and importance of the different factors in each sector. Analysis by the IEA, as summarised below, gives some indication of how these factors differ by sector.

Table 6
Summary of Information Programmes

Policies/Programmes	Primary Goal	Market Limitations Addressed	Implementation Environment	General Conclusions
Publicity Campaigns	- awareness	- lack of information - invisibility	- implemented usually during period of high price increases - many countries have continued them throughout	- valuable for awareness creation
Residential Energy Audits	- awareness - motivation	- lack of information - invisibility	- implemented during period of high price increases	- valuable to increase awareness on part of consumers and show cost-effective options - problem with cost-effectiveness of comprehensive audits
Industrial Energy Audits	- awareness - motivation	- lack of information - invisibility	- initially during period of high price increases	- valuable to create awareness - problem of degree of sophistication and technical rigour

Table 6 (continued)

Policies/Programmes	Primary Goal	Market Limitations Addressed	Implementation Environment	General Conclusions
Appliance Labelling	- awareness - motivation - provide unbiased information to aid purchase decision	- lack of information - invisibility	- initially during periods of high price increases	- biggest effect on manufacturing industry - has been cost-effective means to produce energy savings - has worked well as voluntary programme
Transportation Fuel Efficiency Information	- awareness - motivation - provide unbiased information to aid purchase decision	- invisibility - lack of information	- initially during periods of high price increases	- awareness generally high - credibility problems with fuel economy ratings

Source: Based on *Energy Conservation in IEA Countries*, IEA, 1987.

Table 7

Summary of Financial Incentives Programmes

Policies/Programmes	Primary Goal	Market Limitations Addressed	Implementation Environment	General Conclusions
Industry				
. Grants	- stimulation of discrete conservation investment	- financial attractiveness and access - confidence - lack of information	- largely initiated between two price increases in 1970s - some terminated when energy prices started declining	- expansion and acceleration of investment - introduced new technologies - improved financial attractiveness - good benefit-cost ratio, even given recent price declines - wide range of incremental investment - created awareness - administratively complex

Table 7 (continued)

Policies/Programmes	Primary Goal	Market Limitations Addressed	Implementation Environment	General Conclusions
. Tax Incentives	- stimulation of discrete conservation investment	- financial attractiveness - confidence	- largely initiated between two price increases in 1970s - some terminated when energy prices started declining	- easy implementation - created awareness - application process fairly easy for companies - of little use for non-tax-payers
. Loans	- stimulation of discrete conservation investment	- access to capital - confidence	- largely initiated between two price increases in 1970s - some terminated when energy prices started declining	- in practice, small interference in market - mainly easing access to capital (companies in poor financial situation)

Table 7 (continued)

Policies/Programmes	Primary Goal	Market Limitations Addressed	Implementation Environment	General Conclusions
Residential/ Commercial				
. Grants	- stimulation of discrete conservation investment	- financial attractiveness and access - lack of information - confidence - separation of expenditure and benefit	- largely initiated between two price increases in 1970s - some terminated in early 1980s when energy prices started declining	- popular and visible - created awareness - provided information to consumers - improved financial attractiveness - helped develop conservation service industry - poor results in rental market - poorer benefit-cost ratio than industrial grant programmes - administratively complex
. Tax Incentives	- stimulation of discrete conservation investment	- financial attractiveness and access - lack of information - confidence - separation of expenditure and benefit	- largely initiated between two price increases in 1970s	- lower government involvement - mainly used by higher income groups

Table 7 (continued)

Policies/Programmes	Primary Goal	Market Limitations Addressed	Implementation Environment	General Conclusions
. Loans	- stimulation of discrete conservation investment	- financial attractiveness and access - lack of information - confidence - separation of expenditure and benefit	- largely initiated between two price increases in 1970s	
Energy Transformation Sector . Grants, tax incentives and loans.	- stimulation of investment into CHP and for DH	- financial attractiveness		- subsidies effectively reduced investment risks - benefit-cost ratio similar to industrial programmes - rather high incrementality - often lack of utility co-operation

Source: Based on *Energy Conservation in IEA Countries*, IEA, 1987.

Table 8
Summary of Regulations and Standards

Policies/Programmes	Primary Goal	Market Limitations Addressed	Implementation Environment	General Conclusions
Building Codes	- upgrade efficiency of new building stock	- invisibility of consumption - lack of information - separation of expenditure and benefit	- energy efficiency aspect of existing building codes added after major price increases have been maintained even in periods of declining energy prices	- very effective in overcoming market limitations - low cost means of upgrading thermal quality of new building stock - provide long-term signals - easy to adapt to regional/local conditions
Appliance Efficiency Standards	- upgrade efficiency of new appliances	- invisibility of consumption - lack of information - separation of expenditure and benefit	- initially implemented when energy prices increasing	- insufficient information to draw conclusion - most countries more interested in appliance labelling programmes than efficiency standards

Table 8 (continued)

Policies/Programmes	Primary Goal	Market Limitations Addressed	Implementation Environment	General Conclusions
Fuel Economy Standards for New Passenger Cars	- upgrade efficiency of new passenger cars	- lack of information	- initially when energy prices increasing for specific period - some kept after target period	- directed towards manufacturers and importers work in parallel with transportation information programmes - attribution of effects is difficult yet countries have maintained momentum to improve efficiency even when energy prices declining - both mandatory and voluntary programmes have achieved targets

Source: Based on *Energy Conservation in IEA Countries*, IEA, 1987.

Industrial Sector. Structural adjustments and changes in production levels can sometimes be factored out, though rather imprecisely, to illustrate the relative impact of improvements in efficiency in the industrial sector. The illustration in Figure 2 for Japanese industry in the period 1979 to 1985 provides an instructive example [37]. The figure shows that the lower industrial fuel consumption observed in this case actually represents a combination of: first, improvements in energy efficiency which reduced demand for energy; secondly, changes in industrial structure which in this case decreased demand because the structure became less energy intensive; and finally, changes in the activity level of industry (i.e., changes in its output) which increased demand as output expanded. Thus, in this case, overall reductions for efficiency gains and structural changes were greatly offset by increased activity resulting in a net reduction of about 17 Mtoe in industrial consumption between 1979 and 1985. That is, while energy intensity as measured by the TPER/GDP ratio dropped by 3.7% per annum during the period, it is only by chance that this reflects more or less the rate of enhancements in efficiency achieved over the period. As structural changes and industrial output could have been less or even reversed in direction, this example illustrates the importance of analyzing all three factors in any analysis of efficiency gains in the industrial sector.

Figure 2
Example of Changes in Japanese Industrial Energy Consumption

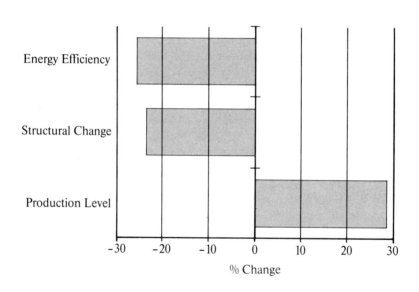

Source : IEA Secrétariat.

Recent unpublished analysis carried out by the IEA for a number of countries' industrial sectors finds that, in general, efficiency gains influenced energy intensity trends (downward) more than did structural changes in the period 1973 to 1985. Production changes, in particular, were found to be likely to decrease overall energy intensity while nevertheless increasing electricity intensity. Regarding the motivations for the changes observed, one estimate prepared for the IEA suggested that government-sponsored energy-saving programmes within the OECD accounted for around 10% of all savings by 1985 in the industrial sector, implying that 90% was due to market effects (e.g., prices and the availability of technologies). However, in the lower energy price environment experienced today, the impact of government-sponsored programmes might be significantly higher as a proportion.

IEA analysis has found that the use of oil is likely to increase if oil prices remain low. Overall gains in efficiency are likewise not expected to continue to the same extent with continuing low energy prices. Although government programmes have acted to minimize them, there are barriers which still remain in the industrial sector to the adoption of more energy-efficient technologies. These include:

-       the invisibility of energy consumption and efficiency gains for all but the largest industrial concerns;

-       the lack of information and technical skills, especially for small and medium size industries;

-       the perception of risk towards adopting newer, innovative technologies or services;

-       the desire to minimize production disruptions; and

-       the access to (competition for) capital for such improvements.

Nevertheless, where certain production changes are being made anyway, for example, those motivated by cost-efficiency and the desire to increase product quality and production flexibility, they will generally also be more energy-efficient and thus will result in lower energy use per unit output than the production process being replaced. For example, the continuing introduction of robotics and computer-integrated manufacturing is likely to lead to more efficient production and less overall energy demand (although electricity demand could increase). Such "incorporated" energy savings can be counted on to contribute to environmental improvement to the extent that industrial activity is robust.

Electricity End-uses. Electricity has the appearance of being environmentally "clean" as it is not evident at the point of use what type of environmental impact, if any, is occurring at the point of generation. Yet electricity end-uses represent an area with possibly high potential for savings that are beneficial to both energy security and environment, especially in light of the recent and continuing strong growth in demand for electricity. Since 1973, electricity requirements in OECD countries have grown by almost 50%, partly as a result of government policies encouraging energy substitution, while oil demand has remained roughly constant. In effect, electricity intensity (i.e., the ratio of electricity demand to GDP) has remained almost constant while energy intensity on the whole has declined 23%. As a result, electricity production now accounts for about 35% of primary energy requirements. The IEA estimates that electricity demand will grow at about 2.3% per year on average up to the year 2005 -

- slightly lower than the assumed rate of general economic growth.

The recently published IEA study of the efficiency of electricity end-use [38], examines historical achievements in electricity efficiency and the opportunities for slowing electricity demand growth by further improving end-use efficiency. A cross section of six technologies representing 65% to 71% of total electricity use and six OECD countries that represent a range of climatic, economic and electricity sector characteristics was selected. In response to market conditions and some existing government programmes, there were significant efficiency improvements in all of the six end-use categories over the past 15 years, even though, as noted above, total electricity demand in these areas has generally increased. In most of these countries, the efficiency improvements are especially evident in refrigerators, where average use per unit declined by 10-20% between 1973 and 1986, and in new buildings, where heat loss from new homes declined by 20-50% or more from the 1970s to 1986. The efficiency of lighting has probably improved by about 10% since the early 1970s, commercial space conditioning systems by over 10% and industrial motors by perhaps 5% or less. In Germany, the electricity use per unit of new refrigerators declined by 39%, and for freezers it declined by 28%.

For each of the six end-use categories, it was found that there is a significant opportunity for additional savings -- perhaps in the range of 10-20% per unit of service -- from economically viable improvements in electricity end-use efficiency. The trend towards improving efficiency on a per-unit basis and resulting electricity savings in new equipment and buildings is likely to continue as the existing capital stock is replaced, although the rate of change appears to be slowing. Because the full achievement of this potential would require the replacement of major existing capital stock, it could be practically realised only over a period of about 20 years or more. Despite these expected improvements, various barriers to efficiency improvements have been identified which mean that there will remain a significant economic potential for even larger efficiency gains which are not likely to be realised in response to the current level of efforts alone.

The barriers remaining to electricity-efficiency improvements are quite similar to those in the industrial sector, described above. In addition, for most end-users the payback period (i.e., the implied discount rate, which in fact reflects the constraints perceived by investors) required to motivate them to act on matters of energy efficiency can be relatively short. There is also the problem of separating the expenditure for the more efficient item from the receipt of the benefit of this expenditure, as is found for example, in landlord/tenant situations [39].

The question remains whether additional workable government, utility or other policies could be developed that would, in fact, help to overcome the remaining barriers and result in the fuller realisation of these objectives. Evaluation of the spectrum of different policies or programmes to increase end-use efficiency which have been implemented by various IEA governments or utilities indicates that a number of them have been effective with regards to promoting electricity efficiency, including: pricing policies, information programmes, incentives and regulations, among others. Finally, in some countries utilities have played an important role, depending on the financial and other characteristics of individual utility systems. Close cooperation among governments and utilities has been found to be the key to designing and implementing effective policies to improve end-use efficiency.

The IEA's analysis considered what particular additional action might be taken to accelerate improvements in the efficiency of electricity end-use. A variety of measures were found to be effective in promoting improved energy efficiency in general. Two of the most important steps for the electricity end-use sector that are open to governments were found to be:

-   ensuring that electricity prices (and metering practices) provide correct market signals to users;

-   establishing a regulatory framework for utilities that, to the extent possible, provides economic incentives for utilities to encourage end-use efficiency improvements when such improvements would benefit the utility system as a whole, including the utilities involved and their customers.

Vehicle efficiency. Vehicle efficiency is an obvious area of concern for both environment and energy security because, unlike other sectors of the OECD economy (i.e., the industry, household, commercial and the electric utility sectors), the consumption of oil in the transport sector rose significantly between 1973 and 1987. This increase, combined with declining oil consumption in the other sectors, raised the transport sector's share of OECD total final oil consumption from 38% in 1973 to 57% in 1987. Road transport is of particular concern since its consumption accounts for over 80% of oil consumed in the transport sector. It is also a high priority target for environmental protection efforts since it contributes substantially to air quality problems, acid rain and global climate change.

Recent unpublished analysis by the IEA examines and explains the trends and the prospects for the future in terms of changes in the number of cars in use, average distance travelled per car and average car fuel efficiency for three representative countries; the United States, Germany and Japan. This analysis suggests that observations of these trends made in a 1984 IEA study on passenger car efficiency [40] are even more pronounced, that is, that the rate of improvement in fuel efficiency has continued to decline significantly. In the more recent work, two separate measures of fuel efficiency were examined: the overall average car fleet efficiency (i.e., the fuel efficiency of all cars on the road) and the average new car fuel efficiency. There were significant fuel efficiency gains in new passenger motor vehicles over the period 1973 to 1986 in all three countries studied and particularly in the United States. However, the rate of improvement in new car fuel efficiency declined in all three countries after 1983, with the trend even being reversed in Japan after 1984. The reasons for this slow-down in improvement, while many and varied, probably include increasing cost of incremental fuel efficiency improvements (least-cost options will have been implemented first), reduced economic incentive because of lower oil product prices and the increased market share of larger and more powerful cars.

As far as overall car-fleet fuel efficiency is concerned, significant improvements were recorded only in the United States. To a large measure, this is a reflection of the fact that United States cars of 1973 vintage were 60% less fuel efficient than those in Japan and Germany. Consequently, in the catching-up process, large efficiency improvements were possible and implemented, thus improving significantly the average car-fleet fuel efficiency. One study performed for the IEA estimated that government-sponsored energy savings programmes within the OECD accounted for almost 50% of fuel savings in the transport area in North America to date (driven primarily by the introduction of automobile efficiency standards in the United States). In contrast to the United States, however, the increased fuel efficiency of new cars which was achieved did not translate into significant improvements in car-fleet fuel efficiency in Japan and Germany because of offsetting factors, such as changing driving habits, a trend towards purchasing larger cars and increased road congestion.

Fuel demand for passenger motor travel is expected to continue to increase as it has since 1973, although demographic factors and saturation effects could eventually moderate these increases. Numerous small efficiency improvements in vehicle and engine design will probably continue but they are not expected to overtake the increase in fuel demand. In the United States, there is the potential for some more improvement in car fleet fuel efficiency. However, it is not clear how much of this potential will be realized. Fuel demand for private passenger motor vehicle transport increased in 1986 and 1987 and fuel efficiency of new cars has been stagnant since about 1986. The trends that have been evident in Japan and Germany in recent years could be surfacing also in the United States as the catch-up phase of its automotive industry is completed. The recent decision to increase the average efficiency of new cars to 27.50 mpg[1] in 1990 models should have some positive effect.

Numerous studies have recently attempted to survey the technical potential for increased vehicle fuel efficiency. For instance, the United States Office of Technology Assessment has concluded that the upcoming car fleet could achieve an average 33 mpg[2] fuel efficiency rate by 1995, without hampering performance or forcing individuals to move to smaller vehicles, if manufacturers adopted more widely technologies already in use in some car models. A recent study based on figures from the U.S. Department of Energy puts the efficiency figure for 1995 at 31.6 mpg[3] on the same basis while taking into account consumer willingness to pay for increased fuel economy [41]. But while these technologies might be cost-effective, they may not be attractive to consumers or be provided by car manufacturers unless there are additional incentives established. Without such incentives the study suggested that new car fleet efficiency might only be a few miles per gallon over the 1987 efficiency of around 27 mpg[4].

In assessing the potential environmental benefits to be gained from greater fuel efficiency in vehicles, it will be important to include the factors mentioned above. That is, trends in vehicle miles travelled, car size and the effects of congestion may be equally important or more so in determining the fuel usage (and emission levels) in this sector. An update of this analysis including improved data and broader analysis would be needed before even a preliminary estimate of the likely contribution of this sector to environmental objectives could be provided. Work ongoing within the IEA, that is, the update of the 1984 passenger car efficiency study, should be able to contribute to such an assessment. More analysis would be also needed comparing the options of fuel substitution and intermodal shifts with fuel efficiency opportunities.

Residential/Commercial Sector *(non-electricity end-uses).* In addition to the potential for electricity savings in equipment used in the residential and commercial sectors, which was already covered above, there is significant potential for such efficiency improvements as

---

1.   i.e. 8.5 l/100 km.

2.   i.e. 7.1 l/100 km.

3.   i.e. 7.5 l/100 km.

4.   i.e. 8.7 l/100 km.

building-shell enhancements and high-efficiency gas furnaces. However, a variety of barriers exist which might hamper the full exploitation of the economic potential of these measures or at least slow down their market introduction. The most important are lack of consumer awareness about potential savings, low technical skills and constraints in disposable income. Furthermore, the split in responsibility in some countries in the residential rental sector for the energy efficiency investment (landlord responsibility) and the operating costs associated with the use of energy (tenant responsibility) is a remaining barrier to the widespread introduction of efficient equipment in this sector. The lack of technical skills in the commercial sector hinders the application of efficient technologies, especially for small enterprises which are often not aware of the possible efficiency improvements and whose energy costs are only a small proportion of their operational costs, as is often the case. In the residential and commercial sector, the most promising gains lie in the incorporation of improved energy efficiency into new structures and equipment in changes of operational procedures and habits.

Electricity Transformation Sector. The bulk of energy transformation losses before final consumption are in the electricity sector. The 1987 IEA conservation study [36], moreover, indicates that electricity generating efficiency has improved very slowly. There are two direct causes. First, as steam turbines are the prime movers in thermal plants, the efficiency of electricity generation is limited ultimately to the efficiency of the heat engine itself. Most of the losses therefore are intrinsic in nature. Secondly, the average lifetime of a conventional steam power plant, with a high quality maintenance programme, is 20 to 30 years. The 1980s were characterised by a significant overcapacity in many industrialised countries, so that the relatively low rate of new plant additions has not over the last twenty years given rise to a significant gain in average steam plant efficiency. The larger share of coal plants during this period reinforces this slow-down as discussed below.

The highest efficiency new single-cycle fossil fuel plants are those fuelled with natural gas or distillate fuel oil and have thermal efficiencies of around 40% under optimal load conditions. Efficient new coal units normally operate in the range of 33-35%. Steam plants fuelled by brown coals or peat tend to have lower efficiencies. Combustion turbine-based combined-cycle plants can be operated with efficiencies of from 45% to over 50%, depending upon the configuration and application. More frequently such units would operate with efficiencies of 40-44%. Combined cycle plants operated as combined heat and power (CHP) plants on the electricity grid can have significantly higher efficiencies depending on the heat/electricity ratio adopted. The use of CHP to provide district heating, in appropriate load circumstances, can significantly enhance the efficiency of electricity production.

Development and demonstration of new configurations or advanced designs of these technologies is still occurring. However, the efficiency gains that might be expected are limited because they are already close to the theoretical limits. Thus, within the range of options above, gradual increases in efficiency of generation would be expected as older units are replaced with more efficient new units and as new capacity is gradually added to meet higher demand. Figure 3 illustrates the experience and expectations of thermal efficiencies of power plants up to the year 2000 for Denmark. As the lifetimes of most generating units are 30 to 50 years, the effect of replacements is gradual except perhaps for some segments of the generation sector, all of approximately the same age and thus needing replacement in the same time period. Where plant life extension is chosen over installation of a new unit (i.e., repowering), there will still be some efficiency gains, although perhaps not as great as those associated with the installation of a new generating unit.

The transmission and distribution grids themselves, which in a modern system lose anything from 8% to 14% of the electricity produced, can have their efficiency enhanced through better grid management, use of high-voltage direct current lines and by improved locations for plants. The potential for achieving such efficiency gains is limited by the rate of replacement and expansion of such grids.

New means for generating electricity, such as advanced fuel cells, magnetohydrodynamics (MHD) and other direct conversion methods, which bypass the thermal or mechanical stages in electricity production, offer the possibility of higher efficiencies along with markedly reduced or no emissions of conventional air pollutants, but not necessarily reduced CO_2 emissions. The timing of their commercialisation is uncertain because they are still in the developmental or demonstration stages. The use of renewable energy forms to generate electricity is discussed in the following section on fuel subsitution.

In summary, electricity transformation, which dominates the transformation sector both in size and level of conversion losses, is undergoing gradual but slow improvement in its conversion efficiency. The commercial advantages arising from even minor improvements in these systems are such that there is adequate incentive to operators to pursue best practice at all times and to incorporate the more efficient new plant (where it has been clearly proven) as quickly as possible. The outlook for the sector is that its relative size is likely to increase with the continued increase in electricity intensity in OECD economies, but that no rapid efficiency enhancements are likely. Rather, losses will either stabilise (reflecting continued expansion of coal use and improved plant efficiency) or decline slowly (representing a gradual shift out of coal and back into gas, oil and nuclear and again improved plant efficiency). Where life extension extends the use of inefficient, older facilities in lieu of more efficient new plants, this might be one area where government encouragement of the more efficient repowering alternative may be warranted.

Figure 3

Historic and Forecast Evolution of Net Thermal Efficiencies in % of Danish Power Plants under Optimal Load Conditions

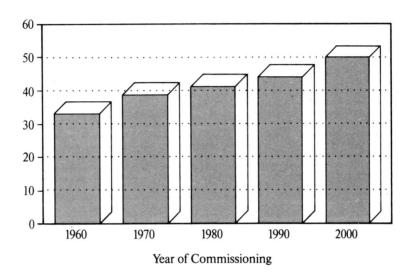

Year of Commissioning

Source : Hostgaard-Jensen, 1989.

(c) The future of greater energy efficiency

Considerable technical potential remains in a number of sectors for improvements in energy efficiency, as shown in Table 9. In particular, the electricity end-use sector and vehicles promise substantial potential. However, if demand for both electricity and transportation fuels continues to increase at current rates, any efficiency gains in these sectors will be offset. From the above discussion it might be concluded that substantial changes in the rate of efficiency improvements depend most critically on the price incentive to different consumer categories and equipment manufacturers as well as on the pace of technological improvements. In the near-term, the opportunity exists for the accelerated introduction of energy-saving technologies in all sectors. National and international collaboration programmes are already in place in the areas of energy-efficient technology demonstration and dissemination and could be extended to place additional emphasis on the environmental benefits of new, more energy-efficient technology.

Price transparency is essential to influencing consumer decisions on energy-efficiency actions. However, historical elasticities indicate that the price of energy would have to rise considerably above present levels in order to hold aggregate energy consumption constant throughout the rest of the century while continuing modest economic growth. The analysis needs to be pushed further in order to determine what price increases would be likely to support major energy demand and corresponding emission reductions or stabilisations. It would be useful to verify that considerable increases are in fact necessary to produce these effects as this would suggest that achieving such goals by improved energy efficiency driven only by prices or their proxies might not be politically acceptable.

While it is widely accepted that the potential for economically viable energy efficiency improvements in member countries is significant even at present low energy prices, the rate of exploitation of energy-efficiency opportunities is largely determined by the payback times involved. Probably the most significant single difference between the decision-makers involved in making investments in supply versus demand-side actions is the higher rates of return applied to such investments by consumers in comparison with those expected by energy production companies for investments in new supply. Electricity supply companies, for example, in many instances operate with rates of return criteria of between 5 - 10%, while the payback period applied by industry and the notional payback period operated by ordinary consumers result in implicit rates of return of between 15 - 40%. This difference has inevitable and observable consequences on investment decisions.

Least cost planning approaches can go some way towards bridging the difference between criteria applied to supply and demand management investments. In addition, if the environmental advantages of energy-efficiency investments (such as emission reductions) are taken into account, for instance, through regulations, the reference to other often less cost effective abatement strategies can markedly modify attitudes towards such expenditure. Some public utility commissions in the United States have begun to recognise the benefits to the environment of energy efficiency achieved in demand side management programmes by allowing these benefits to be included in competitive bids for new electricity supply and in their cost-effectiveness calculations for energy-efficiency promotional programmes proposed for funding with ratepayers funds. The effect of this is to make some previously marginally cost-effective actions more cost-effective. Additional changes to rate regulations will be needed to overcome present disincentives to implementing these cost-effective actions.

Lower prices reduce the consumers' motivation to become informed about and to pursue greater energy efficiency. The private sector promotes the features that are the most attractive to consumers which at present generally excludes or minimises energy efficient features. Some argument could be made for a counter-cyclical effort to increase the visibility of energy efficiency and for emphasizing and explaining the externalities, such as the environmental benefits. However, for numerous reasons, government funding for energy efficiency programmes has been steadily declining. This trend may in fact be near its end with the increased awareness of the environmental benefits of energy efficiency, as a number of governments have started to reorient their energy-efficient technology development and dissemination programmes accordingly. As yet, however, few governments could be counted among those where energy-efficiency programme expenditures have actually been augmented because of perceived benefits to the environment.

In most cases, as analysis of the potential improved energy efficiency has to reduce pollution is still being developed, the action taken usually consists of a renewed impulse given to traditional energy efficiency action originally designed to improve energy security. For instance, the United States' Government has recently decided to impose stronger mandatory fuel efficiency standards through its existing Corporate Average Fuel Efficiency (CAFE) legislation in response to both energy security and environmental concerns. Denmark has actively pursued the introduction of combined heat and power equipment for electricity production and residential, commercial and industrial heat supply, arguing that its greater efficiency provides both energy security and environmental benefits. The Netherlands, which uses natural gas extensively in its energy system, is now subsidising industrial CHP schemes as much for their environmental benefits as for any improved efficiency benefits.

Many governments are of course in the process of reconsidering their policies, including how to restructure old programmes to reorient them to new economic (and environmental) factors. Recognising the benefits to the environment from improving energy efficiency, governments have very recently begun explicitly to develop them as a response to environmental protection needs as well as energy security goals. The government of Sweden has set an ambitious target for the development of a more efficient, environmentally benign energy system. In support of this objective it has undertaken a range of actions in support of greater energy and electricity efficiency: for example, restructuring electricity tariffs, providing extensive R&D and technology demonstration support for more efficient technology and introducing regulations for more efficient use of energy in buildings [42]. The Netherlands [43] and Norway have also recently designed national environment programmes in which energy efficiency developments play an important part in environmental protection efforts. Major metropolitan areas in IEA Member countries are also considering energy-efficiency improvements as part of their responses to growing environmental problems. Greater investment in energy-efficient urban rail systems is one example of these developments. The recently announced plan for the reduction of pollutant emissions in the Los Angeles basin relies heavily on greater efficiency in the utilisation of energy and includes a variety of fiscal, regulatory and other mechanisms to encourage it.

In-depth analysis is needed on the technical and economic potential of energy efficiency improvements that could most benefit the environment (especially in electricity, transportation and industrial uses) and on the design of programmes that would achieve pollutant reduction in the most cost-effective manner, taking into account national differences and broader effects felt throughout fuel cycles. Further analysis of the refinery sector and the transportation and transmission of electricity might also be of use. Such analyses should consider the costs, benefits, timing, trade-offs, barriers, limitations as well as the remaining R&D needs. The relative cost-effectiveness and complementarity of other actions, such as fuel substitution or structural changes, should be also examined. While generally beneficial to the environment as a response to the need to control environmental pollution from a single facility, energy efficiency actions often need to be supported by pollution control technologies or fuel substitution. It is mainly in the aggregate that improved energy efficiency can have an overall major impact on environmental protection.

Finally, in light of the discussion in the following chapter dealing with policy instruments and the experience to date with such instruments in accelerating energy-efficiency improvements, a new look should be given to determine which instruments can be expected to be the most effective in encouraging improved energy efficiency in the present energy and environment situation. The role and limitations of economic instruments and, in particular, market-based instruments (for which definitions vary considerably) should be the subject of particular attention, as should be concepts such as the internalization of environmental costs. These areas of analysis have strong links with work concerned with the potential energy efficiency has to further environmental goals and with the improvement of our understanding of energy demand trends, for instance through the development of energy conservation indicators.

Table 9
Energy-Efficient Technologies and the Economic Potential for Conservation

Energy End Use/Technology	% of IEA TPER	Existing Stock Average Efficiency (Units)	New Stock Average Efficiency (% Savings)	Best Available Technology Efficiency	Best Available Technology (% Savings)	Average Useful Life of Technology
RESIDENTIAL	20-25%					
- U.S. (All electric uses)		1 501 (Watts per capita)		328	-78%	Over 30 years
- Sweden (All electric uses)		1 242 (Watts per capita)		266	-78%	
Heating and Cooling	8-12%					
- Building shell thermal efficiency						Over 30 years
- U.S. (winter)		160 (KJ per m² per degree day)	100 (-37%)	50	-70%	
- Sweden (winter)		135 (KJ per m² per degree day)	65 (-52%)	35	-74%	
Heating	8-12%					
- Oil/Gas - System Efficiency						10-20 years
- U.S.		65-70% (% of TPER converted to useful heat)	75-80% (-13%)	84-94%	-23-26%	

113

Table 9 (continued)

Energy End Use/Technology	% of IEA TPER	Existing Stock Average Efficiency (Units)	New Stock Average Efficiency (% Savings)	Best Available Technology Efficiency	Best Available Technology (% Savings)	Average Useful Life of Technology
Cooling - Central a/c- - U.S.	1-2%	7 (Energy Efficiency Rating)	9 (-22%)	14	-50%	10-20 years
Refrigerators/ freezers - U.S.	2%	1 500 (kWh/year)	1 300 (-13%)	750	-50%	10-15 years
- Germany		About 400 (kWh/year)	(-20%)		At least -20%	
- Japan		35 (kWh/month)	28 (-20%)		At least -20%	
Water Heating - U.S.	3-5%	4 000 (kWh/year)	3 600	1 700	-57%	15 years
COMMERCIAL	15-20%					
Heating and Cooling - U.S.	10-12%	1.31 (GJ per m²/year)	0.73 (-44%)	0.32	-75%	30+ years
- Sweden		1.04	0.76 (-27%)	0.25-0.46	-55-75%	

Table 9 (continued)

Energy End Use/Technology	% of IEA TPER	Existing Stock Average Efficiency (Units)	New Stock Average Efficiency (% Savings)	Best Available Technology Efficiency	Best Available Technology (% Savings)	Average Useful Life of Technology
Large Office Buildings	5%					
- U.S.		270 (KBtu/ft^2 year)	200 (-26%)	100	-63%	30+years
Lighting	3-5%					1-10 years
- U.S.		64 (lumens/Watt)	73 (-12%)	86	(-26%)	
. Ballast/Tubes					(-20-30%)	
. Controls					-40-50%	
. Total						
TRANSPORT	20-25%					
Automobiles	10-13%					
- U.S.		19.0 (miles per gallon)	26.1 (-34%)	31.5	-46%	10 years
- Japan		11 (km/l)	13 (-15%)			

Table 9 (continued)

Energy End Use/Technology	% of IEA TPER	Existing Stock Average Efficiency (Units)	New Stock Average Efficiency (% Savings)	Best Available Technology Efficiency	Best Available Technology (% Savings)	Average Useful Life of Technology
Other road transport	7-10%					
Air Transport	2-3%	25 (passenger miles/gallon)	30+ (-20%)	40+	-40%	15-30 years
- All countries						
Rail/Marine/Other	2-3%					
INDUSTRY						
Chemicals	35-40%					
- U.K. (Inorganic)	6-8%				-13%	
Iron and Steel	5%	22-24 (GJ/tonne)	17-18 (-20-25%)	n.a.	At least -20-25%	10-30 years
- U.S./Japan/U.K./Netherlands.						
Non-ferrous metals	3%	15-17 (mWh/tonne)	13.5 (-10-20%)	n.a.	At least -10-20%	20-30 years
- OECD (Aluminium)						

Table 9 (continued)

Energy End Use/Technology	% of IEA TPER	Existing Stock Average Efficiency (Units)	New Stock Average Efficiency (% Savings)	Best Available Technology Efficiency	Best Available Technology (% Savings)	Average Useful Life of Technology
Paper	3%					
- U.K. (Paper and Board Making)					-30%	
Stone, Clay and Glass	2%					
- U.S./France/Switz. /France/Switz. /U.K. (Bricks/ Pottery)		2.5 (MJ/kg)	1.5-2.0 (-20-40%)	n.a.	At least -20-40%	10-30 years
- France/U.K./ Switz./Germany (Cement)		3.6-3.8 (MJ/kg)	3.3 (-8-13%)	n.a.	At least -8-13%	10-30 years

117

Table 9 (continued)

Energy End Use/Technology	% of IEA TPER	Existing Stock Average Efficiency (Units)	New Stock Average Efficiency (% Savings)	Best Available Technology Efficiency	Best Available Technology (% Savings)	Average Useful Life of Technology
Food	1%					
Space Heating, Cooling, Water, Heating, Lighting	2-3%					
ALL SECTORS *Electric Motors*	20%	75-90% (% converted to motive power)	80-92% (-2-7%)	85-93%	-15-30%	10-20 years
Central and On-Site Electricity Generation	35%					
- U.S. (Gas Turbines)	n.a.	30% (% converted to electricity)	35% (-15%)	39-41%	-25%	

Source: Based on *Energy Conservation in IEA Countries*, IEA, 1987.

3. Fuel Substitution

Substituting fuels to further the achievement of environmental objectives can involve:

- permanent shifts to energy alternatives;

- temporary fuel switching to minimise seasonal or short-term environmental impacts; or

- the use of higher quality (less polluting) forms of the same fuel.

It is the purpose of this section to provide an overview of recent trends in fuel substitution and their implications, and the factors that will determine the potential for fuel substitution to further enhance environmental protection while avoiding or minimising adverse effects on either energy security or economic growth. Some of the potential benefits, costs and risks associated with different types of fuel substitution are discussed qualitatively in this section, but there has been no attempt to draw specific conclusions regarding the net benefits (or costs) that are likely to result or how fuel substitution compares with other methods of achieving these same objectives. The assessment of the existing opportunities focuses on the period up to 2005. While the possible long-term implications are described, the potential effects of more radical long-term changes in energy-supply systems or end-use technologies are not analyzed.

(a) Historical Trends in Fuel Substitution

The historical and more recent shifts in primary energy sources, fuel quality and end-use energy forms are illustrated in Figures 4, 5 and 6 and in Table 10. They were caused by many different factors, although the most important reasons behind the large shifts in primary energy sources were economic and technological. As a result of energy security and environmental objectives explicitly supported by government policy-makers, a number of important shifts in fuel choice occurred after the mid-1970s. Perhaps most significant were the shifts in the utility sector, indicated in Figure 5, but also important were the shifts in fuel choice for residential and commercial building space heating, examples of which are indicated in Table 10. The shifts in industry, indicated in Figure 6, were less significant and often were the result of structural changes within the industrial sector and not of fuel substitution. The impact that government policy measures had on fuel substitution during this period is not well understood.

The historical shifts observed, including the shift towards electricity, are the result of a combination of fuel availability and technological and economic factors. In each case, the new source or form of energy was plentifully available at acceptable and usually declining relative costs. This availability was combined with the development of technologies using the new fuel which provided lower cost means of performing work, provided significantly enhanced levels of service (e.g., greater reliability or convenience) or enabled a totally new service (e.g., television). The results were powerful economic motivations for shifting to new energy sources or forms. The more recent expansion of natural gas, nuclear power and coal in the electricity generating sector were also, in the large part, economically motivated. These shifts have been accompanied by technical developments in electricity generation. The rapidly rising costs of oil in the 1970s provided the major stimulus for these shifts -- although they were also usually encouraged by government policies.

Alternatively, economic forces have, of course, also worked against the unsuccessful competing fuels. In the United States during the late 1970s and early 1980s, rising costs of new nuclear power plants relative to coal-fired plants were a major contributing factor in the drop in new plant orders. Similarly, the high capital costs associated with industrial uses of coal, including investment in storage and handling, were a major factor limiting the re-introduction of coal into these markets following the dramatic rise in oil prices.

Since the 1970s, individual countries and international agencies like the IEA have pursued a range of policies in order to improve the security of energy supplies. The substitution of other, more plentiful and secure fuels for oil has been a central objective of these policies. Most member countries relied primarily on the high world oil prices during the period 1973 to 1985 to provide the motivation for users to switch to other fuels. However, governments have also supported the substitution of other fuels for oil through tax (and related pricing) policies, regulation, incentives and the public support of R,D&D related to alternative energy supplies and distribution systems. For instance, EC member countries and the United States banned the use of oil for electricity generation. These measures are discussed in more detail later in the chapter concerned with policy instruments.

The growing recognition of environmental problems by IEA countries and how they affected fuel choice have been discussed in previous chapters. Improvements in fuel quality have been the main focus of environmentally motivated fuel policies and a variety of government regulations have been promulgated that require the use of higher-quality fuels: low-sulphur oil and coal, unleaded petrol, for example. There are some recent examples of government environmental policies that have required or encouraged the use of alternative "clean" fuels, such as the experiments with non-petroleum based automotive fuels in Southern California and Texas in the United States. The varying actions of IEA countries with respect to nuclear energy and hydropower are largely or partially motivated by environmental or safety issues. Some countries are encouraging the continued or expanded use of nuclear power, among other reasons, to avoid the emission of pollutants from fossil fuels, while others have decided to phase out (or ban) the use of nuclear power to avoid the environmental and safety risks associated with the use of radioactive materials. With respect to hydroelectric power, the main motivations have usually been cost, energy security or regional development, but some countries have stressed the benefits of hydroelectric power deriving from the avoidance of air pollutants. Others have decided against the construction of new dams to avoid loss of natural wildernesses, agricultural land or recreational areas. The various market factors and government policies that influenced fuel substitution have thus had both complementary and conflicting effects on the achievement of environmental and energy security objectives. In other words, because perspectives differ on the environmental effects of the different energy sources, there is often disagreement within and among Member countries as to which policies have basically complementary or conflicting effects.

Figure 4
World Primary Energy Developments Illustrating Fuel Substitution

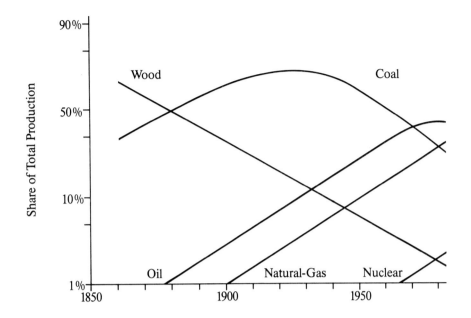

Source: Based on a graph developed by Cesane Marchetti and submitted to the IEA seminar on Energy Technologies for Reducing Emissions of Greenhouse Gas, 12-14th April 1989.

Figure 5
**Shares of Fuel Inputs into Electricity Generation
in IEA Countries**

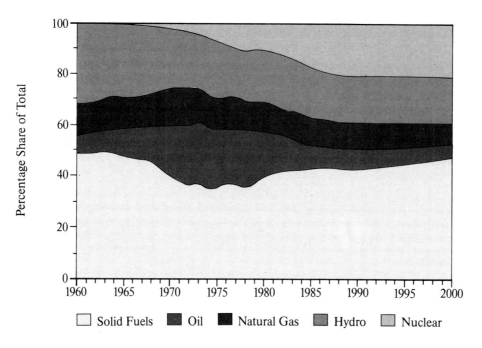

Source : IEA Secrétariat.

122

Figure 6

Shares of Energy Consumption in the Industry Sector in IEA countries

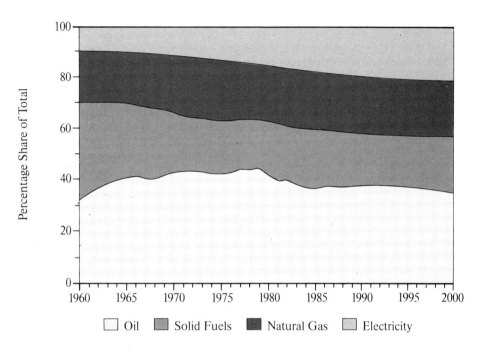

Source : IEA Secrétariat.

Table 10
Principal Space Heating Fuel Choices

Country Year	Dwellings 10⁶ units	Oil	LPG	Piped Gas	Electric	District Heat	Coal/Coke	Wood
				% of dwellings				
Germany								
1960	15.4	14	(a)	1	0	1	84	(b)
1972	21.4	48	(a)	11	4	5	32	(b)
1978	23.4	53	1	15	7	5	19	1
1983/4	24.7	50	1	24	7	8	9	1
Sweden								
1963	2.8	57	0	1	1	4	13	24
1972	3.3	69	0	2	6	17	1	6
1978	3.6	57	0	1	15	24	0.5	4
1982	3.7	39	0	0.5	24	32	0.3	4
United States								
1960	53.0	32	5	43	2	0	12	4
1973	69.3	25	6	55	10	0	1	1
1978	76.6	21	5	55	16	0	1	2.5
1981	83.1	17	5	55	17	(b)	1.7	6.4
1984	86.3	14	5	55	17	(b)	1.7	7.5
1987	90.3	14	5	55	20	(b)	1.3	5.6

Key: (a) Included in gas figures.
        (b) Included in coal figures.

Note: For the United States, the figures reflect occupied dwellings: for Germany and Sweden, all dwellings.
Sources: Lawrence Berkeley Laboratory, Berkeley, California, based on government and private surveys in each country.

124

(b) Limitations and Potential of Fuel Substitution

Some of the anticipated trends in fuel choices and quality up to the year 2005, based on a continuation of current government policies and reasonable assumptions about economic growth and relative fuel prices, are described here to provide an indication of the possible future developments in the area of fuel substitution.

Under one scenario assessed by the IEA [42], which assumes that the price of crude oil increases from $17-18 per barrel in the late 1980s to $30 per barrel by 2005 (in constant 1987 U.S. dollars), the energy requirements of the OECD will grow about 1.3% on average between now and the year 2005. During this period, the price of natural gas is expected to rise slightly less rapidly than that of oil and the price of coal is expected to rise much more slowly. The requirements for all major primary energy sources are expected to increase, but no major shifts in primary energy sources or final energy forms occur. Varying growth rates result only in a slight decline from 1987 levels in the share of total energy requirements met by oil and small increases in the shares of solid fuels (mainly coal) and nuclear power.

However, a significant shift occurs in final consumption, where the demand for electricity is expected to continue to grow more rapidly than the demand for other final energy forms. Consequently, in the year 2005, electricity production accounts for about 41% of primary energy requirements, compared with 28% in 1973. This means that the fuel choice decisions in the electricity sector will continue to be increasingly important from both energy security and environmental perspectives. In 2005, petroleum products are still expected to dominate energy use in the transport sector, accounting for nearly 99% of total final energy demand for transport. Gasoline and diesel fuel used in transport alone represent about 47% of the total consumption of petroleum products. A mix of fuels continues to be used in both the industrial and residential/commercial sectors.

Table 11 summarises the primary energy consumption patterns forecast, under this scenario, for the year 2005. However, the table does not show the anticipated shifts in fuel quality. While shifts in the quality of energy products is significant in terms of their environmental effects, they are not expected to have major long-term effects on energy security, although they may have significant short-term effects on some markets and on some energy industries. Changes in the quality specifications of petroleum products is a major technical problem faced by refiners. For instance, the change in gasoline specifications, such as the reduction of the permissible lead content, has led to octane producing facilities being the largest current area of major investment in the refining industry, particularly in Europe [35].

Table 11
Trends in Total Primary Energy Requirements in the OECD
[Mtoe and (% Share)]

	1973	1979	1987	1995	2005
Solid Fuels	715.4 (20%)	802.0	936.1 (24%)	1 060	1 250 (26%)
Petroleum	1 874.7 (53%)	1 942.7	1 653.8 (43%)	1 800	1 900 (39%)
Natural Gas	692.6 (20%)	741.7	730.0 (19%)	800	940 (19%)
Nuclear	42.2 (1%)	126.7	311.8 (8%)	390	450 (9%)
Hydro/Geothermal	201.5 (6%)	239.8	254.8 (7%)	290	350 (7%)
TOTAL	**3 524.8**	**3 853.0**	**3 886.6**	**4 340**	**4 890**

Source: IEA Secretariat.

The supply and demand estimates indicated for 2005 reflect the results of one scenario, based on a set of assumptions about energy prices, economic growth and other factors. It is likely that actual trends during the next 15-20 years will vary widely among countries and even the average trends for the OECD could differ significantly from those forecast as a result of changing economic forces and government policies. The impact of such changes on the achievement of energy security or environmental objectives could be positive, negative or conflicting.

There is a wide range of fuel substitution options that might be considered: from supply to transformation to end-use or directly from supply to end-use. Substitution is technically possible for most of the energy sources and forms. For example, all primary energy sources can be used to produce electricity or heat, which in turn might be used in all end-use sectors. But there are important technical and economic limitations which, for practical purposes, exclude certain combinations. For instance, unless there are major advances in electric battery technology or in the production of transport fuels from electricity (e.g., hydrogen), it does not appear feasible to substitute electric power for the bulk of the energy now used in motor vehicles. As a result, a number of primary energy sources that can feasibly be used to generate electricity (or heat), such as nuclear energy, hydropower, direct solar energy, wind or geothermal energy, cannot be substituted for most transport fuels (although electricity can be used for propulsion, for instance, for railway transport). Similarly, there is a wide range of end-uses, such as lighting and many motor applications, that are essentially dependent on electricity. The number of fuels that can be substituted on a flexible, temporary basis for each other is also limited. For example, natural gas and fuel oil can usually be interchanged in power plants and both can be used to replace coal or biomass in large power plants. But coal or biomass cannot easily be used in plants not specifically designed for their use. Despite these exceptions, the number of technically and economically feasible ways in which fuels can be substituted is quite large.

The development of effective fuel substitution policies to achieve environmental objectives, without impairing energy security, requires careful consideration of all of the major effects anticipated, as well as the underlying economic factors which might accelerate or slow the desired shifts. The potential environmental benefits of each differ, as do their likely economic costs and energy security implications. In order to develop public policies which maximise the environmental benefits, while minimising any additional economic or energy security costs, a detailed assessment of each option, alternatives and their interactions is necessary. Such an assessment needs to examine the effects of the alternative fuel substitution possibilities on all stages of the production, transport, conversion and final end-use of the types of energy involved. The following section describes some of the fuel substitution options that might be available and the factors that should be examined in the evaluation of their relative benefits and costs. In order to give an indication of opportunities for fuel substitution that may exist, their limitations and the unresolved issues concerning their net environmental, energy security and economic impacts, there follows a brief assessment of four important areas:

- switches to low sulphur oil and coal;

- increased production and use of natural gas;

- substitution in electricity generation and use; and

- the substitution of "cleaner" fuels in the transport sector.

Switches to low sulphur oil and coal. Sulphur control strategies can be expected to have an impact on the use of low sulphur oil and coal (defined as less than 1% sulphur) where the use of such fuels represents the cheapest method for plant operators to meet regulatory requirements. This may arise:

- when limits on sulphur content are the only regulatory control of SO_2 emissions;

- when applicable emission regulations can be met by the use of low sulphur oil or coal;

- when a combination of low sulphur oil or coal and simple control technologies allows emission standards to be met cost-effectively; and/or

- when use of low sulphur oil or coal would significantly reduce the costs of control technologies or advanced combustion.

Such conditions currently exist in many OECD areas. In the case of coal, around 150 GWt of existing and planned units could potentially switch to low sulphur coal to meet agreed SO_2 control regulations [33]. However, since units are designed to suit the combustion of particular coals, many would first need modification. The key factors affecting the use of low sulphur coal in emissions control are its availability and cost relative to other control options.

127

Many of the major coal-producing areas within the IEA, including Australia, the United States and Canada, have indigenous supplies of low sulphur coal [1]. But most other countries would have to increase the level of coal imports to obtain significant supplies of low sulphur coal. Clearly, if the demand rose significantly because of the need to meet emission regulations, there would be an impact on both price and availability. The size of this impact has been the subject of considerable controversy. There are at present no signs that there will be overall coal supply problems in the foreseeable future because of environmentally driven demand for low sulphur coal.

An alternative means of obtaining low sulphur coal is to "clean" higher sulphur coal. The aim of coal cleaning is to remove as much ash and sulphur as is economically possible, while maximizing recovery of heat content. There is little indication that increased coal cleaning has played a major role in sulphur control strategies to date. However should the price of low sulphur coal increase significantly, or techniques for cleaning become far more effective or less costly, it may become economically viable for coal producers or users to carry out more cleaning.

In the case of oil products, low sulphur (light) crudes have for a long period of time been the preferred crude quality, particularly for reasons of demand for products at the lighter end of the barrel, and have achieved relatively higher prices on the market. For SO_2 control, low sulphur crude oil is obviously desirable and regulations prescribing maximum sulphur limits have a direct influence on the crude mix used in refineries. A CONCAWE study of European refineries shows that sulphur intake into refineries decreased by 53% between 1979 and 1985, and that sulphur in products sold for combustion purposes was reduced by 62% during the same period [44]. All crude oils contain sulphur compounds, the amounts of which depend on the crude oil source. During the refining process these sulphur compounds are distributed between the various products, with very little appearing in the lighter products, such as gases and gasolines, rather more in the intermediate products, such as gas oils, and the highest levels in the heavy products, such as fuel oil. As the sulphur content of residues may be twice the percentage of sulphur in the crude, sulphur limits for heavy fuel oil may therefore restrict or limit the use of high sulphur crudes.

Generally, heavy fuel oil is used for electricity generation and ship bunkers. Many utilities use low sulphur crude for electricity generation rather than heavy fuel oil with a high sulphur content associated with modern emission control equipment. If demand for low sulphur oil outstrips its availability, various desulphurisation techniques would have to be considered. Except for the direct desulphurisation of heavy residues, technology developments have been largely limited to solid fuels and the desulphurisation of liquid fuels remains expensive [45]. At present, costs for desulphurisation of heavy fuel oil seem to outweigh additional costs for light crude.

Increasing Natural Gas Supply and Use. Natural gas consumption, which has remained comparatively stable for the OECD region as a whole over the past ten years, is expected to increase about 25% by the year 2005 under the IEA scenario described earlier, but the share of total primary energy requirements would remain approximately the same. Between one half and two-thirds of the increasing consumption of natural gas would be met by increasing imports from outside OECD, but in 2005 approximately 75% of gas requirements would still be supplied by production from OECD countries (against only 30% of oil requirements).

Because of the environmental characteristics of natural gas, the availability of supplies at reasonable costs and the related energy security advantages of natural gas in many areas, private markets and some government policies have in recent years tended to favour the use of gas in most sectors (except electric power generation). But there remain many unanswered questions concerning how much and at what cost OECD and non-OECD production of natural gas could be expanded beyond current levels. Possible market or institutional barriers that are inhibiting these developments should be investigated, as well as the risks of supply disruptions due to increased reliance on natural gas imports.

The combustion of natural gas generates no SO_2 emissions and substantially less NO_x and CO_2 than its two major competing fuels, oil and coal (though the greenhouse effect of methane emissions should be taken into account). It has the added advantage of being able to be substituted temporarily for oil or coal used in plants located in areas experiencing short-term environmental problems. But the production, distribution and use of gas do carry some important environmental impacts or risks, a few of which are unique to this fuel (or its derivatives). It therefore appears less environmentally desirable than most renewable energy sources or electricity generated by less polluting primary energy sources. A comparison of the environmental benefits (or costs) of nuclear power and gas is, however, much more difficult and depends almost entirely on the different perceptions of the environmental impacts of nuclear power. Even with respect to renewable energy sources, individual perceptions of relative environmental benefits and costs are critical. For instance, there is no clear way of weighing the costs of a wilderness valley flooded by a hydroelectric project or a coastal area covered by windmills versus those resulting from emissions of CO_2 and NO_x from the combustion of natural gas.

The ability of OECD countries to produce or obtain from other countries additional supplies of natural gas (beyond those increases already foreseen), at acceptable costs, is extremely difficult to predict. There are several OECD countries that are in the process of increasing production and these increases might be accelerated in some cases, without significantly raising resource costs. It is difficult to estimate, at this time, to what extent such an acceleration of OECD production increases might add to total available supplies prior to 2005. In some regions, such as northern Europe and Canada, the potential may be significant, but in most producing regions the potential for increases appears limited. If such increases in OECD gas production were not sufficient, even larger increases in natural gas supplies could be obtained from non-OECD countries. These non-OECD sources of natural gas are also expected to greatly increase production over the next 10 to 20 years. Finally, there are higher-cost sources of natural gas within OECD countries, such as coal seam gas, geo-pressurised gas and deep water wells which could become economic for some end-uses but only if oil prices increased substantially more than IEA projections.

In terms of market penetration, modest increases in natural gas supplies above those forecast in Table 11 (perhaps 10% above) could probably be substituted for other fossil fuels in the industrial, residential/commercial and electricity generating sectors. Existing or planned natural gas pipelines and distribution networks would be able to supply such additional volumes to any of these three sectors without incurring prohibitively high transport costs or major delays. The end-use technologies to use such additional supplies are either already in place or could be economically installed as existing capital stock and electric generating capacity is expanded or replaced. For example, most electricity generating and industrial oil or coal burning installations could be easily (and inexpensively) modified to use natural gas (temporarily, permanently or as a mix) if supplies were economically available. In addition, by 2005, a major portion of such installations would have been built after 1990. In this regard, recent estimates of the cost of generating electric power by coal (with pollution controls), nuclear power or natural gas (using the new generation of more efficient combined cycle gas turbines), suggest that natural gas could be competitive in many OECD regions. This could be the case for instance, if supplies were available at or below $4 per million Btu (i.e., at 1987 prices), the investment choice was guided by a discount rate of 10% and other fuels generally followed the price assumptions described earlier [28].

Increased penetration in the residential/commercial sector would be slower and dependent, to some extent, on local distribution costs and the pricing of competing fuels. Central hot water or air heating systems can be easily converted to use natural gas, but this normally makes economic sense only when the existing systems require replacement or major repair. In the transport sector, the introduction of fuel-flexible vehicles might permit natural-gas-derived fuels to be substituted for petroleum based fuels for short periods of time in areas experiencing especially severe pollution problems. Substantially increased use of natural gas in the transport sector, however, does raise some questions regarding new distribution and end-use technologies (except for LPG) which would have to be more fully addressed. Some of the characteristics of the fuel may inhibit the introduction of natural gas (or its derivatives) in particular sectors. For example, the widespread introduction of methanol in the transport sector would require a major change in automotive engines (and some new technology) and simultaneously a major change in the distribution system supplying automotive fuels, both in terms of fuel production (e.g., refining) and local distribution (e.g., fuelling stations).

Very large increases in natural gas imports from non-OECD countries might pose some potentially serious energy-security risks. These risks could be mitigated by cooperation between countries and by proper steps taken by individual countries which might include: increases in natural gas storage, interruption tariffs (and hence dual firing) and diversification of the sources of natural gas imports as well as political and economic contacts with natural gas producing countries. Such increased reliance on gas imports, however, could present greater risks from supply disruption or economic manipulation than parallel increases in imports of coal. Natural gas imports can create some unique security risks that might in some situations be even more troublesome than those posed by imports of oil. Gas imports, especially those by pipeline, could be extremely difficult (both time-consuming and costly) to replace if there was a lengthy (or permanent) supply interruption. International gas markets are still very limited and available supplies are usually entirely committed under long-term contracts (outside North America). As a result, gas supply interruptions that endured longer than available supplies of stored gas (the large scale storage of gas being limited by technical, economic and safety constraints) would probably lead to the substitution back to oil in industrial or electric utility gas markets.

Where it has been determined that an accelerated increase in the supply and use of natural gas, as a substitute for other fuels, was desirable, governments have used a wide range of different actions. An important step has been to ensure that existing policies or measures were not placing uneconomic impediments on market forces that might otherwise result in an increase in natural gas supply and consumption. Policies have included eliminating or modifying unwarranted restrictions on gas use, over-regulation of prices or market access and discriminatory tax policies. Questions that have been addressed in some countries are limitations placed on access to pipeline or distribution networks and on the development of gas supplies or the construction of gas transport or storage systems.

Government policies to internalise the environmental and energy security costs of different energy sources can lead to increased substitution of gas for other fuels. The pricing, taxation or regulatory measures necessary to achieve this end require somewhat more government intervention, but still rely primarily on market forces to determine fuel choices. Other policies have included:

- supporting a public information campaign which explains to consumers the benefits of converting to gas;

- modifying tax or other policies to increase further the financial incentive to convert to natural gas or dual-firing capability;

- mandating the use of (or the capability to use) natural gas in certain sectors (such as new homes in urban areas or in new power plants).

These measures are described in more detail in the following chapter concerned with policy instruments.

It can be concluded from the discussion above that there are numerous possibilities for substituting natural gas for other energy forms. It is also likely that modest increases in the use of natural gas, even if they relied on imports from non-OECD countries, would pose fewer energy security risks than increased reliance on oil. But it is not certain to what extent natural gas supplies and use could be increased, without entailing large additional economic costs. If additional gas supplies were available, and there were no warranted barriers to its transport and use, it remains to determine what fuels they would likely displace and what net environmental benefits would result. Natural gas's possible contribution to global climate change makes it imperative to look at the full fuel cycle and determine its real desirability *vis a vis* this and other environmental problems. These are some of the major issues that individual Member countries and the IEA might examine in more detail. Elements of each of these questions and others are being addressed by the IEA in several studies of natural gas resources and markets which are either under way or planned for 1990.

Substitution in Electricity Generation and Use. The potential contribution of substitution in electricity generation and use to environmental goals depends on two factors. The first is the actual environmental benefits that can be derived from changes in the fuel mix used for electricity generation and, taking into account any benefits gained in this way, those that can be gained by substitution towards electricity at the end-use level. The fuel cycle review presented in Annex 1 includes a comparative analysis of the environmental effects (air and water pollution, waste disposal, siting and land-use impacts, etc) and control of a broad range of energy sources currently used for electricity generation, as well as of the various energy forms to which electricity might be substituted at the end-use stage. This review demonstrates that all energy activities have some environmental impact and that the choice of an energy source for electricity generation in particular involves some form of trade-off between different types of environmental effects or different pollutants. Table 16 in Annex I provides comparative data on the emissions of certain pollutants from the combustion of different types of fossil fuels in power plants.

The net environmental benefits (or costs) of substituting electricity for other fuels are particularly difficult to quantify. In some cases, the direct burning of fossil fuels may be less polluting than the use of electricity generated by the same fuel. For example, conventional electric resistance heating often uses about twice the primary energy resources as does direct combustion heating. But this is not necessarily always the case: heat pump water heaters powered by electricity generated by a highly efficient combined-cycle gas turbine could use 50% less energy than a highly efficient gas water heater. Furthermore, the direct burning of fossil fuels by small, dispersed sources is often more polluting because their emissions are difficult to control. Given that the electricity sector presents a number of opportunities for fuel substitution that could also help achieve environmental objectives, such as the limitation of traditional air pollutants (SO_2, NO_x, PM) or of CO_2 emissions, the second factor to consider is the extent of such substitution possibilities, in both technical and economic terms. The discussion developed below covers these possibilities first at the generation stage and then at the end-use stage, on the basis of historical trends and the outlook for 2005.

Although the size and longevity of capital investments in generating facilities mean that opportunities for substitution can only be economically realised gradually over a period of several decades or more, some significant shifts can occur over much shorter periods of time, as recent history has shown. From 1973 to 1987, the share of electricity generated by oil and natural gas dropped from 38% to 17%, while the coal and nuclear share increased from 42% to 64%. However, from 1987 to 2005, such large shifts are not expected. Oil use in power generation is expected to continue to decline, from about 155 Mtoe in 1987 to about 80 Mtoe in 2005, but increases are expected in the use of natural gas, coal, nuclear energy and hydro power. The end result is that the relative shares of these energy sources in the generation of electricity are not expected to change dramatically. Table 12 provides historical as well as some forecast (based on the IEA-developed scenario described earlier) data on these and related trends in the electricity sector.

Table 12
Primary Energy Requirements for OECD Electricity Generation

1973-2005
[Mtoe and (% shares)]

	1973	1979	1987	1995	2005
Solid Fuels	374.8 (38%)	467.3	604.9 (43%)	750	940 (47%)
Oil	240.6 (25%)	230.8	109.5 (8%)	100	80 (4%)
Natural Gas	118.1 (12%)	130.5	126.5 (9%)	150	190 (9%)
Nuclear	42.2 (4%)	126.7	311.8 (22%)	390	450 (22%)
Hydro/Geo/Sol	201.5 (21%)	239.8	254.8 (18%)	290	350 (22%)
Total	**977.3**	**1 188.3**	**1 397.0**	**1 680**	**2 010**
Share of TPER	28%	31%	36%	39%	41%

Source: IEA Secretariat.

Virtually all primary energy sources can be used to generate electricity and many of these sources are competitive in at least some OECD countries. Because of the large number of alternative sources and their many variations in availability and cost, overall economic opportunities for fuel substitution in the electricity sector are difficult to assess. But previous analyses of the characteristics and potential of most of the technologies for generating electricity permit some observations. The following paragraphs review the conclusions that can be drawn on the potential contribution of renewable sources to electric power generation. Hydro and geothermal energy have long been economically exploited for power generation (and sometimes for mechanical power or heat) and these sources currently generate about 20% of total electricity supply, almost all of which comes from hydropower. Electricity production from these sources is expected to increase about 35% by 2005. Some further increases may be economically justifiable, although the remaining hydroelectric sites are likely to be either much more costly to exploit or in more environmentally sensitive areas. There may be some remaining potential for pumped-storage hydroelectric systems, which utilise low-cost electricity produced at night to pump water to a reservoir and later to provide peak power in high-cost production periods. To the extent that these systems can obviate the need for other types of peaking units, such as internal combustion units or gas turbines, they can displace specific fuels, such as more expensive oil or gas.

The economic potential for greatly expanding the use of **wind, photovoltaics** or **solar heat** to generate electricity, prior to 2005, is likely to be limited. At present, the economic exploitation of these renewable energy sources requires atypical climatic conditions and/or situations where the realistic alternatives (e.g., remote power generation or distribution) are costly. Furthermore, the periodic nature of these power sources means that additional investments must be made in storage or backup capacity if such systems are to contribute a significant portion (e.g., 10% or more) to the continuous power requirements of a grid or of an individual user. A further restraint might be the difficulty of rapidly expanding electricity production from these sources given the comparatively low current manufacturing capacity of the solar industries. Because of these limitations, wind, photovoltaics and solar thermal power stations are unlikely to contribute more than a few percentage points of the OECD total power requirements in 2005, although some regions or localities should be able to exceed this level. The potential for increasing, prior to 2005, the contribution to electricity generation from tidal, wave, or ocean thermal energy technologies is also quite limited. While they are more continuous except for a few very specific sites, none of these technologies have been shown to be economically competitive and further development of some of them will still entail major technical as well as environmental problems.

The only renewable resource that appears to be able to make a substantially larger contribution to electric power generation is the direct combustion of **biomass,** ranging from solid waste (including agricultural wastes) to wood. Potential resources are large in a number of IEA countries and the technology for burning such fuels to produce power is well commercialised. But high extraction and transportation costs mean that the economics of such power generation are still not directly competitive with fossil fuels in most areas, especially at current price levels. In addition, the combustion of certain solid wastes poses significant environmental problems, although the combustion of wood or agricultural wastes generally produces relatively little SO_2 and no net increase in CO_2 provided that sufficient replanting or regeneration occurs.

In addition to shifts towards less polluting qualities of the same energy forms, the main sources of energy that are likely to be substituted for other fuels in electricity generation prior to 2005 appear to be **natural gas** or **nuclear power** although land-fill gas does show some potential. The availability and costs of additional natural gas supplies was briefly described in the previous section. The consumption of natural gas in the electricity sector is already expected to increase from about 130 Mtoe in 1987 to about 210 Mtoe in 2005. It appears quite feasible to double 1987 consumption by the year 2005 and even larger increases might be possible within the total range of gas supplies described earlier. Additional gas consumption for electricity generation might either further reduce oil use in this sector (expected to be about 80 Mtoe in 2005) or slow the growth in coal use, which is expected to increase from about 580 Mtoe to 890 Mtoe in 2005. More natural gas could also be used as a temporary replacement for oil or coal in areas experiencing short term environmental problems.

Nuclear power generation can also be increased prior to 2005, although there is still considerable disagreement about its net environmental benefits. In any case, the long lead times and large capital investments required would certainly limit the potential for further increasing the contribution of nuclear power in this time period. Nuclear power contributed about 310 Mtoe to power generation in 1987 and this is expected to increase to about 450 Mtoe by 2005 (most of which would be in place prior to 1995). If the rate of construction of nuclear power plants returned to the levels reached during the 1970s and early 1980s, it is conceivable that an additional 100 Mtoe of nuclear power might be available in 2005 (giving a total of 550 Mtoe). Such an increase would represent a likely maximum, given the comparatively short time-frame and limits in the manufacturing and construction capacity of the industry. However, with the current opposition to nuclear power in some countries, such a re-acceleration of plant construction is not likely. The Nuclear Energy Agency has estimated that, in order to stabilize CO_2 emissions at current levels, the nuclear generating capacity of 1987 would have to be multiplied by 2.7 in 2005 [46, 47].

To the extent that electricity is generated, especially on the margin, by more environmentally benign energy sources, the achievement of environmental objectives would be further accelerated by the substitution of electricity for other fuels **in end-uses**. Since 1973 there have been important shifts in electricity end-use and a continuing increase in electricity's share of energy end-use. Much of this increase in the use of electricity has come as a result of the expansion of services which are, for technical or economic reasons, uniquely provided by electric technologies, such as lighting, refrigeration, most (non-mobile) motorised equipment and all electronic equipment. In a number of non-exclusive areas, electricity has successfully competed, based on its price, convenience and other attributes, with other energy forms used for space and water heating, cooking and certain industrial processes, such as steel-making, pulp and paper, and chemicals.

Many of these recent trends in electricity end-use are expected to continue through 2005. Electricity demand is expected to grow more slowly but still by about 2.3% per year on average, compared with about 1% for other forms of end-use energy. Growth is expected to be most rapid in the commercial/public sector, both because this will most likely be the fastest growing segment of OECD economies and because the energy use in this sector is increasingly dominated by electricity. As a result of this growth, electricity generation is likely to account for about 41% of TPER in 2005, against 36% in 1987 and only 28% in 1973. Further increases above these levels depend largely upon the evolution of energy prices. But relatively small changes in prices, combined with some improvements or cost reductions in certain electric technologies (e.g., heat pumps), might significantly alter the comparative economics in many applications. The rate of increase above forecast levels, however, would probably be limited by the replacement rate of existing capital stocks.

The increased use of electricity and the shift away from oil which took place in the electricity generating sector have significantly improved **energy security**. Many of the electricity substitution options considered to reduce the environmental impact of energy activities, such as CO_2 emissions, are likely to further improve energy security. Higher shares of renewable and nuclear energies to generate power would certainly further enhance energy security. Increases in the use of natural gas are not likely to worsen energy security provided adequate gas stocks and other emergency preparedness measures are taken and gas supplies are diversified.

Electric utilities usually are monopolies, often without any direct competition, and are strongly influenced (and often owned) by governments. Consequently, fuel choice decisions for electric power generation are often affected by a range of non-market factors. Because utilities are usually protected monopolies, some argue that utilities are less likely to be innovative in the development and exploitation of new technology. Alternatively, as protected monopolies, utilities can sometimes assume risks or support experimental technologies to a greater degree than would a private company. Because of their use of discount rates that are lower than those used by private industry generally, utilities are likely to be somewhat more willing to invest in more capital-intensive technologies, such as those based on renewable or nuclear energy sources. But the ability of utilities to pass through to their customers higher fuel costs without fear of competition means that they often have less incentive to develop such alternatives.

The end-use of electricity is, of course, greatly affected by the pricing policies of individual utilities. Most utilities in OECD countries base electricity tariffs on average historical rather than the long-run marginal costs that would be charged by most private companies in other lines of business, although the effect of this policy on price levels and electricity demand remains unclear. Because utilities are generally owned or regulated by governments, there is a wide range of both direct and indirect measures which governments use to control or influence utility fuel choice decisions. With respect to the substitution of electricity for the direct combustion of other fuels, government control or influence is likely to be much more difficult. Tax and pricing policies have been needed to alter the economics of electricity relative to other fuels. Improving electric technologies by supporting R,D&D is another way some governments have tried to encourage greater electricity use.

In summary, the electricity sector does offer some significant opportunities for fuel substitution, although many of these opportunities could not be fully realised until well after 2005. Before 2005, the greatest potential seems to be the increased use of natural gas and nuclear power (in power stations that are already under construction or planned), although increased power production from renewable energy sources, especially hydropower and perhaps biomass, could also make a significant contribution. But it is, nevertheless, not likely that such increases could eliminate continued growth in coal requirements, though these might be increasingly met with low sulphur coal. There are opportunities for further substituting electricity use for other fuels, but these will be largely determined by relative price trends and possible technological advances in certain key end-use areas, such as space and water heating.

Alternative Fuels for the Transport Sector. Transport is the only sector which remains almost entirely dependent on petroleum products. While some small increases in the use of natural gas and to a lesser extent electricity are foreseen, it is expected that oil will still account for almost all transport energy requirements in 2005.

Several of the adverse environmental effects of petroleum products can (and are) being addressed by the use of emission control technologies and higher-quality products. Considerable attention has been placed on upgrading fuel quality and improving motor vehicle fuel flexibility. Most governments have already established requirements to gradually phase out leaded gasoline and to limit benzene content. Recently, the United States has acted to lower significantly the volatility of gasoline sold, especially during the summer months. While such fuel quality requirements may pose some short term difficulties for producers and refiners, there is not expected to be a significant problem in achieving major improvements in these areas before the year 2005.

But the accelerated substitution of other energy forms for petroleum in the transport sector could result in even greater environmental benefits while also improving energy security. Individual countries and the IEA have made at least preliminary assessments of the possible contribution of alternative fuels in the transport sector. The fuels that are perhaps the most likely to be able to make a significant contribution in this area prior to 2005 are: compressed natural gas (CNG) or methanol (which can be derived from natural gas), as well as liquified petroleum gas (LPG). Another important, but generally more costly alternative, is ethanol derived from biomass (largely agricultural products). Electricity could also be used more for rail transport and certain short distance, urban vehicles. Each of these technological options involve a broad range of often uncertain benefits and costs, including investments in fuel transformation and distribution systems and motor vehicle manufacturing, usually with long implementation periods.

Small increases in the demand for LPG products, natural gas, certain fuels derived from agricultural products or electricity could probably be met by existing resources, without major price effects. It is not certain whether, if any of these options were to replace a major portion (e.g., more than 10% of the petroleum products used in motor vehicles), supply constraints would occur or prices might be significantly affected. Ten percent of motor vehicle fuels in 2005 is expected to be about 90 Mtoe, which would equal about 10% of total expected OECD natural gas requirements in that year. As indicated in the earlier section on natural gas, such an increase appears feasible if there are no major, unanticipated increases in the demand for natural gas by other sectors (e.g., electricity generation). The price of these additional natural gas supplies would, however, vary depending on the region (e.g., additional supplies that could be transported by pipelines would likely be less costly than LNG.) If electricity or fuels derived from coal were to contribute 10% of the energy needs of motor vehicles in 2005 there would be less likelihood of supply constraints (assuming sufficient lead times for capacity expansion), but the additional economic costs are likely to be higher than those for natural gas-based fuels. Meeting even 10% of motor vehicle requirements by agricultural products would have a major impact on world markets (e.g., about 360 million tonnes of maize, roughly equal to the OECD's total production, to produce 90 Mtoe of ethanol) and would likely be considerably more expensive, at current commodity and fuel prices, than petroleum or natural gas alternatives. Ethanol can be derived from other forms of biomass, but these non-agricultural sources are even more costly.

Introducing fuel flexible vehicles (capable of using gasoline, methanol, ethanol or fuel mixes) prior to 2005 also appears technically feasible, although the economic costs are likely to be much greater than those involved in producing higher quality fuels. Fuel flexible vehicles would enable the gradual introduction of alternative fuels and the establishment of temporary or special fuel restrictions to respond to local environmental conditions. For these reasons, the United States Government, and certain state and local governments in the United States have been encouraging the development and gradual introduction of fuel flexible vehicles by major auto manufacturers.

Most of the alternative fuels being considered would involve major changes in the systems which transform and distribute transport fuels as well as major changes in motor vehicle manufacturing. To derive methanol from natural gas (or coal) would require new processing facilities. And to distribute methanol through fuelling stations in the same manner as gasoline and diesel are distributed would require new storage tanks and pumps. To use methanol in motor vehicles, other than when mixed in small quantities with gasoline would require modifications to engines and fuel system design. None of these modifications would require radically new technology, but all would involve investments, which in turn would have to be gradually implemented over a considerable period of time. To derive ethanol from agricultural products also involves a proven, but comparatively expensive distilling process. Some modifications would also be required in fuel distribution systems and in motor vehicles (unless mixed in small quantities with gasoline), but the required changes would be somewhat less extensive than for methanol. Powering electric vehicles would require the most substantial changes in vehicle design, manufacture and probably even function, but electricity supply and distribution would not be a major problem (assuming that most vehicle recharging could be done off peak).

LPG, CNG, methanol, ethanol and electricity all have some significant environmental advantages over gasoline and diesel (as described in more detail earlier), although each has some drawbacks as well. LPG produces higher CO_2 emissions than natural gas. CNG would have the same environmental advantages over petroleum products as does natural gas. Methanol derived from natural gas could emit CO_2 and NO_x in similar quantities to that of gasoline (on an energy unit basis) but is considerably more toxic than gasoline if ingested or absorbed through the skin. Furthermore, if the methanol is derived from coal, additional environmental problems would be generated. The environmental effects of electricity depend largely on how it is generated, but electric-vehicle batteries might pose some disposal difficulties. Ethanol has probably the fewest net effects, although its combustion produces some NO_x. The use of methanol, ethanol and CNG often results in higher unburnt hydrocarbon emissions.

Any alternative transport fuels not derived from petroleum would probably offer significant energy security advantages, as discussed before. Deriving alternative transport fuels from energy sources other than natural gas (e.g., from coal, coal or nuclear-based electricity or biomass) would, of course, probably result in greater energy security benefits.

The major barriers to the introduction of alternative transport fuels, other than the absence of an economic incentive to supply and purchase such fuels, are the investments that would be required both by fuel suppliers and distributors and by motor vehicle manufacturers. To design and begin to mass-produce flexible or alternative fuel vehicles (capable of using CNG, methanol or ethanol in high concentrations, or electricity) would take automobile manufacturers at least several, and perhaps more than five, years and it would then require another ten years or more for the existing vehicle fleet to be largely replaced. In order to serve vehicles not capable of using gasoline or diesel, a new large and dispersed distribution network would be needed. And, finally, facilities for producing the alternative fuels, whether it is methanol or ethanol, would have to be greatly expanded. These private and largely independent investments need to be made roughly simultaneously or the process could be halted and the investors would likely experience heavy losses. If the market provided sufficiently large financial incentives to motor vehicle users, manufacturers and fuel suppliers, the risks of such investments might be considered worthwhile. But with only a small financial reward and indirect environmental benefits, such investments are not likely -- except perhaps for urban fleets.

There are several ways by which governments have accelerated the introduction of alternative transport fuels. Perhaps the easiest has been to create or increase the price differential between petroleum-based fuels and alternatives fuels by increasing taxes on petroleum-based fuels and/or reducing them on other fuels. A second approach is regulatory, which has involved, for example, proposed legislation requiring auto manufacturers to make a certain percentage of their annual production flexible-fuel vehicles and requiring distributors to offer certain fuels (if available) or, in some cases, removing certain regulatory controls if the appropriate action is taken. Other ways in which governments have encouraged the use of alternative transport fuels include the support of relevant research efforts on the vehicle technology or the fuel production facilities and direct purchase of alternative fuel vehicles for government use. Experience in the large-scale introduction of alternative fuels in countries, such as New Zealand, Canada, and Brazil suggests that a carefully designed package of measures including several of those mentioned above is necessary.

In summary, there are a number of different fuels which, if substituted for at least part of the automotive fuels now in use, could produce significant benefits for certain environmental problems. But the time and cost of introducing these fuels, as well as their availability, means that their contribution to motor vehicle fuel requirements before 2005 is likely to be limited. The greatest environmental gains during this period appear likely to be made by the accelerated introduction of unleaded and low volatility gasoline (with appropriate emission controls). But some significant contributions might also be made, especially in specific cities or regions, through the introduction of CNG or fuel flexible vehicles. Widespread introduction of such vehicles and the necessary fuel supply and distribution systems is unlikely to occur before 2005.

There remain, however, many unresolved issues, such as the comparable environmental and economic benefits and costs (from fuel production to motor vehicle manufacturing and use) of the different major options available and the potential to exploit limited motor vehicle markets (e.g., fleets). Of course, questions about supply availability -- such as those discussed earlier in the section dealing with natural gas, are also highly relevant. There clearly could be problems of natural gas availability if natural gas and natural gas-based fuels were used massively for substitution purposes in the transport and in the electricity generation sector simultaneously.

4. "Clean" Energy Technologies

(a) The development and use of "clean" energy technologies

For industry, pollutant emission or the production of waste often means a net loss of raw materials, reactants or finished products. Measures which increase the efficiency of the manufacturing processes can prevent pollution as they save or recover these materials. This approach is the basis of the "clean" technologies that have been developed in a broad range of industrial activities, including those related to the production and use of energy. "Clean" energy technologies are defined here as those technologies that combine more energy efficient processes or operation and reduced pollutant production without necessarily entailing a change in the form of energy used. Major examples of "clean" energy technologies relevant to air pollution control are listed in Table 13. These technologies are primarily designed for new equipment and facilities. Their application to existing facilities, such as power stations is possible through repowering. Unlike most add-on technologies, the use of these "cleaner" technologies does not entail a fuel economy penalty. Many of the environmentally favourable energy technologies considered in the OECD COMPASS project [48, 49, 50] derive their environmental benefits from increased energy efficiency, as described earlier. "Clean" technologies are in addition specifically designed to limit emissions to air or water, or waste production, at the process stage. As such, they have been particularly applied to the energy sources that are otherwise among the most polluting. "Clean-coal" technologies, for instance, typically reduce emissions of SO_2 and NO_x by 70-90% and provide improvements in energy efficiency of the order of 6% compared with traditional coal combustion technologies [1].

As compared with more traditional add-on pollution control technologies, "clean" energy technologies may considerably reduce the cost of pollution abatement, particularly as they usually reduce emissions of several pollutants simultaneously. In many cases these technologies also have other positive attributes. In France, a survey of 200 "clean" technology installations showed that there had been energy savings in 51% of the cases examined, savings in raw materials of 47% and improved working conditions of 40%. Such benefits make it possible for some "clean" technology expenditure to provide investment returns [32].

The framing of environmental legislation (particularly regulations) has not always been favourable to the use of "clean" technologies, as emission reductions due to improved efficiency could not necessarily be credited in abatement programmes. Nevertheless, a number of IEA Member countries have included changes in production processes and "clean" energy technologies in their financial support schemes for pollution control. Specific aids have been provided for the development and introduction of advanced, "clean" process technologies.

Coal has been a major focus of the development of "clean" technologies. Oil price rises in the 1970s spurred a considerable research effort into novel coal combustion technologies to allow replacement of oil by coal firing. As oil prices fell during the 1980s, the difference between oil and coal prices became insufficient to justify the costs of many of these technologies. Pollution control strategies are now regenerating interest in advanced combustion technologies, such as atmospheric or pressurised fluidised bed combustion (AFBC or PFBC) and integrated gasification combined cycle (IGCC).

The most widely used advanced combustion technique is AFBC. Coal-fired AFBC is now established in major coal using countries in a wide range of applications. About 15 000 MWt are now installed in commercial applications in IEA countries [33]. The majority of units by number use bubbling beds, although most of the units are small (on average around 25-30 MWt). Circulating fluidised bed units are lower in number but tend to be larger. The technology has been favoured in some countries (in Germany for instance) because of its lower NO_x emissions. PFBC plants are in operation at the pilot/demonstration scale in Germany and Sweden, and are being tested in the United Kingdom. Most PFBC work now includes combined-cycle power generation. In the combined cycle configuration, concurrent advances in gas turbine technology are important, as it is necessary to match the temperature and flow-rate characteristics of the turbine to that of the combustor.

An IGCC demonstration plant has been completed in the United States although its long-term operational reliability is still untested. In addition there are a number of other coal gasification plants at demonstration scale, but none has yet been connected to a combined cycle generation unit. The design of IGCC units, like that of FBC units, are suitable for staged construction through a series of small units that have a high efficiency. Electrical utilities can therefore increase the size of a plant gradually, in line with demand. They can begin by installing a turbine which burns either oil or natural gas. As the load increases, they can add a boiler to recover heat from the turbine exhaust to raise steam followed by a steam turbine to generate more electricity. When the original fuel becomes too expensive, a coal-gasifier can be added. Each stage can be completed in less than two years. As the load increases further, the process can be repeated.

Not all efforts to develop "clean" energy technologies have been fully successful. In the area of pollution control for mobile sources, it was believed that advanced combustion technologies, such as the lean-burn engine, might make the use of catalysts redundant. However, recent experience indicates that low HC and NO_x emissions are not achieved through the use of these techniques alone. An oxidation catalyst would be necessary to reduce emissions.

"Clean" technologies listed in Table 13 also include the so-called "select-use technologies". This term covers technologies that can use natural gas in conjunction with coal in order to take advantage of their combined environmental, operational and reliability-of-supply benefits. Natural gas select-use technologies involve the burning of natural gas with coal in the same or separate combustion units in utility and industrial boilers. Two main technologies are available. Co-firing natural gas in a coal-fired boiler refers to the use of natural gas during start-up and normal boiler operations to provide a fraction of the boiler's total heat input and achieve a variety of boiler performance improvements due to the use of gas. A gas:coal ratio of 10:90 can reduce NO_x and SO_2 by 25% and 12% respectively. Gas re-burn technology involves the injection of natural gas into the upper furnace above the primary region of combustion to produce a fuel-rich zone, thereby improving combustion efficiency and reducing emissions. A 20:80 mixture of gas and coal can reduce NO_x and SO_2 by 60% and 20% respectively. Enhancing gas re-burn systems with sorbent injection can raise SO_2 reduction to over 50%.

"Cleaner" energy technologies have also been developed in order to reduce the amount of waste generated. Minimising waste means introducing improvements or changes at the process stage of industrial production. Such action has long been advocated, for instance, by the UN-ECE in a declaration on low and no-waste technology and by the EC through a programme of "clean" technology pilot projects. At a national level, a few countries, such as Germany and Austria, have introduced legislation stipulating that before a licence is granted for a new industrial activity, the applicant must show that the technologies used will produce as little waste as possible.

Waste disposal is an area where there are many opportunities to integrate energy and environmental goals, with recovery/recycling techniques. For example, a saving of 1 500 kWh results when one tonne of steel is made from scrap instead of ore. For copper the energy saving is spectacular: 1 700 kWh per tonne from scrap, against 13 500 kWh from ore. Other examples include paper and glass. Another opportunity lies in waste incineration. In many instances, energy is recovered, though the proportion of waste incineration where such recovery takes place varies considerably from one country to another (from 100% in Finland to 21.3% in Italy). Composting plays a significant role in the disposal of municipal waste in a number of Member countries (Austria, Belgium, Germany, Italy, the Netherlands, Portugal and Spain). Industrial high-temperature kilns, such as those used in the cement industry, can be used to safely burn hazardous industrial wastes which would be substituted for traditional fuels. The major problem that has plagued recycling efforts has been the sensitivity to the relative prices of the raw material versus the recycled material.

A number of "clean" technologies have also been developed to reduce water pollution at the stage of the industrial process itself. Some of these are applicable to energy activities. For instance, technologies that integrate water saving techniques (e.g., processes that include systematic recycling of waste waters) have proved very effective in pollution prevention [51].

Table 13
Examples of "Clean" Energy Technologies

	Pollutant Controlled	Impact on Energy Efficiency	Status
1. STATIONARY SOURCES			
Fossil fuel combustion facilities			
. FBC	SO_2, NO_x	+	Commercial
. AFBC	SO_2, NO_x	Variable	Demonstrated
. PFBC	SO_2, NO_x	+	Demonstrated
. IGCC	SO_2, NO_x	+	Demonstrated
. High-efficiency gas turbines	NO_x	+	Commercial
. Co-firing	SO_2, NO_x	+	Commercial
. Gas re-burn/with sorbent injection	SO_2, NO_x, PM	+	Commercial
2. MOBILE SOURCES			
Gasoline-fuelled vehicles			
. Changes in compression ratio, combustion chamber design	HC, NO_x	+	Commercial
. High-compression lean-burn engines	CO, NO_x	+	Demonstrated Commercial
. Stratified charge engines	CO, NO_x	+	R&D
. Fast-burn systems	NO_x	+	Demonstrated
Diesel-fuelled vehicles			
. Air/fuel ratio	PM/PAH	Variable	Demonstrated
. Controlled electronic fuel injection	HC, NO_x, CO	+	Commercial
. Four-stroke adiabatic engine	PM/PAH	+	R&D
. Turbo-charger/ turbo-intercooling	HC, CO	+	Commercial
Evaporative losses			
. Modifications to the tank and carburetor	VOC	+	Commercial
. Carbon canisters	VOC	+	Commercial

Notes: .   *Pollutant controlled*: main target pollutants.
         .   *Impact on energy efficiency*: positive (+) or negative (-).
         .   *Status*: technologies are classified here as still requiring research and development (R&D), demonstrated in some locations (demons.), or available on the market in some locations (commercial).

Source: IEA Secretariat.

(b) The limitations of "clean" energy technologies

As mentioned above, most R&D effort and industrial investment achievements in the area of environmental control has been devoted to add-on technologies, particularly in the private sector. The shift of R&D effort and support towards "clean" energy technologies is accelerating their development in member countries. A large number of "clean" technologies are still in their infancy, either in terms of their development or in terms of their demonstration and commercialisation. As a result, the full potential of these technologies is not well known, and uncertainties remain concerning their contribution to energy and environmental goals. A number of technical factors have yet to be examined, or costs to be determined. The time frame for compliance with regulations has also affected available control options. If regulations are implemented rapidly, plant operators tend to turn to technologies that are already commercially available (often simple add-on pollution options) or, in some cases, fuel shifts. Where a longer implementation period has been allowed, there is more scope for developing controls specifically geared to the fuel used and the particular requirements of the plant. The recent proposals for updating acid rain legislation in the United States acknowledge these considerations and a three-year extension to meet standards could be granted to operators installing clean "coal" technologies as part of their compliance strategy.

While "clean" technologies help control a broader range of air pollutants through their inherently more energy-efficient processes, the problems of waste disposal and cross-media pollution remain in some cases. For instance, in some countries, notably Germany, AFBC residues are classified as hazardous wastes and require special disposal, which can add considerably to costs. The United States Environmental Protection Agency estimates that the volume of waste produced by an FBC system would be 40% larger than that generated by a FGD/gypsum byproduct-producing system.

"Clean" technologies are necessarily limited by the rates of growth of new facilities and by repowering/life extension opportunities. In addition, they are not at the moment available to equip even all new facilities: "clean" technologies have not been developed for all scales of facilities and types of applications. Furthermore, like add-on technologies, "clean" technologies can only go so far in reducing pollution levels. This is particularly true in the case of vehicle technology. With current technology, neither engine modifications nor add-on technologies alone can provide sufficient emission reductions to prevent such intractable problems as severe urban air pollution in large cities. Greatest emission reductions and energy efficiency improvements can be achieved through the combined use of advanced combustion technologies and add-on technologies, which still require R&D and demonstration.

(c) Future development of "clean" energy technologies

New capacity and replacements represent a major opportunity for the application of "clean" technologies. The market for "clean" technologies for power generation could be considerably broadened by repowering, particularly where encouraged by environmental regulations. It also depends on cost factors and choices that have to be made for instance, between shifting to environmentally favourable fuels or shifting to environmentally favourable technologies. This market could eventually extend to retrofitting existing plants with advanced combustion technologies.

The commercial application of a number of "clean" technologies is only a few years away.

For instance, most of the technologies discussed above are covered by the United States government/industry "Clean" Coal Technology Programme, which now focuses on applications both for existing and new plants [52]. Clearly programmes at such a high level of funding ($537 million for the 1988 round of the programme) are likely to have a major effect on these technologies in a world-wide sense. Research and development efforts made in the 1970s are coming to fruition as shown by promising technologies such as IGCC. Their potential to advance energy and environmental objectives goes beyond the specific reduction in pollutant emissions and energy consumption and includes opportunities for increased flexibility and diversity. These technologies may reduce some of the economic and environmental impediments that limit the full consideration of coal as a future energy resource. Their introduction onto the market will broaden the range of options from which companies can choose to comply with often increasingly stringent environmental regulations, particularly if these encourage selection from the full range of such options and the optimum control technology can be applied for each facility or category of plant.

The ability of "clean-coal" technologies to reduce CO_2 emissions along with emissions of traditionally controlled pollutants is likely to prove a bonus in the support they are given. For instance, the United States Department of Energy has announced that extra credit will be given in its matching R&D support grant programme to innovative "clean-coal" technology projects that also reduce CO_2 emissions.

X. POLICY INSTRUMENTS

Once it has been determined that certain responses would be desirable for ameliorating or preventing a given environmental problem or a set of problems, but that market forces alone are not likely to produce such a response, the efficacy and need for government intervention might be considered. The tools governments have available for policy purposes are relatively few: information and consultation, standards and regulations, permits and licensing; and economic instruments including taxation, charges, pricing schemes and subsidies.

These instruments are used by governments singly and in combination to implement a broad range of policies. The instruments used for environmental protection are described in Chapter IV dealing with the typology of environmental measures; examples of specific uses of these policy instruments in connection with both energy-related and environmental goals were provided both in that chapter as well as in Chapter IX which discusses responses, such as improved energy efficiency, energy substitution, add-on control technologies and "clean" energy technologies. This chapter describes the mechanics of how such interventions operate to affect producer and consumer behaviour. The discussion assesses and compares the effectiveness and economic impacts of various intervention measures and describes relative trade-offs among them. The different criteria by which policy makers can assess these various measures when contemplating implementation are summarised broadly in Table 14.

In an ideal market operating more or less freely and effectively, the allocation of resources in the economy will tend to be optimally efficient. In such a case, government interventions to change market behaviour would tend to result in less efficient and less optimal allocation of resources, thereby imposing some cost on the economy in terms of distortions and lost efficiency. However, such ideal situations are not always achieved: sometimes the market does not necessarily capture or reflect in full the costs of a certain activity. Put another way, these costs are borne by individuals or groups who are not a party to the market transaction. In these instances, government intervention may in fact operate to reduce existing market distortions and thus result in a more efficient allocation of resources. While pollution is a case in point, it is but one example of an externality: occupational health and public education are respectively other commonplace examples of both negative and positive externalities.

Table 14

Applicability, Effectiveness, Limitations and Economic Effects of Policy Instruments

Instrument	Applicability	Relative Impacts Duration	Relative Impacts Size	Effectiveness I/P/C[1]	Implementations Cost to Govt.	Duration	Limitations	Micro-Economic Effects	Macro-Economic Effects
Taxes	- fuel quality - fuel choice - technology development	as long as in effect and some lags thereafter	depends on magnitude and elasticities	I/P/C	low to moderate	medium	political unacceptability of taxes high enough to be effective	- raises consumer prices so lowers consumption of taxed goods - raises producer costs and so internalises externalities - tax forgiveness does converse	- diversions of investment and consumption and output - redistribution of tax burden creates cross subsidies
Charges (Sub-set of Taxes)	- reimburse common services (solid waste, water treatment) - emissions reduction	--	depends on magnitude and elasticities	I/P/C	low to moderate (self)[2]	--	--	raises producer costs and so internalises externalities	may improve efficiency of investment, consumption and output

Key: (1) I/P/C: Effectiveness to influence, Investment, Producer or Consumer.
(2) self: can be made self-funding.

146

Table 14 *(continued)*

Instrument	Applicability	Effectiveness Relative Impacts Duration	Effectiveness Relative Impacts Size	Effectiveness I/P/C[1]	Implementations Cost to Govt.	Implementations Duration	Limitations	Micro-Economic Effects	Macro-Economic Effects
Sub-sidies	-technology development or introduction -infrastructure investments	--	depends on magnitude and elasticities	I/P/C	high	--	- difficult to eliminate once relied upon - unanticipated spin-off	- inappropriate signal to polluter/users - excess output and demand - inefficient output	- diversions of investment and consumption and output - redistribution of tax burden creates cross subsidies
Market Prices	-commodities; quality or type + technology choice	n.a.	n.a.	I/P/C	n.a.	n.a.	externalities may not be captured initially	efficient pricing tends to result in efficient allocation of resources, i.e., efficient use and production	efficient investment consumption and output
Standards **Mandatory Standards**	equipment and appliances, buildings, "add-on" technologies	medium to long	varies with stringency	I/P/C	moderate	medium to long	implementation and enforcement requires technical expertise, authority	internalises externalities, raises producer costs and prices	can affect trade patterns

Key: (1) *I/P/C*: Effectiveness to influence, **I**nvestment, **P**roducer or **C**onsumer.

147

Table 14 *(continued)*

Instrument	Applicability	Relative Impacts Duration	Relative Impacts Size	Effectiveness I/P/C[1]	Implementations Cost to Govt.	Implementations Duration	Limitations	Micro-Economic Effects	Macro-Economic Effects
Voluntary Standards	equipment and appliances, buildings, "add-on" technologies	medium to long	varies	I/P/C	none	medium	Not enforceable by Government	- internalises externalities - raises producer costs and prices	can affect trade patterns
Licence/ Permit	- siting new facilities - tradeable limits	medium to long	varies	I/P/C	moderate (self)[2]	medium	implementation and enforcement require technical expertise, authority	can create new markets and establish prices for environmental goods	
Information Exhortation	all responses especially those making economic sense	short	small	I/P/C	low	quick	- easily erodes - usually not enough to achieve substantial effects	may alter consumption	n.a.
Negotiation	development of charges, regulations or policies for all responses	long	large	P	low	quick	depends on willingness of industries to be regulated	may alter consumption	n.a.

Key: (1) I/P/C: Effectiveness to influence, Investment, Producer or Consumer.
(2) self: can be made self-funding.

148

Table 14 (continued)

| Instrument | Applicability | Relative Impacts | | Effectiveness | Implementations | | Limitations | Micro-Economic Effects | Macro-Economic Effects |
		Duration	Size	I/P/C[1]	Cost to Govt.	Duration			
Training	services/operations	long	small	P/C	low	quick	getting participation of "needless" groups	may alter consumption	n.a.
Testing	industrial equipment, vehicles and other consumer products	medium	small	P/C	moder-ate	medium	requires facilities, constant update	may alter consumption	n.a.

When markets fail to achieve desired responses and government intervention is considered, such intervention will tend to operate more effectively if it is designed to provide incentives by harnessing market forces rather than counteracting them. Market-based interventions generally permit greater flexibility and efficiency of compliance than do interventions which impose specific outcomes. In this sense, as a response to concerns about the greenhouse effect, an approach that works through the pricing mechanism will generally be preferable to one that mandates, for example, a specific fuel mix for electricity generation or for car fleets.

Environmental resources are generally perceived as being common goods. In the absence of property rights, freely available common goods traditionally have had no established market value. Their use is not reflected in the manufacturer's production costs, even though he is depleting those resources. He uses these commodities and lets others deal with the effects of his use (i.e., absorb the cost of depreciation of the asset). Pollution is one such form of asset depreciation that is often external to manufacturing costs.

"Clean" air and "clean" water over time have become scarce and costly to obtain, and hence valuable. In order to allocate these goods efficiently and bring their use within the discipline of market forces, it is useful to expend effort in finding at least proxy values for now scarce but still freely available environmental resources. Effluent charges, permit fees and taxes are examples of government interventions that can achieve some form of proxy pricing for use of the environment. Such pricing is important in influencing behaviour of, for example, profit maximising manufacturers to reduce pollution.

Government intervention can be used, in effect, to charge a manufacturer for his use of common goods. For example, air quality emission standards and emission taxes can force manufacturers to absorb at least part of the cost of air pollution control. While such measures may initially impose the entire cost on the manufacturer, much of the cost ultimately will be passed on to and paid by the consumer. In the absence of such interventions, the manufacturer would neither prevent or control the pollution nor pay for air pollution damages. The purpose of intervention is thus to place accountability with the manufacturer, that is, to force him to include those costs in his own cost of doing business. Producers react to costs just as consumers respond to prices. Market interventions will generally modify costs and so will affect production. Any measure which raises net costs will move the producer to the point where he produces less and so pollutes less, even if no additional incentives are provided. If further incentives are provided, pollution can be reduced even further. When polluting costs more than not polluting, polluters will have an incentive to stop.

Government interventions thus can be -- and often are -- used to assign costs, accountability and risk where they properly belong and can be most easily managed, with the manufacturer who occasions the costs. This internalisation of external costs is therefore viewed as an essential aspect of economic efficiency and hence of efficient pricing. In general, wherever accountability can be established, it is most efficient for society to make the polluter pay for his own pollution and to try to recover the cost in the price of his product. The notion of holding a manufacturer accountable for his own pollution costs and allowing this cost to be passed on to consumers, provides clearer market signals of the true total cost of producing and consuming the polluting product. This is the theoretical basis for the Polluter Pays Principle (PPP), a legal expression of polluter accountability, which was initially and formally defined by the OECD Council in May 1972, and subsequently updated in 1989 with respect to hazardous substances.

Regulations will generally effect internalisation indirectly, by requiring manufacturers to change behaviour in a given way to reduce pollution. Economic instruments tend to operate more directly. For example, by taxing a polluter, the government raises his costs, ideally, bringing his cost curve up to the true social cost curve (including the costs of pollution), thereby internalising the externality. The distinction between regulatory and economic instruments is in reality blurred by the fact that regulatory instruments often have a monetary component attached to them and that some economic instruments, such as emission trading schemes, do not necessarily involve a financial component. In addition the confusion about what to regard as an economic instrument or a so-called "market-based" instrument is substantial. The following discussion develops according to the typology of environmental measures presented earlier in the study and goes beyond examples of their application to examine in more detail the costs and/or relative advantages of various measures, as well as their broader economic effects.

1. Evaluation of Policy Instruments

(a) Taxation schemes

Governments can change the relative cost of consumption or corporate behaviour through taxation schemes. Whether initially levied on production or consumption, taxes will, by raising costs, tend to induce less production of the taxed product. They will also, by raising prices, tend to induce less consumption of the taxed product. By reducing the discretionary income available to consumers, assuming no offsetting tax forgiveness is granted, an increase in taxes also tends to reduce personal consumption levels. Because of these price and income effects, taxation can induce more efficient use of energy.

Taxes on business, including taxes levied to compensate for pollution damage, simply raise the cost of doing business and a proportion can be expected to be passed on to consumers in the form of higher product or service prices. Taxes levied directly on consumption -- sales taxes -- also raise the price of a good or service, although production costs (and ultimately investment decisions) for the taxed good are only affected indirectly and after a lag, to reflect tax-induced changes in demand. Who ultimately and really bears the burden of the tax depends upon the elasticities of supply and demand in the market for the affected product.

Differential taxes levied on the sales/consumption of substitutable products will tend to affect consumer choices among products. Tax differentiation can lead to relatively lower prices for "cleaner" or less environmentally damaging products, such as unleaded gasoline. Differential taxes tend more to bring about substitution among goods consumed rather than reductions in overall consumption levels, particularly when demand for the basic class of goods affected has a relatively low elasticity. Differential taxes for different fuels, which result in no net tax increase, for example, are thus more likely to produce interfuel substitution rather than an overall reduction in fuel use. While these tax differentials directly affect only consumption at first, the shift in effective demand will ultimately and indirectly affect production and investment decisions as well.

The other aspect of taxation policy involves *tax forgiveness* -- as a reward or incentive to engage in certain behaviour. Tax forgiveness simply means absolving one group of taxpayers from all or some of their obligations to provide their share of the general revenue (which implicitly must then be made up by other taxpayers). Tax incentives of this nature tend to be quite effective in channelling investment, albeit not necessarily to its most efficient use. However, lower overall tax levels can make more money available for investment, which in turn could affect the rate of turnover of capital stock, perhaps, in the case of environmentally-related taxation, thereby facilitating investment in future pollution abatement technology.

Some practical caveats about implementing taxation schemes include the following:

- implementation of specific taxation schemes will tend to have spin-off effects whereby ways, often creative, are found of avoiding or using the tax scheme to advantage. This is not necessarily always undesirable. Avoiding a pollution tax by reducing pollution is, after all, the hoped for result of the tax. Careful structuring of individual tax schemes is sometimes required to minimise their undesired and unintended effects;

- furthermore, because the design of taxation schemes can significantly affect investment decisions, perhaps even making profitable otherwise inefficient business investments, changing, reducing or eliminating a tax reduction scheme generally meets with resistance from those who benefit from the existing scheme. In the same way, the implementation of new taxation schemes usually meets with considerable resistance.

(b) Charges

In their simplest form charges can be viewed as fees for the use of public goods or services. User fees for canal traffic or for parks, and collective municipal sewage treatment charges are examples of such charges. Publicly provided services can thus be enjoyed by specific client groups and funded by charges to those client beneficiaries, rather than by funds from general revenues. Such charges thus generally reflect a government choice to take on the responsibility of providing a service, but not necessarily to subsidise it. Charges and fees can also be imposed for the use and pollution of the environment, considered as a public good. Charges are then additional costs imposed on polluters by government authorities. Such charges may be considered the "price of pollution", which polluters have to pay for use of the environment. In this sense, charges are broadly a reflection of the Polluter Pays Principle. Rather than being reactive, as are fines to pay for pollution damage after the fact, they are anticipatory and imply the purchase of pollution rights or user rights in advance.

Charges can be used to establish in a relatively transparent way, market prices and values for the use of the environment. In the case of air pollution control, charges levied on emissions constitute a price for use of "clean" air and provide incentives for polluters to reduce the amount paid in charges by reducing emissions. Charges too can be set differentially and can be variously based: for example, on the cost of pollution control, the cost of damage from different pollutants or the production cost function of different technologies. Fees and charges can even be set to vary over time so that higher charges at peak periods discourage pollution surges. Charges can also be based on the quantity or potential quantity of pollution discharged or on the pollutant content of the input material, or both, with appropriate rebates calculated for abatement. Of these, input-based charges may be the easiest to administer, but may or may not by themselves provide motivation for efficient pollution control. Such incentive effects of systems have been to date minimal, partially due to the desire not to economically burden industry, and hence the setting of relatively low charges.

Charges can be effective as revenue raising mechanisms to fund directly pollution control activities, thus accomplishing yet another aspect of internalisation. Charges can then have a redistributive effect, since revenues are used for collective treatment, research on new abatement technologies or for subsidising new investments. In fact in some instances, charges have been created for this very purpose. This is the case in Canada where a levy was imposed on every tonne of imported petroleum between 1973 and 1976 in order to build an emergency fund to meet the cost of oil spills. The fund and the interest it is earning is now being used to pay the Canadian contribution to an international fund set up for the same purpose.

The Netherlands in 1988 reformed a former system of product charges, implementing a new general fuel charge. It has been compared to an effluents charge where fuels are used as a proxy base for the charge [23]. The former system included five different types of charges and most of the revenue from the system was rendered by fuel charges that were excise in character. The new charge system reflects an interpretation of the Polluter Pays Principle where groups of polluters are levied specific taxes through fuel prices that will be used to cover the costs (of environmental policy and programmes) that are attributable to that group. Under the new programme, total revenues from charges increase by roughly 170% and will finance the majority of environmental programme costs. While the programme's charge system is explicitly revenue raising, one incentive feature allows a rebate for the use of certain SO_2 abatement technologies.

A fee or charge is often attached to the obtaining of a permit or licence, sometimes in the form of a performance or surety bond, sometimes to cover government monitoring costs and sometimes to limit the number of participants. In most of these cases, the cost of the license and the cost of meeting its established conditions, if any, become a cost of doing business and are included in the production function. To the extent that licensing is used to ration the use of common resources, the licence fee becomes a proxy valuation for use of the resource or public good and hence a mechanism for internalising the external costs entailed by that use. Air pollution emissions permits, for example, usually involve a fee.

In the case of *tradeable emission permits,* markets are created where actors can buy "rights" for actual or potential pollution or where they can sell their "pollution rights". The initial price of the permit can be set so as to provide motivation for development and use of emissions reducing technologies. To the extent that new firms wish to enter the market, the price at which permits are traded will reflect the cost effectiveness of abatement technologies. The difficult part, however, is setting the terms and conditions of the permits/licences appropriately so that overall pollution levels under the permit system actually decrease (or at least do not increase); the initial price must also be set so that businesses do not pay significantly more for the permits than the damage being caused by the pollution.

If such a balance is found, emission trading can allow economic growth to continue while making simultaneous improvements in air quality in "dirty" areas. Technology innovation can be facilitated if industry uses the market and profit incentives to seek cost-effective control solutions. The environmental and economic effectiveness of emission trading schemes may be limited by the quality of baseline emissions data which include problematic emission factors, point source inventories and site operation characteristics. Unless good baseline data exist, a correct evaluation of the effectiveness of emission trading is not possible.

In practice, charges which are not directly service related (user fees) are usually coupled with some set of standards to be complied with. Such charges generally have to be set to be sufficiently onerous so as to encourage compliance with appropriate standards, including the introduction of innovative abatement or process technologies. If too onerous, however, they can lead to surreptitious pollution and involve enforcement costs. The effectiveness as a deterrent to polluting depends on the severity of the charge and hence likelihood for it to become a noticeable and avoidable cost of operations. In fact, where the charge is equal to the firms profit from operation in violation of regulations, the firm should theoretically be left indifferent as to the compliance versus non-compliance choice.

Such *non-compliance* fees are judged to be strongly compatible with the PPP, but, as would be expected, enforcement is problematic. Some laws in fact are so structured that it is more attractive to pollute and face legal costs (which in some tax jurisdictions can be written off at 100 per cent as a component of operating expense), than to install capital equipment required for compliance (which receives only a partial capital cost allowance). In cases where infringements are observed, sanctions, such as fines, add to the cost of repairing whatever damage has been caused and preventing further pollution. Though such sanctions are found in the laws of most Member countries, they are often difficult to apply in practice. Of all infringements on environmental laws, only a fraction are actually sanctioned. Environmental cases in state courts are often abandoned because of difficulties in establishing guilt, particularly for air pollution, and to a lesser extent for water pollution and damage caused by waste disposal.

In practice, governments may find high charges politically unattractive, or there may be marginal, high cost firms that will threaten to close rather than continue to operate under the charges/standards regime. Governments will also most probably not have sufficient knowledge of a company's production cost function to set a single charge at an optimum level for every firm. Nevertheless, charges that tend to be properly set will operate to reduce target pollution. By raising costs to producers they will tend to reduce output; by raising prices to consumers they will tend to reduce demand, which will ultimately be reflected in lower production levels and hence lower pollution emissions. Such fees will also provide incentives to reduce costs through compliance with pollution abatement schemes. To be most effective, fee schemes need to be somewhat flexible and to reflect technological change, changing cost functions and changing pollution levels. It is also important that the scheme be understandable so that the appropriate actions result. Charges cannot thus be considered a fully self-administering form of control; they are not usually designed to be so.

In summary, while charge systems may require monitoring and enforcement, they lend themselves to being self-financing and provide considerable flexibility in how industry meets environmental protection requirements. This in turn may provide more impetus for new technologies. However, the effectiveness of charges in providing such incentives will depend on how they are set.

(c) Subsidies

Subsidies are direct or indirect payments to an individual, or to a class of producers or consumers, giving them a financial incentive to produce or purchase, respectively, some good or service. Subsidies given to one group of market participants ultimately will affect others. Producer subsidies, if passed on, affect consumption through pricing that reflects lower (subsidised) costs; consumer subsidies ultimately affect production decisions by stimulating demand for subsidised products. Subsidies are generally given to producers as compensation if their costs are higher than profits under prevailing market prices (so that the subsidy makes up the difference between profit and market price), or in order to elicit some activity or additional production that, for some reason, is deemed a policy priority. Consumer subsidies are generally given to induce certain behaviour, such as the installation of more energy efficient equipment.

Producer subsidies can be direct or indirect. They can also be distinguished between those that are designed to help maintain current domestic production and those that provide no benefit to current production. Direct subsidies that provide support for production can take the form of price supports and/or direct monetary payments. Indirect production support would include import restrictions (which can function as price supports) and contracts guaranteeing markets to domestic producers (e.g., between utilities and energy producers). Subsidies that are not designed to affect current production would include assistance for research and development and forgiveness of or assistance with inherited liabilities, including environmental damages.

Subsidies also include *government funded R&D* work and subsidies for the demonstration and commercial introduction of emerging technologies. In this context it is worth highlighting that subsidies can be used to capture positive externalities, that is, benefits to society which result from some productive process but are not necessarily reflected in the producer's cost and pricing structure. Private sector or government funded R&D can be an example of an economic activity with positive externalities. In such cases, increased production activity as induced by a subsidy can indeed be efficient and will tend to be socially optimal.

Governments can also, through combined regulation and pricing, effectively create or sanction *cross subsidies* outside of the public finance sector, such that one group of consumers or producers will pay more than efficient market prices for a given good or service, while another group of producers and consumers will either enjoy greater revenues or pay less, respectively, for the same goods or services. Such cross subsidies can frequently be found in utility tariff structures.

Except in cases where positive externalities are being realised, the more effective a subsidy is in altering market behaviour (which may in fact be the intended goal), the greater the divergence from market efficiency it will tend to cause. In this respect subsidies can run directly counter to the other economic incentives for efficient production. Subsidies will also reduce incentive for accountable corporate responsibility in minimising pollution and/or pollution control costs. Firms that receive subsidies for treatment of pollution, for example, may have an incentive to treat pollution to realise their subsidy, but have little if any motivation to minimise pollution or the costs of pollution. Subsidies also tend to undermine the PPP. The PPP recognises this fact, but nevertheless provides for exceptions to the principle in this matter permitting, for example, provision of limited interim financial assistance to small firms to meet environmental standards.

Subsidies can be expensive and, once established, can be quite difficult to withdraw as the subsidized group becomes used to operating under the lower cost condition. If adopted as an intervention strategy, subsidies tend to require careful and judicious management to prevent a snowballing effect. For this reason, subsidies for infrastructure development as a one-time effort and for temporary market assistance for new technologies, which will tend to capture positive externalities, are preferred to long-standing, broader subsidy schemes.

(d) Pricing schemes

Governments can affect consumer and producer behaviour by fixing the prices of goods or services at levels other than those set by the market. Prices that are set low will encourage consumption, but will discourage supply and investment if they are set below cost or so as to jeopardise profitability. Conversely, prices that are set high will discourage consumption, but encourage production and investment, particularly if they result in high profit margins. Price setting schemes almost always result in serious imbalances between supply and demand.

The effects of both kinds of pricing practices, although not initiated for environmental reasons, can be found in the energy industries. The price of natural gas, for example, was set below market value in North America until the 1980s, and in Japan prices for popular petroleum products -- particularly kerosene -- have also been kept low. In the case of natural gas, a shortage and glut cycle resulted in North America as a result of historical price setting, the last effects of which are only now disappearing. Conversely, oil prices have periodically been set or perceived -- in individual countries and in world markets -- above the marginal or resource cost of crude oil; such pricing has invariably resulted in supply/demand discrepancies. Utility services have also been variously priced both above and below the cost of delivering those services to different markets.

The alternative to governments setting prices is for governments to let the market set them. To this end, government policies might foster the deliberate introduction of market-driven and transparent pricing. Such market pricing can reflect the internalisation of external costs, for example, where market interventions, such as charges and/or standards have effectively set a price or created a market for the use of otherwise freely available goods, as is the case for instance, with tradable emission systems.

Efficient pricing can thus include market values or at least proxy prices for the use and depletion of the environment. Using proxy values for scarce and costly "clean" environmental resources can facilitate bringing the use of freely available common resources under the discipline of market forces. Effluent charges, permit fees and, to an even greater degree, tradeable permits, are examples of proxy pricing for use of the environment. Proxy values can also, for example, be based on some expression of "willingness to pay" to preserve or to pollute, or some notion of acceptable avoided cost.

Achieving transparent and efficient pricing which internalises environmental costs entails a certain amount of effort on the part of government and industry. Fostering market driven pricing along with the internalisation of external pollution costs will require some study of the costs of the specific economic activities and social goals at stake. This will permit the government to clarify the choices to be made and the costs and trade-offs involved. While it is impossible to do a completely exhaustive analysis with exact costs and prices, the more transparent the choices are and the more straightforward the pricing, the more efficient the decisions will tend to be.

Capturing externalities in the pricing system is an iterative process; externalities initially and by definition exist outside of the producer pricing scheme and must be brought into it, usually by government intervention. The process may never be complete or perfectly accurate: market prices may never be established for all uses of environmental resources, even after judicious use of economic interventions. This is one reason why the use of such economic measures are usually coupled with the use of standards and regulations which can create or reinforce markets and market prices for environmental values and for R&D on such technologies as pollution control, more energy efficient processes and equipment, "clean" energy technologies, and even new materials and processes.

(e) Standards and Regulations

Standards and regulations can be set either by the government, or by industry itself. Their purpose can be to prescribe to industry an objective bench mark against which to measure acceptable performance, or to provide common reference points or quality control. Common sizing for construction materials and the grading of coal and crude oil are examples of self imposed standards. Standards can also take the form of guidelines or voluntary limitations, which generally are non-enforceable government suggestions or negotiated agreements between government and industry concerning products or business behaviour.

By dictating some aspect of product composition or performance, standards affect producers -- and so ultimately consumers -- in several ways. They can either limit or expand consumer choices and can modify the price of available goods. Standards can change the cost of production for any product or business not already meeting or exceeding the standard by specifying or effectively requiring certain input and process changes which do not necessarily have a net cost. By imposing different costs, standards can affect the relative competitive position of producers subject to different standards regimes. Standards can also be used deliberately, by governments and by industry, to restrict competition and to limit trade in selected markets. The development of international convergence or harmonisation of standards, discussed in the corresponding section of Chapter XI, is one response to these considerations.

Standards and regulations can also have unforeseen spill over or side effects. The Public Utility Regulatory Policy Act (PURPA) in the United States, while aimed largely at removing barriers to the development of small, independent renewable energy projects, has spurred development of large as well as small natural gas fired co-generation facilities, overshadowing the renewable resources eventually tapped by the regulation. This market response, while unintended, has not necessarily been inappropriate given the prevailing market conditions in United States fuel and electricity generation markets.

Standards can also have the effect of encouraging the development and introduction of new technologies. In other cases, standards have been used in non-competitive markets to preclude new entrants or the commercial application of new technologies. Finally, unless regularly revised or upgraded, standards can fail to encourage producers from adopting new technologies to fulfil or improve upon existing minimum requirements. This is one aspect of the flexibility allowed by regulations examined in the following chapter.

The use of energy efficiency standards and of emission standards is well established as a policy instrument. The introduction and upgrading of such standards pose technical and economic problems, though there are many instances where cost-effective technologies exist. The mandatory use of such technologies is nevertheless usually the centre of a debate involving issues such as market choice (leaving it to users to decide the trade-offs between convenience features, purchase price and operating costs) and the commercialisation of new technologies (particularly reliable, low-cost mass production). These familiar issues are being revived by the need to reconsider new energy standards and technologies in terms of their potential for reducing polluting emissions.

While standards and regulations can be fairly effective and easy to promulgate, their initial design often assumes and requires considerable technical knowledge. For this reason it is not unreasonable to expect that standard setting is likely to be an iterative process, whereby standards are promulgated and revised to reflect current experience and technology. Finally, if standards are set without full appreciation by government as to enforcement requirements, including the maintenance of government expertise, enforcement staff and testing equipment, they can be ineffective and lead to inequitable application. Enforcement of standards once they are enacted also requires good faith efforts by industry, as does compliance with guidelines or voluntary standards. As discussed earlier, standards are often enforced by being coupled with charges, such as non-compliance fees that are set so as to provide motivation for compliance.

(f) Information and Consultation

Economic decisions as to consumption, investment and production, and social decisions that require continued support for or compliance with government policies, all ultimately rest with the individual. Governments use economic measures, and such measures as information programmes, to influence these individual economic and social decisions. Several types of information programmes are available to governments, appropriate to the various phases of socio-economic decision-making.

Governments can use public *information programmes* to help to clarify the nature, costs and benefits of the choices to be made. A government could indicate, for example, that, if a nation or a region wants to bring urban air quality to a certain more healthy limit, this would require certain actions, such as reductions in the amount of high sulphur coal burned, with a certain loss of or shift in jobs in the domestic coal industry, or some curtailment of private car transport. In this context, the government might provide information on the options being considered and could solicit input from the general public and industry on the accuracy of the government's analysis and the acceptability of the various options. Governments can thus both clarify the choices to be made and establish objective boundaries for debate, compromise and consensus.

Once a policy has been agreed, government information programmes can urge compliance with and continued support for the chosen policy. This is perhaps the most common type of information programme and can take a variety of forms: training, product labelling, media campaigns, or information brochures. The government can provide information about available benefits that might not otherwise be widely known. Apart from government circulars, for example, consumers might not know of the availability or the advantages of solar hot water heating for home use or about differences in efficiency among appliances or insulation. Industry as well may not be aware of new techniques or equipment available to make pollution abatement or process changes cost-effectively. While providing such information is most often more the domain of the private sector, governments may nonetheless, choose to supplement such efforts with their own, especially where an industry's information dissemination systems are deemed insufficient for the public good. Governments may also choose to exhort the industry to disseminate more information.

Government may also provide unbiased comparisons of available products and technologies through its own *testing* of products. Alternatively, it may resort to the requirement of independent testing and certification of products as part of its regulatory approach. Informing energy users about the energy consumption of equipment is a well-established policy in Member countries. In addition to energy efficiency *labelling*, West Germany, Canada, Italy, Japan and Norway have introduced the "eco-label" which guides consumers to products that are "environmentally friendly", at a time when green consumerism is becoming a major force in the marketplace.

Training programmes by governments have also been used at times to help increase the effectiveness of commercial operations (e.g., energy management) or to facilitate the design and construction of buildings in more energy-efficient ways. Testing and training can entail substantial costs and one alternative to government involvement is to shift such tasks to industry. Such industry programmes by themselves, however, might not be sufficient to achieve a specific government goal, especially if the government's goal goes beyond the economic self interest of affected parties.

Information programmes tend to work best on actions that make good economic sense for an industry or for the consumer, but that may not be widely known. Such schemes offer opportunities to the individual to become better informed about the choices required, their probable benefits and costs, and the alternatives available. On the one hand, to the extent that a government wants to implement a certain policy or influence certain actions, information programmes are probably an essential part of any such effort. On the other hand, to the extent the government wants to influence more directly or more persuasively the individual's choices, direct market interventions in addition to some form of information programme are probably necessary.

2. Broad Economic Effects

The preceding sections have indicated some of the various instruments available to governments that could be used to encourage improved environmental protection. Implementing any one of these measures can directly affect the costs of individual producers and so affect both the firm's behaviour and consumer behaviour. These same government interventions -- using market and non-market instruments -- also impose costs and benefits indirectly on the economy as a whole and could have impacts on economic growth. The preceding sections have focused on the micro-economic effects of interventions, that is, on the behaviour of the affected polluting industries. This section discusses in brief the general macro-economic implications of government interventions. Both the macro- and micro-economic effects of an intervention are a function of the cost changes that result from the intervention. Supply and demand, and flows of investment, consumption and employment will change in response to intervention-related cost changes. Such basic responses are described very generally in this section and without reference to economic theories about taxation, regulation or welfare.

No government intervention in markets, however well designed or properly targeted, is without cost. These costs arise from economic inefficiencies resulting from the misallocation of resources and from trade distortions, as well as problems of implementation. Government interventions in markets are generally undertaken when the perceived public benefits outweigh the anticipated costs; the benefit, in the case considered here, is a desired level of environmental protection. The difficulty in assessing this cost/benefit trade-off objectively lies largely in the problem of measurement. Economic and trade impacts can, for the most part, be specified and to some extent quantified, while a benefit, such as environmental quality, can be a more nebulous and often imprecisely defined concept. Furthermore, even when the concept can be defined, it is sometimes difficult to establish an agreed value for specific environmental goods, or to quantify the benefits of environmental protection measures. Some assessment of these trade-offs is nonetheless important, since certain government interventions could constitute a policy decision with significant implications for the economy as a whole.

If government interventions are relatively minor and affect producers and consumers on the margin, they will probably not have significant economy-wide effects; these might even be irrelevant and unmeasurable in the case of minor policy measures. Small taxes on certain energy products would raise revenues, but would not alter behaviour. In contrast, government interventions that are major and significant enough to change behaviour will have major impacts on the economy as a whole.

This section concentrates on describing the general macro-economic implications of various market interventions. It does not attempt to offer a detailed and quantified cost benefit analysis of any specific market intervention. Such a quantitative analysis must necessarily be country and policy specific, and would depend on the particular circumstances prevailing at the time policy action is implemented.

(a) Inefficiency Costs of Interventions

When markets are reasonably efficient, general fiscal policies ideally should tend to be neutral in the way they redistribute the tax burden for revenue raising purposes, since changes away from a reasonably efficient allocation of resources will tend to create inefficiencies. Taxation schemes in fact are rarely neutral and indeed are often deliberately not so, particularly where governments use taxes to influence behaviour or to implement certain policies, including environmental protection. Despite this potential for inefficiency, taxation is probably the preferred policy tool of most governments, including primarily various forms of fiscal relief from government revenue obligations. These various tax forgiveness measures include oil and gas depletion allowances, lower corporate income tax rates for resource income and special investment tax incentives. Taxation of final consumption of certain target commodities is often the preferred tool for influencing consumer behaviour.

Governments may seek to influence behaviour through taxation without raising overall revenue levels. Such schemes result primarily in transfers of income as discussed below; the efficiency losses associated with such schemes will depend primarily on the elasticities of demand and supply for the affected products and services. Alternatively, taxes can be levied solely for the purpose of raising government revenues, but such tax measures do still ultimately affect consumer behaviour, although for revenue purposes governments will usually tend to tax those commodities with the lowest price elasticities of demand, such as gasoline rather than fuel oil. In this same vein, revenue raising taxes will also generally seek a broad tax base. In general, the broader the tax base for a given tax, the lower its overall impact will be in terms of market distortions.

The way in which a tax works its way through the economy over time can be illustrated with a consumer tax on energy. Consumer taxes which raise energy prices will reduce consumption and generate government revenues (providing there is no compensation through the reduction of other taxes). However, since the higher consumer prices resulting from end-use taxes will not directly and initially affect the net-back price producers receive, the supply distortions created by a tax on consumption will be less and will occur with a lag. An end-use tax will still -- as with other price-raising interventions -- create some inefficiencies and distortions in consumption among taxed and non-taxed fuels, between fuels and other consumer goods and between consumption and savings. Industrial responses to reduced consumption, and the increased cost of taxed fuel as an input to manufacturing, will cause drops in production, employment and investment in the affected industries. Some substitution may result from changed relative prices, occasioning shifts in output, employment and investment, and occasioning transfers of income. Fuel taxes can, if sufficiently high, contribute to inflation and possibly an increase in interest rates. Tax forgiveness for consumers tends to have similar but opposite effects.

Again it should be emphasized that taxation schemes may also be designed to effect the internalisation of external costs or to capture positive externalities. To the extent such schemes are successfully implemented, the supply and demand mechanism described above will operate identically, but with the end result of reducing distortions and inefficiencies instead of creating them.

Charges paid for services rendered, such as collective pollution treatment or user fees, are included as production costs and will be reflected in consumer prices. Higher costs will tend to reduce both output and consumption of the affected product, as well as production-associated pollution levels. To the extent that charges internalise external costs of polluting activities, they will also tend to increase the efficiency of the economy by raising the producer's private costs of doing business to approximate the social cost of his activities.

Subsidies and grants, by altering producer costs and consumer price signals, result in supply and demand in excess of that which would have occurred under competitive and transparent pricing. These measures also create inefficiencies as investment funds are diverted from more efficient but unsubsidized enterprises to less efficient but subsidized ones. Unless the subsidy is designed to encourage a positive externality, the changes in investment, employment and consumption that result from the subsidy will create inefficiencies for the economy as a whole.

Price support programmes raise the price of a good to the domestic consumer and for the domestic producer without raising the cost of producing the good. This provides higher profits for efficient producers and permits the profitable operation of inefficient producers. Investment will be channelled into the affected industry, to otherwise (i.e., absent the price support) inefficient investments and away from more efficient investments. Consumers (including industrial users) must pay higher than market prices for the good subject to the price support, reducing their income disposable for other goods and services, perhaps reducing overall demand. Price supports can thus in certain circumstances affect trade, by raising the cost of a country's exports and inducing imports of cheaper competing goods. They may also contribute to inflation if the good is of economic significance (as is oil) and to higher (i.e., above those faced by foreign competitors) production costs for industries that use the good as an input. Inflationary impacts and higher interest rates may or may not develop.

Where that compliance with standards and regulations occasions costs, this may, depending on the elasticity of demand, affect prices and may affect profitability and investment decisions. Standards may also mandate inefficient outcomes or processes, or preclude the use of more efficient ones. By raising the cost of doing business, standards will discourage inefficient or marginal producers, who may go out of business. And, to the extent that consumers (and intermediate manufacturers) ultimately pay additionally imposed net costs, they will have less discretionary income available to spend on other goods and services. In general, however, because these measures are usually designed to internalise costs, they may actually tend to reduce distortions and inefficiencies.

To the extent that different producers or producers in different regions or countries are affected by differential costs or by inability to meet various standards, trade flows may also change, shifting towards the more efficient and adaptable producers. This may occur whether or not, as noted earlier, standards are used overtly as a tool for trade policy per se. Conversely, if a market is created for new products geared to compliance, such as pollution control devices or new, more efficient manufacturing equipment, there can be economic growth for new or expanded industries and opportunities for increased trade, as well as technological innovation.

Efficiency effects of market interventions will thus be reflected in both the macro-economic and the trade performance of a country. Market interventions that raise domestic prices of traded goods above world prices can reduce exports, while higher prices for non-traded goods can have an inflationary effect, raising the overall prices of domestic goods and services. Inefficient interventions will thus tend to reduce the potential for future growth in discretionary income, saving and investment. In contrast, market interventions that successfully internalise externalities and/or correct inefficiencies may sometimes lead to an overall increase in discretionary income. To the extent that such interventions do increase overall economic efficiency, they will tend to reduce the prices of both traded and non-traded goods and so will tend also to improve a country's trade position. It is unclear whether they would actually contribute to overall economic growth. Income and welfare as measured by conventional indices may fall as resources are diverted from productive activities to environmental improvement, but society could still be better off. This reflects largely a problem of measurement. The intangible benefit of "clean" air is valuable but not necessarily reflected in national income measures. Some policy makers have recognised this problem and are considering ways to bring environmental benefits into the national account framework, in order to show the results of investment in environmental improvements.

(b) Income Transfers and Trade

The efficiency or inefficiency effects of market interventions will fall unevenly among the various parties and sectors of the affected industries. Market interventions will thus invariably make some groups better off while others will be worse off, at least temporarily. Significant governmental interventions which can change behaviour and which will have measurable effects on the economy necessarily imply a government willingness to let the efficiency effects of their intervention run their course. This means that initially producers and ultimately consumers, will bear the impact of the changes and the costs involved. Measures such as subsidies, taken to counteract or cushion the impacts of the intervention, will limit its effectiveness and create further inefficiencies in the economy.

As markets respond to interventions, redirecting investment, consumption and costs in response to efficiency, transfers of income occur among market participants. Such transfers represent costs to individuals or to sectors, but -- unlike inefficiencies -- do not constitute a net loss to the economy. For example, differential taxes can be designed so as not to increase the overall total tax burden but they will nevertheless create a shift in the distribution of that tax burden (creating in effect cross subsidies among classes of taxpayers). Differential taxation or tax forgiveness will thus tend to increase or reduce differentially the amount of disposable income available to certain classes of citizens. Charges that internalise external costs will shift income eventually from producers to others in society. This will act to redress income losses to parties previously bearing external costs. Subsidies entail the same kinds of income transfer and distributional inequities as do differential tax forgiveness schemes. Redistribution of income by subsidies can be either from general revenues to a given group, or from one group to another. Price support schemes also constitute a form of cross subsidy from domestic consumers to the domestic producers of the good whose price is held high. Such schemes result -- at a minimum -- in transfers of income from consumers to domestic producers.

Large transfer payments or income redistributions can be as significant to the national economy as are real efficiency losses. They can induce effects, including regional imbalances, that are perceived to be detrimental. The transfer of income between consumers and producers, and possibly between regions within a country, raises equity issues as well. Income distribution also affects individual and societal valuations of various social goods, including environmental resources. For example, the environmental concerns and impacts associated with poverty are different from those associated with affluence. The *relative* value of environmental quality also varies with income. Income transfers to some extent might aggravate or compensate for and/or alleviate part of this gap, whose persistence and implications will continue to pose serious considerations for government policy makers.

XI. IDENTIFICATION OF AREAS FOR IMPROVED POLICY-MAKING

The wide variety of approaches to and instruments used for environmental control in Member countries makes it possible to draw lessons from past experience and consider improvements that might be made to policy-making. In particular, early efforts may have over-emphasized technical and administrative convenience at the expense of considerations, such as flexibility, efficiency, cost-effectiveness or equity. In addition, approaches are often based on different views of the theory of environmental policy which may not even be held consistently within one country. Underlying these differences are a number of unresolved issues which have fuelled debates on improvements that might be made to existing policy and to the design and implementation of new approaches and instruments.

In considering areas for improved policy-making, it is important to keep in mind the four major developments or trends which have been identified in this study:

- increasingly more stringent, systematic and comprehensive environmental control of (inter alia) energy activities, to which has been recently added a new sense of urgency;

- more emphasis on preventive rather than curative approaches, as exemplified by response strategies that comprise achieving greater energy efficiency and switching to less polluting fuels or processes and implementing inherently "cleaner" energy technologies, especially where required reductions cannot be achieved by the use of add-on pollution control technology alone;

- the development of cross-media (i.e., water, land, air) and multi-pollutant approaches, acknowledging the interactive effect of pollutants at different scales (local, regional, global) and on different environmental media (air at tropospheric and stratospheric levels, surface and ground waters, soil and vegetation); and

-   increased efforts towards the international harmonization of environmental control policy and instruments under the combined effect of concerns about trade and competition and about the transboundary nature of pollution problems.

Environmental policy already plays a significant role in shaping energy choices. The need to improve policy making so that this role furthers energy and environmental goals is becoming more apparent as environmental issues gain even more importance. The trends described above are largely inter-related and could bring about significant changes in the energy systems of Member countries. As such, they highlight the importance of choosing approaches that are comparatively cost-effective and will actually achieve environmental goals as fast as possible, within the limits of energy supply and demand systems that can ensure greater energy security. Perhaps of greatest importance is the problem for combining environmental effectiveness with the flexibility that energy systems need in order to preserve sustainable development.

While environmental control can introduce new constraints in the development and operation of energy systems, it also offers opportunities for reconciling energy and ecological security. A number of areas for improved policy making can be singled out as worthy of further analysis in this respect. Such areas include:

-   allowance for flexibility in responses to environmental requirements;

-   co-ordinated decision-making procedures in a variety of policy areas, including clearer definition of environmental objectives, better information and public awareness and more integrated R&D efforts; and

-   improved approaches for international/transboundary problems, such as harmonization, competition and equity.

1. Flexibility and effectiveness in environmental control

Flexibility is an essential component of energy systems which need to adapt to the constantly evolving framework in which energy activities are carried out. In particular, they need to be sufficiently flexible to withstand changes in non-energy factors which can have major impacts on patterns of supply and demand and thus on the availability and price of energy. In order to preserve the adaptability and diversity of energy systems, environmental approaches need to integrate the concept of flexibility in order to allow energy producers and users to use a broad range of available techniques to meet requirements to reduce environmental impact. But allowing flexibility is not only a desirable goal for energy security reasons. It is also increasingly being recognized that using rigid environmental instruments can rule out cost-effective control strategies and prevent the development of technological innovations that are ultimately the key to a lasting reduction in pollution. It is, therefore, also a matter of making the best use of financial and technical resources at a time when they are increasingly stretched for many competing reasons.

Flexibility has not necessarily been an explicit goal of environmental control measures, nor has it been specifically built into control strategies. As a result it can be difficult to assess or generalize about the flexibility they allow. It is the choice and design of instruments that will actually determine the flexibility that will be possible as well as the overall relative performance of environmental approaches. The pages which follow outline two areas where more detailed analysis might lead to improvements in the flexibility permitted by regulations and by economic instruments.

(a) Flexibility in the application of regulations

Policy makers are becoming increasingly aware of the importance of allowing polluters to implement as wide a range as possible of responses to meet environmental regulations, if only to ensure that cost-effective options are not excluded and that industry is allowed to innovate. Table 15 shows, for a range of regulations commonly used for the control of air and water pollution from energy activities, which of the four response options (add-on pollution control technologies, fuel substitution, increased energy efficiency or "clean" energy technologies) are generally encouraged.

The combination of regulations adopted can limit the use of certain control methods even when they are capable of achieving the required efficiency of pollution reduction. In the case of SO_2 control, for instance, there is a trade-off between removal efficiency, initial fuel sulphur content and the use of add-on control technologies. Where emission standards alone are specified, plant operators have a choice of responses to achieve the required control: either low sulphur coal (alone or in combination with sorbent injection), or high sulphur coal and FGD. A percentage removal requirement, by contrast, limits the operator to using only control or combustion systems which provide the specified removal efficiency regardless of the initial coal sulphur content, thus eliminating access to add-on technologies, greater efficiency and "clean" energy technologies.

The electricity generation sector and the example of improved energy efficiency provides an illustration of the issue of how flexible approaches allowing different responses can be important. Environmental legislation will, perforce, affect utility demand and supply planning. Whether greater energy efficiency can be used to meet emission reduction requirements depends largely on the tailoring of the relevant regulations. A utility confronted with substantial emission reduction requirements might greatly benefit from the contribution that cost-effective energy efficiency actions can make toward these reductions. If it decides to take full advantage of the opportunities presented by end-use efficiency in an integrated energy and environment response to pollution control, it can only get that full advantage if emission reductions resulting from energy efficiency are in some way specifically accounted for and credited in environmental control. Least-cost utility planning, that is, planning which integrates demand-side and supply-side planning into a comprehensive evaluation framework that seeks to provide energy services at the lowest possible cost, could well be the appropriate vehicle to incorporate greater energy efficiency as an environmental response, but only as long as the environmental regulations allow for its contribution to overall emission reductions.

Table 15

Regulations and Pollution Control Options

REGULATION	Add-On Control	Energy Substitution	Energy Efficiency	Clean Energy Technologies
. Fuel Quality Regulation (e.g. sulphur content of fuels)	No	Yes	No	No
. Technology standards (e.g. BAT, BPM, MATC, etc.)	Yes	Yes	Variable	Variable
. Emission limit per unit of flue gas or waste water	Yes	Yes[1]	No	Variable
. Emission limit per unit of energy output	Yes	Yes	Yes	Yes
. Emission limit per unit of energy input	Yes	Yes	No	No
. Emission limit per unit of time	Yes	Yes	Yes	Yes

Key: Yes: Option is supported by regulation.
      No: Emission reductions obtained through the option cannot be credited.

(1) Except when expressed as a percentage removal requirement.

There are, however, instances where greater energy efficiency and environmental regulations may in fact be conflicting to a certain extent. For example, under normal economic dispatch, electricity demand reduction will cause a utility to reduce the operation of plants that are the most expensive to operate [53]. For most utilities, plants that burn low-sulphur coal are more expensive to operate than plants that burn high-sulphur coal because of the differential in coal prices. But in many cases the contradiction stems from the fact that although improved energy efficiency reduces emissions, the environmental legislation is not designed to provide full credit for emission reductions resulting from cutbacks in power plant use.

Most legislation uses one or both of two mechanisms for obtaining emission reductions from power plants. The first is the point source standard. The second is an emission ceiling. Point source standards are expressed in a variety of ways:

- amount of pollutant per unit of flue gas volume (mg/Nm3, ppm);

- amount of pollutant emitted per unit energy output (g/GJ, Llbs./MMBtu);

- amount of pollutant emitted per unit fuel input (g/GJ, Llbs./MMBtu).

These limits need to be examined closely in order to establish whether they allow "clean" energy technologies, fuel substitution or greater energy-efficiency efforts to be taken into account. In the case of the first standard, it is clear that unless otherwise specified, emission reductions due to energy efficiency achievements or "clean" energy technologies cannot be so considered whereas fuel substitution can. In the case of the two other standards, it is more difficult to establish the outcome, which depends, for instance, on the type of energy activity (either energy transformation or end-use). Where the limit is expressed in terms of amount of emissions per unit of heat input, changes in usage of a particular power plant in response to lower electricity demand will have no effect on the emissions rate, even though cutting usage and thus the heat input would reduce emissions. Careful drafting of legislation is needed in order to allow the flexibility required to attain the result closest to the optimum in terms of cost, emissions and energy security.

The form and application of the emission standard may also influence the rate of early retirements of facilities, life extension and construction of new plants. This depends on whether the same standards are applied to new, existing and refurbished facilities, and whether the standards within each of these categories are set on a case-by-case basis or are uniform. For instance, less stringent standards applicable only to existing plants can discourage construction of new plants, such as those using "clean" energy technologies. Depending on demand (and demand management), this could result in the continued use of old, inefficient plants rather than new, more efficient and "cleaner" plants. Flexibility to choose the preferred option may perhaps be restricted by such differential standards.

Alternatively, an emission ceiling, that is, one limiting the total volume or mass of pollutant produced over a given period of time, may be set for individual plants, for a given utility or for a geographical area. This would allow greater flexibility to choose "clean" energy technologies or improved energy efficiency to reduce the usage of existing power plants which will lower total emissions and move the operators closer to the reduction goal. If an emissions ceiling encompasses all of a utility's generating units (i.e., both new and existing plants), the utility benefits further by avoiding emissions via "clean" energy technologies or improving energy efficiency, because the cost of construction of new plants is deferred.

In some cases, environmental legislation specifies both emission standards and emission ceilings. These provisions need to be examined on a case-by-case basis in order to establish whether energy-efficiency efforts and the use of clean-energy technologies can be fully taken into account. It can be particularly difficult to adjust emission standards such as point source standards, to include emission reductions due to improved efficiency. This is because estimates of savings arising from specific demand-management programmes are often uncertain. As well, the programmes may take considerable time to be fully implemented and there is usually no way to account for such deferred environmental benefits.

Technical change and innovation are essential for progress in environmental protection (e.g., add-on pollution controls), in energy security (e.g., energy efficiency and fuel substitution) and integrated technologies (e.g., "clean" energy technologies). Regulations, through the reference they often make to technology, have a strong influence on the choice of technologies and ultimately on their availability. This is a direct result of the regulation's effect on the rate of stimulation of innovation and the dissemination of new technologies.

A regulation may take the form of an "average standard", that is, it refers to a technology applied by most firms which can be easily adopted by others. This practice, which is often justified on economic grounds ("economically feasible technology"), has the effect of encouraging the wide dissemination of existing technologies. However, this allows the least choice of technology and would thus not have much of a stimulating effect upon innovation. The standard may instead be a "model standard" stemming from a technology applied by the most advanced and innovating firms. This again restricts choice and flexibility, but at least this innovation is disseminated and consequently has a more beneficial effect upon technical change. Taking the search for technical efficiency further, the "technology-forcing standard" is determined by reference to a technology at the experimental stage, but which has not yet reached the industrial exploitation stage. As the name implies, this is again most restrictive of choice but has an innovation-forcing effect which may nevertheless run aground if unreliable technology becomes forced into commercialisation too soon.

These various types of standards have very different implications for operators, in terms of costs and in terms of perceived technical reliability. Even though standards promoting innovative technologies can help overcome the reluctance of most polluters to use anything but proven, established control technologies, they still impose a pre-defined solution that cannot be adapted on a case-by-case basis according to the relative cost-effectiveness of a broader range of control options.

Efforts aimed at upgrading the level of environmental control technology used by polluters and promoting the use of innovative technologies can allow more flexibility through, for instance, the provision of time extensions. This could allow the installation of up-to-date control technologies to be scheduled during plant modernizations. Time extensions can also be used as an incentive to use new, "clean" technologies, as is the case in the acid rain legislation proposed in 1989 in the United States: operators would be allowed a three-year extension to meet stricter emission standards if "clean" coal technologies were used to control air pollutants.

Mandating the use of a given technology or group of technologies may not result in a least-cost control solution. For example, depending primarily on the ease of retrofitting at a specific site, the cost of installing FGD can vary from being a moderately attractive option to one which is totally non-economic. A least-cost solution is more likely to be attained if those aware of all site-specific variables are given flexibility to select the optimum control technology for each facility. In general, the greater the number of different regulatory instruments applying to a single plant, the more restricted will be the operator's choice of control approaches. The number of instruments in place varies considerably between countries. Utility plant operators in Denmark legislated one total SO_2 emission target for all power plants to meet (although additional individual actions may be negotiated) and thus have a wide range of possible responses available. By contrast, large new plants in the Federal Republic of Germany must meet emission standards plus percentage emission reduction requirements, and are also subject to coal sulphur limits and BAT requirements.

(b) Flexibility in the application of economic instruments

As shown earlier in Chapter X, economic instruments are usually used, and are indeed most effective as complements to, rather than substitutes for, regulatory and other measures. Economic instruments can help to simplify regulatory systems, to promote early voluntary compliance before a regulatory requirement becomes mandatory and to underpin compliance programmes. In the context of the present discussion, it is therefore appropriate to examine how economic instruments can be used to reinforce the flexibility allowed by environmental control measures.

Financial support for environmental control investments provided through subsidies, soft loans or tax relief has been used for a number of reasons in IEA Member countries. One of these is the encouragement of the introduction of new technologies, such as "clean" energy technologies, which will ultimately make it possible for energy systems to be more flexible and able to adapt to more stringent environmental requirements. For any form of economic incentive to become a real stimulus for innovation, a delicate balance must be found between the technological preferences imposed or suggested by the authorities and the freedom of innovation that is allowed. Financial aid can, therefore, act in a manner similar to the case of technology-based regulations: it can greatly affect the technological response capabilities of industry and the dissemination of these innovations. Allowing flexibility in financial support programmes to encourage development of preferred energy systems, such as the development of new production processes or the re-organisation of an energy activity to minimise environmental impact, requires that the financial support programmes be specifically designed for this purpose.

Financial aid schemes are also provided to accelerate environmental investments, having both environmental and economic benefits. A case study of financial aid schemes in Germany shows that while certain schemes have produced considerable acceleration, there is evidence that operators apply for subsidies only when regulatory action forces them to take environmental measures. An analysis made by the State Industrial Inspectorate for North Rhine-Westphalia shows that 20 to 40% of emission control measures taken by industry were "economically justifiable" without financial aid rising to 50 to 70% with financial aid. The benefits that such schemes can provide by facilitating early compliance is debatable and their environmental effectiveness is limited.

Pricing schemes and charges can lack flexibility in some respects; while they might be effective in influencing the quantity and quality of pollutants discharged, they cannot affect other factors, such as the location of the waste storage and outlet points, the timing and rate of output, or the risk of accidental and highly polluting discharges. Seasonal emission/effluent fee structures incorporating a variant of peak-loading pricing can curb pollutant emissions at certain periods. In the case of water pollutants, this could be at times of the year when the absorptive capacity of the steam is lowest, and in that of urban air pollutants, in summer, during the ozone-producing period. In the utility and industrial sector, legislation in the State of Texas places a seasonal surcharge of U.S.$20 per MMBtu for fuel oil burned between April 15 and October 15 in boilers that could otherwise burn natural gas in urban areas that have not attained national ambient air quality standards. Over 1 400 utility and industrial boilers are covered by the legislated surcharge. The effectiveness of this approach has yet to be compared to that of the more traditional view which is to set seasonal standards, such as lower volatility level for transport fuels in summer months.

The so-called "market-based" economic instruments include a variety of policy instruments that use the power of the marketplace to achieve environmental goals. Tradable permits (i.e., emissions trading schemes) have been specifically developed to increase the cost-effectiveness of environmental control and allow industry maximum flexibility in choosing a technical solution. Environmental goals are pursued by creating conditions (markets) where economic actions are developed and the actual application is left to the polluters. This means that all the options listed in Table 15 can be used and their emission reduction benefits fully credited. The United States is the cradle of emissions trading policy and the vast majority of the applications of this instrument are found there. Schemes involving "bubbles", "offsets", "netting" and "banking" of emissions have emerged as a consequence of regulations being perceived as too rigid in some respects. Though a relatively recent approach, experience is sufficient to examine whether emissions trading does make it possible to achieve flexibility and effectiveness in the environmental control of energy systems.

The main feature of emissions trading is a partial shift of decisions about environmental control from public authorities to plant operators. Thus the flexibility allowed by emissions trading implies a greater responsibility for industry. Though emissions trading is often presented as an alternative to direct regulation, this is hardly conceivable in practice. On the contrary, the basis of emissions trading is regulation, as the first step is to set an environmental quality standard for the area considered. It is the prefixed total emission level that causes artificial scarcity leading to prices above zero where demand for and supply of pollution rights meet. In its subsequent stages, the introduction of emissions trading does not, however, necessarily reduce the involvement of public authorities. Approval of abatement technologies for individual sources is replaced by approval of emissions trading transactions. As a result, emissions trading in its present form may not be readily suited to countries, such as the Netherlands and Scandinavian countries, that have structured their environmental policies on the basis of negotiations with licence applicants.

The level of the environmental quality standard should be balanced to ensure sufficient flexibility (i.e., the standard should not be too constraining) and effectiveness (i.e., it should not be too lax). An often stated problem is the lack of precise emission inventories, making reliable assessments of baselines and reductions achieved difficult. It is sometimes argued that the achievement of better, or at least equal, air quality is too uncertain under market-based instruments, since authorities lose control over the application of control technologies. A recent OECD study of the application of economic instruments for environmental protection concludes that, where the environmental effects of emission trading are neutral to positive, then lower pollution abatements costs have been achieved and technical innovation has been encouraged [23].

Further development of the use of emissions trading as a control instrument rests largely on the related issues of implementation strategies and environmental effectiveness. The long preparation period of emission trading policies in the United States, and policy amendments that are still under way, indicate that authorities are confronted with a substantial workload in implementing this new approach. In general, administrative costs of setting up individual emission trading cases have been high. But it is expected that, as the practice develops, a partial transfer of technical knowledge will take place from authorities to operators, since firms themselves search for efficient and effective abatement technologies. This would ultimately ease the administrative burden, at least in sectors, such as industry and electricity generation where experience in emissions trading is greatest. Application to other sectors, such as transport, would be breaking new ground. Recent proposals in the United States as part of the revision of the Clean Air Act have raised the possibility of using emissions trading for vehicle emissions although there are substantial obstacles to their use. Formulation of equitable and effective regulation would be a challenge.

The use of emissions trading for air pollution control is for the moment still limited to the United States and a few minor applications in Germany. Broader applications of market-based instruments are still being explored and a variety of schemes are proposed particularly for those environmental concerns, such as CO_2, emissions for which no control technology is currently economically feasible. As described earlier, there is scope with such instruments for integrating non-energy environmental approaches, such as reforestation, using the concept of "emission compensation", similar to that of emission trading, but on a global scale or "global bubble" although the substantially greater difficulties with international implementation remain unsolved. Nevertheless, this instrument, and its application, deserves further study and development as it seems to offer opportunities to achieve balanced and integrated responses for some of the most intractable environmental problems.

2. Better decision-making processes

The need for more balanced and integrated responses to energy and environmental interactions was highlighted in Chapter VIII. Responses will not be achieved in this optimal manner until there are improved and more co-ordinated decision-making procedures in place at all levels of decision making, that is, from the individual facility planner or operator up to the global level. A number of observations can be made here to highlight some specific areas where decision-making might be improved.

(a) Objectives

Having clearer and more timely environmental objectives with predictable lifetimes might smooth the legislation-enactment and enforcement efforts in environmental protection. For energy project planners and developers, one of the most troublesome aspects of dealing with environmental control requirements to date has often been the constantly changing objectives and the apparently piecemeal way that they have been instituted and subsequently enforced. Many delays in siting and licensing of energy facilities can be attributed to the disruption caused by planning for the "wrong" (i.e., inappropriate, outdated or insufficient) pollution control techniques or technologies. Vehicle and equipment manufacturers (i.e., both of potentially polluting and of pollution control equipment) find that rapidly changing requirements (i.e., relative to the time needed to design, implement and recover investment in technological changes required) reduce their profit margins and lead them to resort to less expensive, easier implementation options which may not be as effective in the long run.

Chapter II described the developments which have contributed to this situation: the most recently identified pollutant becomes the "pollutant-of-the-day" for which new environmental protection measures must be implemented. The urgency of the environmental problem identified has often led to rapid enactment of a new regulation regardless of how long other (often conflicting) requirements had been in effect. Furthermore, pollution control authorities have been given wide discretion in authorising legislation to tighten limits as new effects or concerns have been documented. Regulations requiring BACT often compound the perception of an ever-changing playing field where what was an acceptable limit or technological fix one day turns into an unacceptable one the next. Where there is a lot of room for interpretation in a regulation, there is likelihood of uneven application and time-wasting disagreements about what should be installed.

Implementation timing and decision timing are important factors in developing clearer, more timely objectives and better decision-making processes. Compression of the time to respond to environmental concerns will, in general, negatively affect energy-security goals. Longer planning horizons for the development and introduction of environmental protection measures could help to reduce costs and delays but assurance that environmental concerns are adequately addressed would be needed. To accomplish this, it might be preferable to react somewhat earlier to environmental concerns, while at the same time providing a greater certitude of exactly what will be required over a set time period. This implies taking some risk of being wrong about the magnitude of the response needed in return for less disruption to the energy system later at a more environmentally pressing moment.

There are few, if any, examples illustrating where such an approach has been developed and successfully implemented. It is not even clear that such a concept could be integrated into present approaches or whether there are specific limits or control techniques which could be handled in such a way. Perhaps the most likely and fruitful application would be in the area of prescriptive (or de facto) technology regulations on products, such as equipment or vehicles. In the recent debate over stricter emission limits for vehicles in EC countries, some countries have tried to soften manufacturers opposition to the new limits by promising guarantees of no change in the limits for a set period of time.

Much more analysis would be needed to develop a rationale and mechanism for having longer planning and implementation times which could be traded off for certitude in specific requirements for set periods of time. Any such analysis should include consideration of the trend to set broad environmental objectives and subsequently to search for the most cost-effective ways to meet those objectives.

(b) Improved, co-ordinated technology dissemination and R&D efforts

A number of opportunities exist in the extension of energy policy and technology development approaches to include environmental priorities. Least-cost supply and demand planning approaches which have been used to reduce the cost of electricity supply could help minimize the cost of emission reduction efforts if a co-ordinated least-cost, least-emissions, maximum energy-security planning approach were used. For example, fuel flexibility was originally developed to provide the built-in capability to switch fuels readily when necessary. It can also be considered, perhaps with some additional technology R&D effort, as part of a strategy to meet environmental requirements, particularly when these are set on a seasonal or temporary basis.

It is vital to maintain national and international energy R&D, demonstration and dissemination efforts. These are required both to provide incremental improvements in the efficiency, economics and impacts on human and environmental health and safety of energy technologies for environmentally sustainable energy policies and programmes beyond 2005. Recent heightened concern over global climate change and other environmental issues has raised questions about priorities for R&D efforts as they are presently structured. More integrated and co-ordinated work is needed, including a comprehensive technology assessment to identify "robust" energy technologies and systems and a regionally sensitive database on the technology characteristics and needs. A number of recent initiatives are responding to this need for reassessment of R&D priorities. These include work under way and being planned by the IEA.

(c) Improved Information and Public Awareness

Numerous recent opinion polls and studies indicate fundamental changes in public attitudes towards environmental issues. Better information on environmental characteristics of consumer goods and better communication of environmental objectives to industry and the public could help stimulate voluntary actions (i.e., either individual or in the form of consent for government enaction of policy instruments to achieve energy/environment goals) which would be of benefit to both environment and energy security.

There seem to be two large problems with public information as it stands today. First, in major purchase decisions other factors may weigh more heavily than environmental considerations. Secondly, consumers may not yet be willing to pay substantially more for more environmentally benign products. For example, consumers in many countries still prefer the larger, higher performance cars which can be simultaneously more polluting per passenger mile than smaller cars. The inability to achieve shifts to unleaded gasoline without a price differential provides a substantive example of the second problem. Much more information should reach the public about how the external costs of environmental protection can be most efficiently internalised and what this might mean for the prices of some products.

Hand-in-hand with the above is the need for the public to know how much is already being done or under way to protect the environment as well as energy security. Such efforts may not seem as newsworthy as, for example, articles on accidental environmental disasters. Some argument could be made for a continuing and vigorous joint government and private industry campaign to publicize this more positive side of the situation. Consumers may be further convinced by such information that, as government and industry action is under way, the problem is not merely one of government regulation of private industry.

Industry, too, has been responding to increased concern over environmental degradation and to environmentalists efforts to rate their products. Making industry aware of public concern and environmental objectives allows them to act to their best competitive advantage. Most companies recognise that their image is a major commercial asset. With public opinion running high on environmental concerns, many more companies may act to appear progressive with respect to the environmental aspects of their products. There are numerous examples of voluntary initiatives. Two, concerning lead-free or reduced-lead gasoline, illustrate the point:

- introducing unleaded gasoline or reducing maximum gasoline lead levels below those required by law;

- a petroleum company reducing the price of unleaded gasoline prior to government action to reduce the tax paid by petroleum companies on unleaded gasoline.

Better information about environmental problems and plans to deal with such problems spurs activity to develop new products and services to meet expected market demand. One example is a Virginia consortium of government and private industry formed expressly to develop and market natural-gas fuelled vehicles in expectation of the need to reduce urban air quality problems. A group of Belgian companies have become specialists in recycling of all sorts, from scrap metals to toxic chemicals, as problems of waste disposal have increased.

Better information about the connection between energy use and environmental degradation might help to both spur energy-efficient actions as well as reduce some opposition to new energy facilities. There exists a conundrum of continued increasing demand for certain fuels in the face of opposition to the facilities which make such consumption possible (e.g., refineries, pipelines, etc.). While such opposition may well achieve important concessions to production costs in favour of environmental protection, inaccurate information can often lead to sub-optimal decisions. As just one example, consider the situation where residents in some areas oppose offshore drilling. As a result oil must be brought in by ship. Recent statistics for the coast of California indicate that tanker spills amount to about 60-100 barrels per day while offshore oil platform spills account for only 10 barrels per year. This phenomenon of the "not-in-my-backyard" (NIMBY) consumer has been recognised but no good solutions have been found. Much more study of the attitudes and habits of energy consumers would be useful to elucidate how best to ensure maximum understanding of the choices available.

There are still many cases where no amount of information will be able to change consumers purchase decisions. The most striking example is that of electricity where no distinction can be made regarding the fuel that was used when viewed at the point of end-use. Additionally, it is argued that some decisions may become too complicated for most purchasers of products especially in light of the numerous criteria that the consumer might have to weigh. This problem has already been well illustrated with the less complex decision to be made considering higher first cost versus lower operating cost of a more energy-efficient product.

3. International Harmonization and Co-ordination of Environmental Control Efforts

As shown in Chapters IV and V of this study, environmental standards vary considerably within the OECD region, though there is a strong tendency towards increasing stringency.

International activities relating to environmental problems have multiplied recently and are increasingly affecting the formulation of local and national environmental goals and standards. These efforts have developed along two major lines: harmonization on the one hand and co-ordination on the other.

The major drive towards the *harmonization* of environmental control efforts is fuelled by concerns that large differences in environmental control standards and costs would restrict trade and competition. International action in this field has been particularly intense in the EC and the United States/Canada free-trade area. Regional or international *co-ordination* efforts have been essentially motivated by environmental degradation that transcends local or national boundaries. Acid deposition, maritime pollution, ozone depletion, global warming and radioactive releases are on a growing list of environmental problems for which action can no longer be considered merely on a local scale.

Obviously, the principles of international co-ordination and harmonization are related, and their application to international energy and environmental policy follows similar processes involving the exchange of information, the negotiation of agreements and the subsequent implementation at a national level of commitments made to meet targets or requirements. Nevertheless, these principles have been developed (sometimes simultaneously) to meet two quite different goals, with co-ordination fulfilling essentially an environmental goal and harmonisation basically an economic one. Their frontier is the issue of the allocation of effort and costs and therefore involves questions of equity and competition.

One primary difficulty in many such international efforts is the significantly different philosophies of environmental control upon which national approaches have been built. To recall from Chapter IV (typology), these approaches fall into three general categories:

- the "cost-optimised" approach, which seeks to reduce emissions wherever it is cheapest to do so, with sources controlled in order of increasing marginal cost, until a desired level of emission is reached;

- the "deposition-optimised" approach which seeks to reduce emissions so as to reduce pollutant effect or deposition at a particular receptor site, with sources controlled on the basis of lowest cost and greatest contribution to deposition until a desired deposition goal is reached;

- the "emission-optimised" approach which seeks to reduce emissions wherever emissions are greatest until a given emission limit is reached, with costs taken into account in so far as the emission limit is usually set in the context of economic (and technical) realities, though not on a case-by-case basis.

Such radically different basic approaches are not easy to reconcile on an international level. This section will examine how harmonisation and co-ordination might be pursued more effectively through improved policy-making and how they could be reconciled within the framework of national and international efforts to control the environmental impact of energy activities whilst preserving energy security.

(a) Harmonization of national environmental control efforts

International efforts to harmonize national control efforts have focused on avoiding large differences in environmental control standards and in some instances in environmental control costs as well. The theory is that the concerted definition of environmental standards and their uniform application to internationally traded goods, such as cars or refrigerators, can ensure that environmental standards do not represent or cannot be used as trade barriers. This economic argument in favour of such harmonization is generally accepted by environmental experts, providing that the choice of the "common denominator" does not result in increased environmental degradation. To avoid the pitfall of the lowest common denominator, it is necessary to take as a base a high level of environmental protection, as does the Single European Act.

The level of economic effort needed to achieve a certain environmental quality goal is strongly dependent upon local factors, such as geomorphology and climate or industrial activity and location. The original choice of control approach is, after all, largely based on differing national situations. This inevitably results in significantly different effects in terms of the level of effort required which in turn affects choices of technologies and costs, but, more importantly, in terms of who bears the costs of such efforts. For instance, the British cost-optimised approach to pollution control is based on BPM by reference to environmental quality standards. While accidents of geography (length of coastline, short rivers and strong tides and prevailing winds) may have encouraged this approach, it has proven adequate for resolution of most localised pollution problems. By contrast, countries, such as Germany and the Netherlands, which not only feel the effects of the pollution generated on their own territory but, due to their geography, also receive pollution from other areas (through westerly winds or the Rhine), favour deposition-optimized approaches.

If harmonisation resulted in measures that were uniformly set and overly rigid in their application, there would be no way to account for the natural advantages or disadvantages of geography and other regional differences in the assimilative capacity of the environment. For such cases, harmonisation might in fact be internalising costs which were not actually incurred or discouraging development or continued production which might be environmentally sustainable in certain locations. Alternatively, harmonisation to the lowest common denominator might result in increased environmental degradation in some geographic areas and thus fail to internalise environmental costs incurred in that locality. This is the case for most transboundary pollutants. However, for pollutants where there is no regional difference in assimilative capacity, such as greenhouse gases, this is not a problem and, in theory at least, harmonisation would be possible.

However, the harmonization of environmental control costs represents an even more complex but related issue and remains widely debated. The implementation of uniform international environmental standards would not necessarily achieve equal control costs even if they were expressed as percentage reductions, because this would tend to penalize those countries that have low baseline emission levels. Conversely, those countries with high emission levels for historic or structural reasons, could also be penalised if forced to adopt uneconomic measures to reduce emissions to essentially arbitrary levels. In terms of energy activities, the costs of implementing pollution control or fuel quality requirements, of necessity, vary significantly according to the physical characteristics of the energy resources produced, transformed and consumed. This issue was raised recently in the context of developing an acceptable agreement to limit the use of CFC. Assuming that the standards are flexible enough to allow it, the most cost-effective action will largely depend on the local calculation of costs and benefits which will inevitably be different for different polluters. Financial support, which may be implemented at a national level to help spread costs and smooth equities, may nevertheless increase the differences in costs among countries and possibly distort international competition.

The points made above indicate that issues of harmonization of either environmental control standards or costs cannot be considered in isolation or independently of the particular environmental problem under consideration. Further work and analysis is needed in this area in order to explore possibilities for integrating the related, but often conflicting, factors of cost-effectiveness, cost-benefit and environmental effectiveness. Efforts to coordinate environmental control aimed at transboundary and global environmental problems, covered immediately below, are likely to add to the debate surrounding the allocation of effort and equity.

(b) International co-ordination of environmental control efforts

International activities to improve the co-ordination of environmental control efforts are motivated by a need to increase the effectiveness of strategies aimed at tackling regional or global environmental concerns, such as transboundary pollution, while obtaining or maintaining an equitable balance of effort. In the case of agreements that relate to the risk of major accidents, such as radioactive releases or oil spills, goal setting is relatively straightforward. The main focus of international co-ordination efforts in these cases is obtaining agreement on the preventive or clean-up measures to be taken and their enforcement.

In the case of low-level chronic pollution, however, the first step is usually to agree on the reduction target or level. This process alone is complex and often lengthy, especially where numerous existing but varying national standards and instruments have previously been instituted. Indeed, in many cases, agreement on such targets is the only object of the co-ordination efforts and the definition of specific implementation measures and their enforcement is left to national authorities.

As a result, new concepts are being developed and used to deal largely with transboundary air pollution problems. One of them, the concept of a total national emission limit, is often expressed more precisely as a percentage reduction by a future date over total emissions at some previous date. This is sometimes referred to as a "national bubble". One of the attractions of using national bubbles as a basis for international measures is that this approach avoids any specification in the international agreement of the exact means each signatory will use for achieving the stated objective.

Until recently, such national emission limits consisted of uniform percentage reductions, such as the 30% SO_2 reduction target formalized in 1985 by the Helsinki Protocol to the UN-ECE Convention of Long-range Transboundary Air Pollution (1979) and the NO_x stabilisation target agreed in its Sofia Protocol of 1988. The disadvantage of such formulations in these agreements is that the target reduction cannot be exactly correlated to the prevention of a given amount of damage or to a given improvement in the environment. It is essentially a political commitment to move in the desired direction.

The concept of national bubbles increasingly appears to be the key to handling air pollution in an international context and is now being widely used in such fora as the EC and the UN-ECE. Their use as an international air pollution control strategy imposes very different burdens on signatories. Therefore, further steps are likely to meet growing difficulties for reasons of elementary marginal cost calculations and consequent perceptions of equity. Nonetheless, this approach is one of the most flexible international means to limiting pollutants which are subject to long-range transport and which contribute to environmental degradation independent of the exact location of the source.

A trend to move from uniform percentage reduction targets to defining different percentage reductions for different countries is also becoming apparent. The EC used this approach to define national reduction targets for SO_2, NO_x and PM emissions for existing large combustion plants. The Directive on large combustion plants is more refined for this reason, as well as for its inclusion of technology-based emission limits for new plants. Yet, neither approach is directly related to the effects on the environment. Thus, the problem remains that some countries or polluters may be paying either too much or too little for ameliorating an environmental problem. More refined and equitable approaches can only be achieved using reliable information on emission volumes and locations, as well as patterns and mechanisms of transport and deposition. It may be that future agreements of this sort will have to build in the flexibility needed to adjust adopted targets as better information or analysis is forthcoming.

The development of the concept of critical loads can be seen, at an international level, as an attempt to go further than the national-bubble approach while avoiding immediate difficulties which exist in confronting technology-based obligations. The elaboration of an approach based on critical loads is aimed at the establishment of an effect-oriented scientific basis for decisions concerning the limitation and reduction of transboundary pollutants. The critical-loads concept aims at the protection or restoration of areas or regions which are already highly polluted while allowing increases of pollution in unpolluted areas (up to the critical load). The use of this concept might contribute to the migration of polluting industries to unpolluted areas and, eventually, air pollution would be spread more evenly. The concept could be expanded to postulate a global bubble for greenhouse gases and a critical load beyond which it would be unwise to go.

There is also a trend to use the principle of critical loads to complement BAT and vice versa. The critical loads approach is applied when known environmental tolerances are exceeded by known sources, whereas the application of BAT treatment is favoured in more complex situations, for example, unknown critical loads, complex dispersion, unknown sources, or no source-receptor relationship available. The application of the critical-loads concept requires that the technical and economical feasibility of measures be taken as the control variable; whereas, when BAT is applied, critical loads is the control variable. The BAT principle, which covers all polluters including already existing sources, results in the most significant improvements in highly polluted areas and, as a consequence, benefits immediately all areas.

The definition of a control policy based on critical loads could address the cost-effectiveness issue. As the use of the concept of critical loads develops at a national and international level, it will become apparent that further uniform percentage reductions in emissions will not, in general, be the most economical means of reaching target critical levels. The use of BAT can play an increasingly important part in the development of cost-effective strategies which will necessarily need to be coordinated at an international level.

If the reductions needed are based upon critical loads, the nature and scale of resulting reduction measures would vary considerably from country to country (posing new problems for the harmonization of environmental standards). Compliance with the requirements of any major programme to control problems, such as acid deposition or ozone levels, will inevitably be costly. An important policy issue is, therefore, how the costs should be shared among different geographical areas and what flexibility should be allowed for allocation among different sources. The RAINS model developed by IIASA suggests that larger and more cost-effective reductions in acidification in Western Europe can be achieved by controlling emissions in Eastern Europe, whereas across-the-board reductions of SO_2 and NO_x emissions in countries that have signed the UN-ECE protocols would have a limited impact on pollution levels. Several analysts and legislators have acknowledged that the poorly understood source-receptor relationship of many pollution problems (especially air pollution) renders the idea of a culpable "polluter" inappropriate. Instituting policies involving very different levels of abatement investment in different countries implies the need to consider the equity of and need for arrangements for financing abatement policies. The geographical disparity between the parties experiencing the costs and the parties receiving the benefits argues for broader distribution of the cost burden. As a result, cost-sharing schemes analogous to the Superfund for toxic waste clean-up which is funded from feedstock tax revenues or emission trading schemes used in the United States have begun to be considered, either nationally or internationally, as a part of an integrated and equitable approach to international environmental problems.

As shown by the discussion presented here, the difficulty of improving and developing existing and future international co-ordination efforts is a growing challenge for national governments and relevant international organisations. The balance that has to be achieved between the performance criteria of environmental control on the one hand (environmental effectiveness, cost-effectiveness, equity and flexibility) and of energy security on the other (reliability, availability, adaptability and diversity) should now be considered at the international level as well as at the national and individual polluter's level. More analysis is needed on what has worked well in the past in developing and implementing coordinated, flexible and equitable approaches. It is imperative that all concerns, including, inter alia, energy interests, are represented in the process of development and implementation.

XII. CONCLUSIONS

Environmental policy and instruments for environmental control already play a significant role in shaping some of our energy choices, from production to end-use. The energy sector, which spreads a complex web of activities throughout the economy of industrialised countries, is participating in this evolution. There is growing acceptance, by energy and environmental policy makers alike, that environmental issues, and the measures designed to alleviate them, will gain even more importance in the years ahead. While the current economic growth in OECD countries increases the volume of activity which in turn generates possible threats to the environment, it also improves the capability for carrying out sometimes costly environmental control actions and expands in many ways the opportunities for technological innovation in the area of pollution prevention and control.

The potential environmental impacts of energy activities are pervasive but so, by now, are the systems devised by governments in conjunction with industry to prevent, minimise, control or eliminate such impacts. Environmental protection approaches are evolving rapidly as new challenges appear, but the basic tools available are well known. Despite sometimes considerable uncertainty, improved scientific methods and information are supporting major efforts to tailor approaches and responses to a very broad range of complex environmental problems. In many instances, further scientific evidence and data to verify the connection between the sources of pollutants/hazards and the effects are still needed. In some cases, governments feel that the environmental risk involved justifies taking action based only on partial, but convincing evidence. This can be a matter of anticipating environmental risk by taking preventive action. Given the complexity and magnitude of current and emerging environmental concerns, expert opinion (considered alongside reliable information) is increasingly valuable in the provision of advice to policy-makers.

Several complementary and mutually supporting policy instruments are usually combined to ensure increased effectiveness. The instruments used, the limits imposed and the extent of coverage still vary among countries or even within countries. The trend towards stricter limits, broader coverage and harmonisation of approach on transboundary and global problems will ultimately reduce some of these disparities. Regional solutions are also being sought where it might be less effective to further tighten an individual country's regulations and for global and transboundary problems. International co-ordination efforts are leading to much more reliance on the development and implementation of protective action, via international bilateral or multilateral agreements.

Response strategies also differ according to the varying environmental effects of different energy sources and end-uses. This ensures that efforts are as effective as possible, both in environmental terms and in economic terms. It also implies careful comparative analysis of alternative responses (when they exist) as well as a consideration of interactive effects. Thus, national action plans will naturally contain different elements and stringencies even while contributing to solutions to global and transboundary environmental problems. Yet, it is important that these individual plans add up to an adequate and equitable overall response. Assurance that this is so requires active exchange and co-ordination at the international level.

Actions to protect the environment have, of course, affected energy activities by internalising some of the environmental costs and thus changing some patterns of energy supply and demand. However, even the extensive actions taken to date have been developed and implemented in a fashion that has not significantly affected energy security. The effect of commitments already made for further action could be more significant and needs better quantification. Examination of the implications of further actions on future energy security leads to a number of notes of caution.

Energy and environmental objectives must be taken into account together to avoid imbalances between supply and demand. Through the implementation of mutually beneficial responses, environmental concern and measures can provide major impetus for the implementation of policies supporting energy security. Improved energy efficiency and conservation as well as the promotion of renewable energy and other non-fossil resources are priority options for environmental protection that have strong positive implications for the energy security of Member countries. Many complementary actions can be taken in promoting a higher degree of diversification in transport fuels which would in turn improve the environmental performance of vehicles.

Heightened concern about the environmental impacts of energy activities has thus created not only a mandate but more importantly an opportunity for governments, producers and consumers to implement optimal solutions supporting the goals of economic growth, energy security and environmental protection. There are numerous options available which the study examines under the categories of the use of add-on pollution control and "clean" energy technologies, greater energy efficiency and fuel substitution. At least in the case of actions considered in the short to medium term (e.g., up to the year 2005), it is a question of a more directed and improved application of familiar actions rather than one of entirely new responses, though any such responses should also be considered. However, because of the potential gravity and extent of many environmental problems and the complexity of their interactions, the scale of action that will be needed in order to reach economic and energy security and environmental goals simultaneously is not yet clear. The combinations of policy responses and instruments that will be best suited to achieving these goals also require further analysis.

It is widely accepted that the potential for economically viable improved energy efficiency in Member countries is significant even at the present, relatively low, energy prices. Such improvements are in the interest of the sustainable development of Member countries, their energy security and, through the potential energy conservation which helps to reduce the overall environmental impact of fuel cycles as well as the direct pollution caused by energy use, their environmental quality. Nevertheless, substantial changes in the rate of efficiency improvements, such as those that would be necessary to make a more significant contribution to regional or global environmental problems, depend critically on the price incentive to different consumer categories as well as on the pace of technological upgrading.

There are numerous opportunities for fuel substitution in most end-use sectors and for electricity generation. For instance, in the transport sector, fuel switching options that could make a contribution probably by the turn of the century include compressed natural gas, methanol and ethanol, especially if the transition can be facilitated by flexible-fuelled vehicles currently under development. Dual-fuel and multi-fuel electricity generation, where economic, can likewise contribute to energy security by the added flexibility provided by fuel-switching possibilities. Increased interest in, and development of, environmentally beneficial multi-fuel systems (used to comply with seasonal environmental requirements, for instance), could augment such flexibility and therefore improve energy security.

Regardless of the particular response chosen, the reconciliation of conflicting needs remains a major problem. On the one hand, society needs to ensure that environmental damage will be prevented or limited to acceptable levels and such certainty is most often obtained through regulation. On the other hand, economic (and energy) systems work best when there is adequate flexibility. While this study does not attempt to settle these differences, it provides insights into areas where improvements could be made to make the balancing process a little easier.

For example, better policy co-ordination and better decision-making procedures, at both national and international levels and involving a wide range of actors (governments, private industry and individual consumers), can contribute substantially. In particular, such co-ordination must be implemented throughout the full cycle of technology development and commercialisation and must extend to the selection of responses and policy instruments. Like energy decisions, decisions on environmental protection are often necessarily made under conditions of uncertainty. Precautionary action taken before achieving full scientific understanding or evidence can be less traumatic for the energy sector and energy security than delayed, drastic implementation. The early engagement of implicated decision-makers smooths this process.

Better methods are needed to deal with the increasing resistance to the siting of coal, nuclear and hydro generation facilities and waste disposal facilities which adds to the uncertainties about future electricity planning. For example, to the extent that environmental concerns restrict the siting of mining and drilling operations, the development of indigenous energy supplies may be restricted. Given such siting difficulties, together with an uncertain regulatory situation for many utilities, there is a threat to system reliability in some countries. As available lead times are shortened, this may result in shifts to generating fuels which might then pose energy security problems in the medium to longer term. Efforts to develop technological solutions for any environmental problems posed by the development of indigenous fuels could be expected to continue, although acceptable solutions to all of the emerging environmental problems may be costly and long in coming. New or revised approaches may be needed to facilitate siting decisions without sacrificing public involvement. For example, compensation in some form to those likely to be affected may be necessary and could in turn be internalised into the cost of the project and passed on equitably to the full, benefitting population.

There are increasing constraints on the use of fossil fuels with the emergence of a variety of environmental concerns (acid deposition, respirable particulate matter, photochemical oxidant pollution and, more recently, global climate change). Efforts to avoid or minimise the narrowing of fuel choice could begin with a better understanding and quantification of the environmental effects of energy use throughout the full fuel cycle. Such quantification could support decision-making in respect of efforts to establish an energy system that will supply and use a diverse range of energy forms that are also environmentally favourable. This is a key area for future research.

Designing appropriate responses and improving policy-making means addressing the constraints that commonly result in efforts and programmes involving large numbers of organisations and individuals at various levels. That is, responses and policy instruments should be tailored to take into account the specific characteristics and the multiple goals of the various economic actors and groups, such as private industry or consumers. Knowledge of these particular aspects and how to use them to advantage in the case of environmental concerns is still developing.

Environmental measures have the potential to modify, significantly, patterns of energy trade and investment. Increased demand for environmentally preferable fuels could create additional motivation to relax trade restrictions, where they exist, on these fuels. The trend towards the international harmonization of environmental approaches along with other related efforts should help to reduce competitive inequities. While lack of harmonization in some countries was not a major factor in causing the structural changes observed over the last decade, divergence in stringency of environmental requirements among countries, combined with continuing or increasing siting difficulties, could eventually lead to migration of energy intensive industries, such as refineries, within and out of OECD, countries with some resultant effect on energy security.

Technologies and techniques have been developed which have met both requirements without much sacrifice to either goal. The key to avoiding incursions on energy security because of environmental concerns may well be careful "implementation timing", in conjunction with careful co-ordination of energy and environmental concerns. Constantly changing conditions and scientific information should be acknowledged by designing approaches with greater flexibility built in to allow modification as conditions change or new information surfaces. There has been progress on integrated pollution control approaches based on full-fuel-cycle, least-cost analysis. These are well suited to identifying the benefits, costs and trade-offs that may have to be made.

Suggestions for Further Work

The study found considerable variation in the availability, level of detail and reliability of information and analysis on the possible responses and the effects of the application of policy instruments. The study considered only the data available on OECD countries. Including data from non-OECD countries would help to complete the picture. In general, even for OECD countries, further country and sector-specific analysis on the contribution of all of the possible responses to the achievement of national and international environmental goals is needed in order to formulate and evaluate specific proposed responses. More specifically, in the areas of greater energy efficiency and fuel substitution in the sectors of industry and of buildings, basic information is still needed on past achievements, barriers, and remaining potential. For the sectors of transport and electricity generation and end-use, comparative analysis of the full range of responses (e.g., greater energy efficiency, fuel substitution and "clean" energy technologies) should be undertaken, taking as a basis the generally better information available on these sectors.

There are numerous questions raised in the study's sections on policy instruments and on responses which need to be addressed within the context above. With respect to policy instruments (e.g., taxes, subsidies, etc.), a more thorough examination of all applicable economic and administrative policy instruments is needed. Such analysis should consider the instruments in the context of specific environmental problems, such as climate change or acid rain, and should assess, and, as far as possible, quantify, the likely impacts of the application of such instruments on energy consumption, energy efficiency and intensity, and fuel mix and their combined effect on the energy sector in general.

There are also major questions raised for each of the responses considered by the study. Further analysis of strategies to increase energy efficiency should include examination of how policy instruments can be applied to encourage very specifically those energy-efficient actions that are most beneficial to the environment because of their emission reduction potential. A first step would be a thorough analysis of how effective regulations and standards have been in supporting greater energy efficiency.

Analysis of strategies to substitute more environmentally benign fuels should consider the availability of these fuels in light of the likely demand for them over time as well as some of the difficult trade-offs between environmental goals and energy security involved in some substitution options. For "clean" energy technologies, analysis of strategies must include establishing more up-to-date information on their rate of commercial uptake and finding ways to achieve better integration of R&D, demonstration and dissemination efforts of the energy and environment interests to better promote these technologies. Questions of flexibility in environmental control and its timing become paramount in decision-making regarding environmental problems where "clean" energy technologies are nearly ready for commercialisation. More work is needed on the development of a mechanism (i.e., some sort of staged strategy) to allow the penetration of "clean" energy technologies which are not yet fully commercial but which have great promise. It will also be important to determine the capabilities of these technologies (as well as of add-on technologies) and their manufacturing industry to keep up with the imposition of stricter regulations.

In designing responses, it will be important to understand better how industry and energy-production facility operators will respond when it becomes time to make decisions with respect to the energy/environment/economics frontier with which they are faced. It will be important to know, for example, how least-cost planning can contribute to achieving optimum "least-cost, least-emissions and maximum energy-security" results. Questions relating to the ability of industry to take advantage of market-based instruments, such as emission trading, will be of particular interest.

More analysis is needed of the responses designed primarily to alleviate single air pollution problems in terms of their positive or negative impact on other air pollution, solid waste and water pollution problems. Such work could also extend to examining the opportunities offered by cross-media or integrated pollution approaches and should in particular consider how the bundle (and the costs) of responses and instruments would vary depending on whether a piecemeal or an integrated approach were taken.

To assure an unimpeded ability to respond to environmental problems, there needs to be continuing supply of technologies capable of providing the responses needed. This will require the effective prioritisation and design of RD&D programmes, including their integration, along with accompanying policy instruments, into a coherent overall policy. This would be essential for implementation of the concept of the phased approach to "clean" energy technology development and integration into the energy/environment system. The extended time horizons required for some technological responses to environmental issues, such as climate change, can exceed the time-frame used by industry in evaluating its technology investment decisions. The role of government in ensuring adequate and timely resources for R,D&D programmes needs to be addressed in formulating response strategies.

At the international level, increasing attention is focusing upon improved co-ordination to deal with transboundary and global pollution problems. The analysis and development of basic concepts, integrating factors, such as cost-effectiveness, equity and environmental effectiveness, represents a major area where further work is essential before acceptable solutions are realised. In this context, it will be important to examine the applicability in an international context of new concepts on abatement strategies, such as the critical loads concept and market-based instruments, such as emission trading, to a variety of OECD countries for transboundary and global environmental problems.

ANNEXES

ANNEX 1: FUEL CYCLE REVIEW OF ENVIRONMENTAL CONTROL

In order to make a full assessment of the capacity to control or eliminate the environmental impacts of any energy decisions, it is necessary to:

-        know the nature of all environmental and impacts at all stages of the fuel cycle;

-        be able to quantify in comparable terms each of these emissions and impacts; and

-        know the full range of control measures available.

To identify the nature of all environmental impacts, it is necessary to look at all stages of the cycle, namely:

-        production;

-        refining/processing;

-        transformation and conversion;

-        transport and distribution to consumer; and

-        consumer usage (including disposal).

In making this assessment it will not be possible to use standard factors since the environmental impacts will inevitably be site-specific and will depend on the precise chemical composition of the energy source. The conversion of environmental impacts into some comparative measure presents great technical problems as illustrated by the debate about the appropriate technical factors for converting methane emissions into carbon dioxide equivalent emissions in a greenhouse context. The following sections therefore concentrate on outlining available environmental control processes for the fuel cycle relating to oil, natural gas, coal, nuclear, renewable energy and electricity generation.

1.   The Oil Fuel Cycle

(a) Production of Crude Oil

Accidental spills, blow-outs and fires are controlled by safety regulations. They extend to inspection, maintenance and emergency procedures. Strict licensing of facilities is implemented in Member countries. Regular monitoring of marine ecology around platforms is often mandatory and procedures are set out at the licensing stage.

Brine from onshore drilling is not usually considered to be hazardous but can effect surface and ground-waters. The re-injection of brine and used waters from on-shore drilling activities is a well-established practice in order to comply with ambient water quality standards.

(b) Transport and Storage of Crude and Refined Oil

Maritime oil pollution from accidental spills or discharges from tankers is controlled by the

International Convention for the Prevention of Pollution from Ships (MARPOL) signed in 1973 and backed up by nearly 30 international treaties which lay out standards and technical requirements, as well as economic disincentive schemes (fines, compensation). The use of tankers with double hulls is mandatory in only a few areas in the OECD region.

In the case of *VOC control*, as a consequence of the MARPOL 1973/78 Protocols requiring all new crude carriers to have segregated ballast tanks, the emission of HC vapours during ballasting should ultimately be eliminated. But growing concern about VOC emissions means that releases from storage facilities, which had not been singled out in the past, might be subject to specific emission limits. Techniques, such as sealing or floating roofs on storage tanks, ensure that 90% of HC emissions are controlled and can in fact be very cost-effective for operators [18].

(c) Oil Refining

The control of the disposal of *waste waters* from refineries is covered by ambient water quality legislation which typically sets concentration limits and may prescribe the use of continuous sampling devices to monitor compliance. Waste water treatment systems are universally applied since the value of the oil recovered by gravity separation ensures that such systems are now established as good refinery practice. More advanced, expensive treatment (extending to biological treatment) is being made increasingly necessary by stringent limits for discharged waters set by local or regional authorities. There are considerable differences in these point-source limits, as ambient water quality standards vary according to the nature (river, estuary, bay, coastal waters) of the medium.

Air-borne pollutants are controlled by ambient air quality regulations which are applied to refineries as to all large combustion plants. Fuel quality specifications concern the sulphur content of the fuel oil used for the distillation and reforming process and are also those defined for all combustion facilities. Point-source limits that are applicable depend in some Member countries on whether the refinery is situated in a highly polluted area:

- for new refineries, in addition to constraints imposed by siting and licensing regulations, SO_2 and NO_x limits usually follow those set out for combustion facilities in most Member countries. They are point-source emission standards which vary according to plant size; in the Netherlands a single emission limit applies for the refinery as a whole, independent of the fuel used and of plant size;

- for existing refineries, SO_2 and NO_x emission limits are usually less stringent when they exist. The strictest emission standards are found in Germany, particularly for NO_x, where there are "technology forcing" standards.

Other controlled pollutants include PM, CO and more recently for many Member countries, VOC. Recent PM emission limits set in Member countries are usually met by current dust removal equipment (cyclones). More stringent standards would necessitate the use of baghouses. In the same way, future CO standards would require catalytic cracking units to use secondary combustion. In Europe, so far only Germany has set specific VOC emission limits for refineries which require the installation of vapour recovery units at loading installations. It is anticipated that the regulation could be made less restrictive to allow the use of technologies, such as activated carbon absorption, which offer a high recovery efficiency. The Netherlands has set a target of 50% VOC reduction by 2000. A package of measures has been negotiated with the refining industry.

At the moment there are still large differences between national environmental legislations [54]. But environmental control in refineries is clearly becoming stricter in all countries, as is apparent from the laws planned by national governments and the EC.

2. The Gas Fuel Cycle

(a) Production of Natural Gas

Because natural gas is often produced in association with crude oil, it can be difficult to differentiate precisely between controls applied to the environmental impacts of gas and oil production. The risk of accidental *blow-outs* is covered by a set of safety regulations. This had led to improvements in both technology and practice, which have reduced these risks.

(b) Gas Treatment

Ambient air quality standards in most Member countries do not allow the *emission of SO_2* from sour gas treatment into the atmosphere. It must be converted to elemental sulphur which can then be used as a raw material. NO_x, PM and liquid residuals, such as condensate from gas stripping, are controlled through broader air and water quality standards. Liquefaction facilities and LNG receiving terminals are subjected to strict siting and safety procedures in order to minimise the risk of *LNG leaks*.

(c) Transport and Storage

The siting and construction of *pipelines* is controlled by environmental impact assessment procedures, particularly for areas characterised by extremely sensitive, ecological systems, such as Arctic regions. Pumping stations burn gas and emit NO_x and CO. They are subject to standards applicable to combustion facilities. The transport, storage and distribution of natural gas can cause *methane releases* which are now attracting attention as possible contributors to the greenhouse effect, though no controls have been designed or implemented in this area.

3. The Coal Fuel Cycle

(a) Coal Mining

In the case of new coal mines, siting and licensing procedures include provisions at the design stage for minimising dust, noise, nuisance and health effects as well as occupational hazards. Mining operations are required to implement land rehabilitation schemes, as well as pneumatic backfilling for deep mines. Remedial measures for existing mines are more difficult to design and implement and are usually set out by local authorities following national guidelines. Abandoned coal mines can also be a source of methane emissions.

Acid mine drainage control measures have developed along with concern about groundwater pollution. In order to comply with ambient water quality standards, some form of chemical treatment and of drainage control in the mine area is usually necessary. This is an area where there is still substantial scope for development and control measures are not uniformly applied throughout the coal-producing IEA countries, despite the development of new control techniques, such as ion-exchange technology, reverse osmosis and flash distillation [55].

(b) Transport and Storage

Fugitive coal dust releases are still a common problem as the technology for handling and storing is poorly developed in many countries [56]. Inland coal transportation by slurry pipelines will be more common in the future; water or oil slurries could be transported by sea. This would solve dust and spontaneous combustion problems, but the water used in coal slurry pipelines is contaminated with suspended material and could cause water pollution problems if discharged without proper treatment.

(c) Treatment and Beneficiation

Coal treatment includes operations such as upgrading, washing or sulphur removal [57]. Water quality standards ensure that re-circulation and treatment of *waste water* are now usually integral parts of the operation of coal cleaning plants. *Air pollution* from coal drying is related to the combustion of coal which causes emissions of SO_2, NO_x and PM. Legislation developed to control air pollution from industrial combustion plants is applicable to coal treatment facilities (see section on industrial end-uses).

Coal gasification has evolved over the last ten years into various competitive second generation technologies which have the advantage of low SO_2 and NO_x emissions. Advanced coal processing offers important improvements in efficiency of energy use. The possibility of meeting environmental requirements is strongly supporting interest in the development of the "coal refinery concept" and of integrated gasification combined cycle (IGCC) power plants, even though SO_2 and NO_x removal operations at the syngas fabrication stage could lead to solid waste disposal problems and eventually more stringent regulations [25].

4. The Nuclear Fuel Cycle

(a) Uranium Mining

Uranium mining is controlled essentially by case-by-case licensing and monitoring and inspection procedures. There is, for instance, no practical means of trapping *airborne radon*; control of this occupational hazard is effected by careful design of mining facilities and by adequate ventilation, though the problem can only be considered solved if there are no human settlements close to the mine vents. Milling operations are controlled by licensing and prescriptive technology standards concerning the use of particulate filters and appropriate containment and storage procedures to comply with ambient radioactivity limits as well as water quality standards which could be affected by process effluents and tailings [58].

(b) Enrichment and Fuel Fabrication

Controls of *non-radiological pollution* are aimed at fluoride (in gaseous or liquid effluents) from UF_6 production and fuel fabrication, as well as combustion emissions due to the use of energy for process requirements. Point-source toxic pollutants standards require that gaseous fluorine be removed from air effluent streams by scrubbing and filtration systems. Water from the air scrubber systems is combined with process liquid wastes, and sometimes treated with lime to precipitate fluoride ion before being stored in settling ponds. Safe disposal of this waste requires careful packaging and burial as low activity solid waste subject to mandatory regular monitoring procedures.

Ambient *radiological controls* concern radionuclides discharged from UF_6 production, uranium enrichment and fuel fabrication (airborne or waterborne). Although these operations contribute to the radioactive content of the environment, the incremental exposure is not considered to be significant. Licensing systems and inspection procedures developed in all Member countries specifically for nuclear installations are applicable to uranium enrichment and fuel fabrication plants.

(c) Transport of Radioactive Materials

Safety regulations for the transport of radioactive materials have evolved with the development of national nuclear programmes and are now relatively elaborate. They are backed by various international agreements, such as those signed by the Member countries of the IAEA. Specific requirements cover packaging, labelling, requirements for loading, handling and carriage and emergency procedures. National regulations also include licensing and permit procedures to obtain authorisation for the transport of radioactive material, to ensure that internationally-agreed guidelines are respected.

(d) Nuclear Power Production

The major focus of environmental control is the risk of *accidental releases of radioactivity* into the environment. Environmental protection and the safety of nuclear power production is regulated primarily through licensing systems. Though institutional arrangements for licensing procedures vary from country to country, they have grown more comprehensive and stringent, sometimes contributing to long lead times. In addition to these national regulations, international legislation is playing an increasing role through requirements for emergency reporting and planning, or consultation prior to licensing facilities in border areas (Euratom Treaty, for instance). Regulations cover the entire lifetime of the plant, during which general or specific inspections are designed to verify that the requirements of the licence are met, and that the safety measures taken are effective [26].

Three principles govern the management and control of *radioactive wastes*:

-     dilute and disperse wastes into the environment in effluents containing radionuclides in amounts below authorised radiological protection limits, defined by national legislation and based on recommendations of international organisations, such as the International Commission for Radiological Protection and the World Health Organisation;

-     delay and decay wastes which contain only short lived radionuclides in appropriate sites;

-     concentrate and confine wastes which contain significant amounts of long-lived radionuclides in appropriate sites.

Low and medium-level wastes are disposed of in shallow ground and rock cavity repositories, the siting of which is controlled by national licensing procedures. The option of sea dumping is subject to the provisions of the London Dumping Convention and to close co-operation within international bodies, such as NEA and IAEA. The disposal of low-level liquid and gaseous wastes by disposal into rivers, coastal water and the atmosphere can only be considered suitable for limited amounts of radioactive waste. As the amount of waste to be disposed of increases, the balance between dispersal and containment will shift towards containment, increasing the volume of waste that needs controlling during storage, while decay takes place.

High-level and long-lived wastes disposal basically involves storing and isolating the waste in a manner and for a period of time sufficient to ensure that any residual activity making its way back to the environment would not lead to unacceptable levels of exposure of man or any other biological species. The most favoured solution is disposal into deep, stable geological formations. Reprocessing and the use of fast breeder reactors would alleviate radioactive waste problems as well as make more efficient use of the energy contained in nuclear fuel, thereby reducing the environmental burden due to uranium mining and milling, though these technologies raise the question of new environmental concerns due for instance, to the liquid sodium used in fast breeder reactors. At the moment, the only technique available for waste disposal is storage and the approach for environmental control remains, and will continue to be, siting approval and licensing of storage and disposal facilities aiming at an almost total isolation of the waste from the biosphere. There are both economic and safety reasons for using a minimum number of disposal sites and their use might in due course be approached on a regional or international basis.

(e) Decommissioning of Nuclear Power Plants

Specific legal provisions on the manner of decommissioning and removing an installation are being developed. Though experience is limited to the few plants that have been decommissioned, knowledge and understanding of the environmental problems posed by the decommissioning of nuclear power plants is constantly progressing. Legislation should develop as practical experience increases, and decommissioning procedure requirements could intervene at the stage of licensing for construction. Such requirements would include, as it does already in the United States, that the utility demonstrate that it has the financial resources to carry out the decommissioning operations.

5. Renewable Energy Sources

(a) Hydropower Plants

Licensing and siting procedures usually include environmental impact assessments, covering aspects such as flooding and loss of land; eutrophication of the reservoir, silting, impact upon the biological regime of rivers; barriers to fish migration; aesthetic impact, though this varies considerably from site to site, and hazards from dam failure. Requirements can be met by improved reservoir management and the use of dams with "stairs" to allow fish to pass through. There is also a trend towards a preference for small-scale applications of hydropower, with more limited local impacts, rather than large-scale schemes, though this shift is at least partly due to the limited availability of new large-scale sites.

(b) Biomass

Biomass energy includes a variety of energy sources, such as wood (or charcoal) as well as methane or alcohols (methanol or ethanol) produced from various agricultural, industrial or domestic wastes. Though the uncontrolled combustion of wood produces more *air pollutants* (NO_x, CO, HC and PM) in weight/Btu than that of oil or coal, regulations concerning small, usually domestic combustion facilities using biomass fuels are limited. Some IEA countries (the United States and Germany in particular) have introduced standards for wood heaters. In the United States, legislation also stipulates that only untreated natural firewood can be used in open-hearth fire places. In some areas of heavy wood use, legal restrictions have been placed on wood burning. For larger combustion facilities, the NO_x, CO and PM standards applicable to solid and liquid fuels also extend to biofuels.

As for the use of methanol and ethanol for transportation, concern that recourse to biomass-based fuels for transportation may increase HC, aldehydes and PAN levels is very recent and no responses have been considered so far. The environmental impact of these fuels is still being studied and this could lead to the introduction of environmental controls. Overall, there is insufficient data on the environmental impact and emissions from biomass-based energy production and use. Further environmental controls could be developed as information improves or as the production and use of biomass fuels increases, emphasizing the scale of possible environmental impacts.

(c) Solar and Wind Energy

Solar energy (thermal and photovoltaic) and wind energy have space and location requirements that can be difficult to meet, as these resources are site-specific and compete with other land uses. So far, the environmental impact of solar and wind energy has been limited, as they have been mostly used on a relatively small scale. Formal controls aimed at limiting visual impact or regulating land use have been implemented in a few cases, particularly in the United States, where siting is subject to licensing procedures for wind parks and solar power stations. The visual intrusion of domestic solar installations can be controlled by local building codes.

(d) Geothermal Energy

Licensing and environmental impact procedures are applicable to geothermal facilities. The re-injection of brine and used water is usually necessary in order to comply with air and water quality standards. Temperature limits applied to discharges of cooling water from power stations must also be met.

6. Electricity Generation from Thermal Power Stations

Thermal power plants share a number of areas of environmental concern where controls have been implemented or are being considered:

-   concern over thermal pollution from power station cooling systems in the 1970s led to regulations limiting the temperature of water discharged into rivers in order to protect local ecology;

-   the visual impact of power stations, due in particular to cooling towers, as well as that of fuel loading and storage facilities, are generally regulated through siting and licensing procedures;

-   visual air quality and visibility are more recent concerns, for which remedial measures are proving difficult to design;

-   the issue of the environmental effects of high voltage transmission lines remains unresolved. In a few cases, such as the State of Florida since March 1989, rules have been adopted for the design and development of new transmission lines. Public authorities are seeking to help utilities alleviate public concerns about health effects in transmission siting disputes, as well as minimising the visual impact of towers.

In other respects, such as air pollution, different types of power plants span a wide range of pollutants and environmental control approaches: a comparative table of emissions from utility boilers by fuels is presented in Table 16 at the end of this section [59].

(a) Oil-fired Power Plants

In the area of *air pollution*, SO_2 is the most controlled pollutant: in addition to ambient air quality standards, all Member countries have set sulphur content for fuel oil used for power generation. Most have also introduced point-source emission limits for SO_2:

-   for new plants, the limits are set according to the size of the facility;

-   for existing plants, emission limits are usually less stringent when they exist. The strictest standards are found in the Netherlands and Germany: medium capacity installations can meet requirements by using low sulphur fuel oil, but most existing power plants are having to install FGD units or convert to natural gas if technically and economically feasible.

In the case of NO_x control, most Member countries have also set point-source emission limits for new plants and less widespread and stringent ones for existing plants. Over and above common standards agreed by EC Member countries, the strictest standards are implemented in Germany, where they are in fact "technology forcing" standards. As for PM emissions, they have been regulated for many years and standards are regularly upgraded, though they are still well within the capacity of current dust removal equipment.

Solid waste from the control of PM, SO_2 and to a lesser extent NO_x emissions poses a disposal problem that is directly related to the scale of use of fuel oil. As fuel oil has lost over the last fifteen years most of its outlets in power generation in Member countries, industry is now the main sector concerned by controls on the disposal of this type of waste (see paragraph 9 on industrial end-uses, below).

(b) Gas-Fired Power Plants

The main target for environmental control of the combustion of natural gas is NO_x emissions, though gas generally emits less NO_x per unit of delivered electricity than conventional oil and coal technologies. Gas-fired plants could be affected by NO_x emission limits if these were set at below 200 mg/Nm^3, as is planned only in Germany at present. SCR or low NO_x burners have been installed in a few cases on dual oil and gas-fired installations. NO_x emissions considerably below 200mg/nm3 are possible using in-furnace NO_x reduction. Sulphur emissions are much lower than that for oil and coal. Recourse to SO_2 control technologies, such as FGD, are not necessary for natural gas combustion.

Natural gas releases one-third to one half CO_2 for the same amount of delivered electricity compared with coal. Compared with residual oil, gas combustion releases about one-third less. Gas is not a prime target for CO_2 controls that might be more readily considered for other sources of electricity generation, though its use produces higher emission levels of methane, particularly in older distribution networks.

(c) Coal-Fired Power Plants

As in the case of oil-fired power plants, SO_2 and NO_x are the most controlled emissions [60]. All Member countries have set point-source emission limits for new plants. The SO_2 limits usually imply the use of desulphurisation techniques which perform as well as FGD -- 85 to 90% reduction. In Canada and the United States, SO_2 emission limits are less stringent and can be met by using low-sulphur coal. In the case of NO_x control, control technology requirements have been spelt out in only a few IEA countries, due to technical and economic problems. Most plants rely predominantly on low-NO_x burners to meet emission standards, though the technology is less efficient and also much less costly than selective catalytic reduction (SCR).

The question of whether or not to apply strict emission standards for existing power plants is a matter of on-going debate in many countries. Countries such as Japan and the United States which have applied strict standards since the 1970s have less of a retrofit problem compared to other countries. Relatively strict regulations for existing power plants have also been issued in Germany, the Netherlands and Sweden (for SO_x only). In Denmark, an emission ceiling for the electricity generation sector has been set in order to meet the targets of reducing SO_2 emissions by 60% and NO_x emissions by 50% in 2005 compared to 1980 levels.

The problem of PM emissions was thought to have been widely solved, as electrostatic precipitators with a very high recovery efficiency have been developed and installed at relatively modest cost. National and EC legislation has ensured their widespread use for large combustion facilities. But recent concern about the highly respirable, smaller particulate matter that is not captured by these systems could lead to requirements for 100% recovery. Baghouses would then have to be installed.

Many Member countries are planning stricter emission standards for SO_2, NO_x and dust emissions for new coal-fired power plants and extending or upgrading those for existing plants. At the EC level for instance, the Commission will be presenting before 1993, new proposals for a second stage of emission standards in the light of technological developments.

Such emission standard upgradings are often part of policies aimed at achieving overall SO_2 or NO_x reduction targets, for which control of emissions from existing plants will play a major role. Effective emission control has become an issue in the consideration of plant life extension, particularly in the United States where life extension is regarded by utilities as one of the most cost effective means of meeting capacity requirements. Some electric utilities (in North America in particular) have come around to the view that improved efficiency both in the production and the use of electricity can avoid or delay the construction of additional capacity which would be constrained by environmental considerations [39].

Finally, it is worth noting that concerns about visual air quality and visibility, particularly in North America, has the potential of further shrinking acceptable levels of and tightening emission controls on SO_2 and PM emissions for large combustion facilities. The problem of PM is more compelling in the case of large coal-fired facilities, such as power stations.

High volume *solid wastes* produced by coal-fired utility boilers (fly ash, bottom ash, boiler slag and more recently FGD wastes) are usually not classified as hazardous waste in national legislation. Regulation of these wastes may exist at a local level and it is difficult to generalize about extent and stringency. It can include requirements for design and operating standards, as well as on-site and off-site permit requirements. Historically, wet ponding has been the most widely used disposal method used by utilities. In recent years, regulations requiring liners and long-term water monitoring have increased wet ponding costs, making it less attractive as a disposal option compared with landfills.

The number of FGD plants installed in Member countries is increasing rapidly [61]. In the Netherlands and Germany FGD is required on plants over 300 MWt capacity in addition to an emission limit in order to save the use of low sulphur fuel for smaller plants. Most FGD systems are of the lime/limestone type, producing either a product sludge or gypsum. The remaining capacity is divided between regenerative (producing SO_2, sulphuric acid or sulphur) and spray-dry processes. In all cases, the scale of operation of a typical power station means that large quantities of products are generated. There is increasing interest in the utilization of by products from flue-gas cleaning systems and in particular gypsum from FGD, and fly ash from FBC. These products can be used in the cement, construction, and building industries, provided that the flue gas cleaning system is optimised with regard to the by-products these users require. It is predicted however that in the case of gypsum, supply will exceed demand and hence there will be a requirement to dispose of the surplus gypsum. As markets for product utilization become saturated, there may be a swing to the more complex and expensive regenerative technologies. The limestone-gypsum method has in addition been criticized by environmentalists worried about large-scale quarrying of limestone. It is worth noting also that there seems to be growing concern with possible future problems with the disposal of de-NO_x catalysts. Finally, there is recent concern that the reduction of SO_2 performed by lime/limestone type FGD systems releases CO_2, and that there might have to be a trade off between SO_2 and CO_2 emission reductions.

The problems posed by waste from pollution control in power stations, which is particularly acute in the case of coal-fired facilities, raise the issue of the isolated development of air, waste and water pollution legislation applied to electricity generation. So far legal controls on solid coal-derived products have been determined by controls introduced essentially for management of other detritus-generating industrial processes. Gradual pollution liability indemnity to ensure that post-operative reclamation does occur according to waste disposal permitting requirements is increasingly likely to feature in Member country regulations. The general trend towards upgrading of landfill standards and the difficulties of siting new disposal facilities might, over time, penalize the use of coal versus other fuels. Emphasis on integrated pollution control, which the United Kingdom for instance, is about to introduce at large industrial sites, would mean a more balanced approach to the environmental impact of coal-fired power stations, as the levels of discharge to all three environmental media (air, water, soil) would be assessed for each facility.

Concern about *CO₂ emissions* from large facilities, such as power plants, relates to all fossil fuels; coal combustion is most conspicuous in this respect. Utility boilers using conventional coal technologies emit between 2 and 2.5 times as much CO_2 per GJ of delivered electricity than gas-fired or oil-fired boilers [59]. Damage limitation efforts are being discussed amid continuing speculation of the cause and effect relationships involved. The most frequently mentioned important step is increased energy efficiency. A recent scheme adopted by an American electric utility is the first practical measure implemented by a power station operator to offset the effect of its emissions in adding to possible global warming by planting in Guatemala enough trees to absorb the 387 000 tonnes of CO_2 the power station should emit over its 40-year life.

(d) Waste Incineration Plants

Environmental regulation of municipal waste incineration plants producing electricity, and in some countries often in association with heat for district heating networks, is recent and still developing. Emissions of traditional pollutants produced by combustion (SO_2, NO_x, CO, PM) are controlled by ambient air quality standards as well as point source limits for combustion facilities. The growing use of plastics and chlorinated paper products in consumer goods is causing toxic air pollution emissions from municipal incineration. The control of non-conventional air pollution from waste incineration plants is a new area where standard approaches are still being defined in many parts of the OECD.

Table 16
Representative Rates of Air Pollutant Emissions from Typical New Power Plant Configurations

Column:		A	B	C	D	Sulphur-oxides			
						E	F	G	H
Energy Source	Plant Type	Net Plant Efficiency (%)[a]	Thermal Content of Energy Source (MJ/kg)	Sulphur Content of Fuel (% by weight)	Emission Controls (Type)	Abatement Efficiency (%)	Plant Efficiency Penalty (%) [b]	SO₂ Emission Factor (mg/MJ)	SO₂ Emissions (tonnes per MW-yr)
Coal (3% sulphur)	dry bottom, wall fired	34.0%	28	3%	none	0%	0%	1929	180
Coal (3% sulphur)	dry bottom, tang. fired	33.1%	28	3%	FGD	90%	2%	1929	18
Coal (3% sulphur)	AFBC (Deep bubbling bed)	33.8%	28	3%	--	85%	0%	1929	27
Coal (3% sulphur)	PFB, combined cycle	38.9%	28	3%	--	92%	0%	1929	13
Coal (3% sulphur)	IGCC	38.0%	28	3%	--	99%	0%	1929	2
Coal (1% sulphur)	dry bottom, wall fired	34.0%	28	1%	none	0%	0%	643	60
Coal (1% sulphur)	dry bottom, tang. fired	33.1%	28	1%	FGD	90%	2%	643	6
Coal (1% sulphur)	AFBC (Deep bubbling bed)	33.8%	28	1%	--	85%	0%	643	9
Coal (1% sulphur)	PFB, combined cycle	38.9%	28	1%	--	92%	0%	643	4
Coal (1% sulphur)	IGCC	38.0%	28	1%	--	99%	0%	643	1
Municipal solid waste	mass feed boiler	20.3%	11.3	0.13%	none	0%	0%	199	31
Fuel oil, residual	boiler, opposed wall	35.2%	43	3%	none	0%	0%	1395	126
Fuel oil, residual	boiler, front wall	34.4%	43	3%	FGD	90%	2%	1395	13
Fuel oil, distillate	combustion turbine	28.7%	45	0.3%	none	0%	0%	133	15
Natural gas	boiler, opposed wall	35.2%	51	0.002%	none	0%	0%	1	0.07
Natural gas	conv. boiler	35.2%	51	0.002%	none	0%	0%	1	0.07
Natural gas	GT, simple cycle	28.1%	51	0.002%	none	0%	0%	1	0.09
Natural gas	GT, combined cycle	44.7%	51	0.002%	none	0%	0%	1	0.06
Geothermal	steam condensing	n.a.	n.a.	[c]	[c]	[c]	[c]	[c]	[c]
Enriched uranium	converter reactor	32.0%	465200	0%	--	--	--	0	0

Note: Endnotes and data sources are given at the end of the table.

203

Table 16 (continued)

				J	K	L	M	N	P
						Particulate matter (P.M.)			
Energy Source	Plant Type	Net Plant Efficiency (%)[a]	Thermal Content of Energy Source (MJ/kg)	Ash Content of Fuel (% by weight)	Emission Controls (Type)	Abatement Efficiency (%)	Plant Efficiency Penalty (%)[b]	P.M. Emission Factor (mg/MJ)	P.M. Emissions (tonnes per MW-yr)
Coal (3% sulphur)	dry bottom, wall fired	34.0%	28	8.8%	none	0.0%	0.0%	2514	234
Coal (3% sulphur)	dry bottom, tang. fired	33.1%	28	8.8%	ESP	99.5%	0.2%	2514	1
Coal (3% sulphur)	AFBC (Deep bubbling bed)	33.8%	28	8.8%	ESP	99.5%	0.2%	2514	1
Coal (3% sulphur)	PFB, combined cycle	38.9%	28	8.8%	ESP	99.5%	0.2%	2514	1
Coal (3% sulphur)	IGCC	38.0%	28	8.8%	--	99.5%	0.0%	2514	1
Coal (1% sulphur)	dry bottom, wall fired	34.0%	28	8.0%	none	0.0%	0.0%	2286	213
Coal (1% sulphur)	dry bottom, tang. fired	33.1%	28	8.0%	ESP	99.5%	0.2%	2286	1
Coal (1% sulphur)	AFBC (Deep bubbling bed)	33.8%	28	8.0%	ESP	99.5%	0.2%	2286	1
Coal (1% sulphur)	PFB, combined cycle	38.9%	28	8.0%	ESP	99.5%	0.2%	2286	1
Coal (1% sulphur)	IGCC	38.0%	28	8.0%	--	99.5%	0.0%	2286	1
Municipal solid waste	mass feed boiler	20.3%	11.3	1.5%	none	0.0%	0.0%	1327	207
Fuel oil, residual	boiler, opposed wall	35.2%	43	0.4%	none	0.0%	0.0%	93	8
Fuel oil, residual	boiler, front wall	34.4%	43	0.4%	ESP	99.5%	0.2%	93	0.04
Fuel oil, distilate	combustion turbine	28.7%	45	0.2%	none	0.0%	0.0%	44	5
Natural gas	boiler, opposed wall	35.2%	51	0.015%	none	0.0%	0.0%	2.9	0.3
Natural gas	conv. boiler	35.2%	51	0.015%	none	0.0%	0.0%	2.9	0.3
Natural gas	GT, simple cycle	28.1%	51	0.015%	none	0.0%	0.0%	2.9	0.3
Natural gas	GT, combined cycle	44.7%	51	0.015%	none	0.0%	0.0%	2.9	0.2
Geothermal steam	steam condensing	n.a.	n.a.	0	--	--	--	0	0
Enriched uranium	converter reactor	32.0%	465200	0	--	--	--	0	0

Note: Endnotes and data sources are given at the end of the table.

Table 16 (continued)

Energy Source	Plant Type	Net Plant Efficiency (%) [a]	Thermal Content of Energy Source (MJ/kg)	R Emission Controls (Type)	S Abatement Efficiency (%)	T Plant Efficiency Penalty (%) [b]	V NOx Emission Factor (mg/MJ)	W NOx Emissions (tonnes per MW-yr)	X Carbon Content of Fuel (% by weight)	Y CO$_2$ Emission Factor (mg/MJ)	Z CO$_2$ Emissions (tonnes per MW-yr)
					Nitrogen oxides					Carbon dioxide	
Coal (3% sulphur)	dry bottom, wall fired	34.0%	28	none	0%	0.0%	438	41	65.0%	84964	7919
Coal (3% sulphur)	dry bottom, tang. fired	33.1%	28	Lo-Nox+SCR	85%	0.5%	313	4	65.0%	84964	8139
Coal (3% sulphur)	AFBC (Deep bubbling bed)	33.8%	28	staged comb.	n.a.	0.5%	250	23	65.0%	84964	7975
Coal (3% sulphur)	PFB, combined cycle	38.9%	28	--	n.a.	0.0%	240	20	65.0%	84964	6922
Coal (3% sulphur)	IGCC	38.0%	28	--	n.a.	0.0%	240	20	65.0%	84964	7082
Coal (1% sulphur)	dry bottom, wall fired	34.0%	28	None	0%	0.0%	438	41	65.0%	84964	7919
Coal (1% sulphur)	dry bottom, tang. fired	33.1%	28	Lo-Nox+SCR	85%	0.5%	313	4	65.0%	84964	8139
Coal (1% sulphur)	AFBC (Deep bubbling bed)	33.8%	28	staged comb.	n.a.	0.5%	250	23	65.0%	84964	7975
Coal (1% sulphur)	PFB, combined cycle	38.9%	28	--	n.a.	0.0%	240	20	65.0%	84964	6922
Coal (1% sulphur)	IGCC	38.0%	28	--	n.a.	0.0%	240	20	65.0%	84964	7082
Municipal solid waste	mass feed boiler	20.3%	11.3	none	0%	0.0%	133	21	26.7%	86480	13491
Fuel oil, residual	boiler, opposed wall	35.2%	43	none	0%	0.0%	395	36	85.6%	72860	6560
Fuel oil, residual	boiler, front wall	34.4%	43	Low-NO$_x$	50%	0.0%	191	9	85.6%	72860	6708
Fuel oil, distilate	combustion turbine	28.7%	45	none	0%	0.0%	203	22	87.2%	70923	7837
Natural gas	boiler, opposed wall	35.2%	51	none	0%	0.0%	290	26	70.6%	50666	4562
Natural gas	conv. boiler	35.2%	51	Lo-NOx+SCR	60%	0.1%	240	9	70.6%	50666	4567
Natural gas	GT, simple cycle	28.1%	51	Stream inj.	70%	2.0%	169	6	70.6%	50666	5713
Natural gas	GT, combined cycle	44.7%	51	Steam inj.	70%	2.0%	168	4	70.6%	50666	3591
Geothermal steam	steam condensing	n.a.	n.a.	--	--	--	0	0	[d]	[d]	1875
Enriched uranium	converter reactor	32.0%	465200	--	--	--	0	0	--	0	0

Note: Endnotes and data sources are given at the end of the table.

205

Endnotes to Table 16:

Key: [a] Net of efficiency losses imposed by pollution-control devices.
 [b] Number represents percentage by which gross plant efficiency is decreased.
 [c] Geothermal steam often contains high amounts of hydrogen sulphide (H_2S), depending on the source reservoir.

Note: Numbers in Columns A, G, H, N, P, W, Y and Z have been calculated using the following formulae (letters refer to column numbers):

Column A: (Net plant efficiency without pollution control devices) x (1 - F - M - T)

Column G: 0.9 x (2 x C/B) x 10^6[Assuming 10% of sulphur is retained in the bottom ash]

Column H: 0.03171 x (G/A) x (1 - E)

Column N: For coal-fired plants: 0.8 x (J/B) x 10^6[Assuming 20% of the ash ends up as bottom ash.]
 For all other plants: 0.9 x (J/B) x 10^6[Assuming 10% of ash ends up as bottom ash.]

Column P: 0.03171 x (N/A) x (1 - L)

Column W: 0.03171 x (V/A) x (1 - S)

Column Y: (3.66 x X/B) x 10^6

Column Z: 0.03171 x (Y/A)

where 2 = ratio of molecular weight of SO_2 to elemental sulphur;
 0.03171 = factor for converting mg/MJ to tonnes/MW-year; and
 3.66 = ratio of molecular weight of CO_2 to elemental carbon.

Data Sources: **SO_2 and Particulate matter**——U.S. Environmental Protection Agency, *Compilation of Air Pollutant Emission Factors Volume 1: Stationary Point and Area Sources*, Report No. AP-42, Supplement A (Research Triangle Park, North Carolina: U.S. EPA, October 1986); International Energy Agency, *Emission Controls in Electricity Generation and Industry* (Paris: OECD, 1988); **NO_x and CO_2**——Radian Corporation (for the U.S. Environmental Protection Agency), "Emission and cost estimates for globally significant anthropogenic combustion sources of NO_x, N_2O, CH_4, CO and CO_2", Draft (Research Triangle Park, North Carolina: Radian Corporation, December 1987); Economic Commission for Europe, NO_x Task Force, *Technologies for Controlling NO_x Emissions from Stationary Sources* (Karlsruhe, F.R.G.: Institute for Industrial Production, June 1986); discussions with Dr. Jan Vernon, IEA Coal Research, London.

7. Transport End-Uses

(a) Gasoline

For gasoline-fuelled vehicles, there are emission standards for CO, HC and more recently NO_x throughout the IEA Member countries. They are regularly upgraded [62]:

-   NO_x emission limits involve the issue of the use of catalytic converters. Historically, the United States has played a leading role in the mandatory introduction of exhaust purification systems (with a concomitant effort on unleaded gasoline). Sweden, Switzerland, Austria, Japan, Australia, Norway and Canada have now introduced similar if not more stringent NO_x limits with accompanying control technology requirements. The situation is more diverse in EC Member countries, and a new EC point-source directive has only recently been adopted;

-   CO emissions have been controlled for many years and regulations have been gradually tightened. For instance, EC emission limits have reduced maximum vehicle carbon monoxide emissions by 60% between 1970 and 1983. In the United States, the effect of existing CO emission limits for new cars is expected to cause a 45% reduction of transport-related CO emissions between 1980 and 2000 [ANL, 1986];

-   total HC emissions are usually dealt with along with CO and NO_x emissions. It should be noted that HC stands for all hydrocarbons without making reference to any specific compounds, such as aromatics, benzene, or aldehydes. Evaporative limits exist in the United States, Japan and Australia, but not in the EC. Benzene is controlled through fuel quality specifications rather than emission limits. The EC Council has adopted a 5 per cent limit for benzene content and Norway, Sweden and Switzerland impose similar limits [63];

-   PM emission limits for gasoline-fuelled cars exist only in the United States.

Other measures include the control of lead pollution which has been tackled by two policies which have been developed simultaneously: on the one hand, there has been an effort to make unleaded gasoline available, and this has been supported in EC Member countries by an EC Directive, stating that unleaded gasoline must be marketed throughout the EC by 1989. Other IEA Member countries already market unleaded gasoline. On the other hand, regulations limiting the lead content of gasoline have been implemented. The lowest level of lead which will allow continued operation of older engines (0.03g/l) has been adopted as a standard in the United States. In Australia, all new gasoline cars have to be designed to use unleaded petrol. Unleaded gasoline tax incentives (tax reductions compared to lead gasoline) are commonly used to encourage the move towards unleaded gasoline, though not in the United States. In some countries (Austria, Germany, the Netherlands, Sweden, Switzerland) lower tax rates are applied to "low-emission" vehicles. Tax incentives are also used to compensate for the conversion costs to LPG and CNG fuelling, as LPG and CNG-fuelled vehicles, when optimised, have lower CO, HC, and NO_x emission levels.

(b) Diesel

Diesel-fuelled vehicles usually have lower CO, HC and NO_x emissions than gasoline-fuelled cars, but more aldehydes, SO_x and much higher PM emissions, as well as increased noise and odour. Standards are well developed for light-duty vehicles, for which measures cover CO, HC and NO_x emissions. Particulate standards have been enforced in the United States. One reason for adopting relatively relaxed standards for diesel-fuelled vehicles is the recognition that diesel engines have specific problems in meeting stricter standards, particularly regarding NO_x. PM emissions can be reduced by 40 to 60%, but this tends to increase NO_x emissions. Several IEA countries have standards concerning smoke opacity of diesel engine exhausts. On the whole, Europe, where diesel-power vehicles held 18% of the new car market in 1986, has lagged behind Japan and the United States in controlling diesel pollution.

It is clear that in most IEA Member countries, vehicle emission standards are and will be further tightened, at a national level and/or through international legislation, such as the new EC Directive ("Luxembourg standards"). This means that the use, mandatory or not, of technologies such as three-way catalytic converters and oxidation catalysts will become more widespread and will concern all categories of gasoline-fuelled vehicles. Particulate emissions standards will be increasingly applied to diesel-fuelled vehicles, the first target sources being light-duty vehicles.

Ozone exposure is an area of growing concern. In the United States, where ozone pollution is a major issue, many urban areas have failed to meet O_3 ambient air standards set for late 1987. It has also become apparent that internationally-accepted health and environmental guidelines for short and long-term ozone exposure, such as those defined by the World Health Organisation, are exceeded in many parts of Europe. Recent research shows that a combined NO_x/VOC reduction strategy is more effective at reducing ozone levels. The transportation sector would therefore be a prime objective, as it is the largest single source of both NO_x and VOC emissions. In the area of VOC, damage limitation efforts are still in their infancy in many countries. In the United States, recent regulation imposes the use of gasoline with a lower volatility level in summer. This measure is projected to reduce urban area VOC emissions by 13%. Emissions from transport vehicles are being tackled by the EC and various Member countries by progressively tightening up legislation limiting total hydrocarbon and other gaseous emissions (with the increased use of catalytic converters for instance). The proposals considered by the EC would lead to a 30% reduction of hydrocarbon emissions for cars by the end of the century [64]. Proposals for heavy-duty diesel vehicles are expected in the near future. As VOC is considered to be, after SO_2 and NO_x, the next most important transboundary pollutant, national control measures might follow from international action and commitments, such as a possible UN-ECE protocol on VOC following that on NO_x.

Experience seems to indicate though that applying best available control technologies for NO_x and VOC would not necessarily assure that guidelines for short-term ozone levels would be attained in some areas. Banning of motor vehicles in downtown areas at times of high pollution levels is already a common practice in some cities, such as Athens, and developing in some German and Italian cities. United States' emission standards are the strictest, but the nation's enormous traffic volume is overwhelming its pollution control efforts. More drastic and lasting action is being considered in California and includes extensive vehicle fleet conversions to "clean" fuels, methanol or even electricity. Volume-oriented measures are under study in the Netherlands [43].

(c)   Alternative Fuels

During the last decade, petroleum supply disruptions and cost increases have accelerated interest in fuel extenders and alternative fuels for motor vehicles. Environmental concerns are now providing a considerable part of the impetus for a diversification of transport fuels, and this could lead to the more widespread use of alternative fuels. But some environmental uncertainties remain to be resolved. The use of alcohol fuels will result in lower emissions of CO, NO_x and unburned fuel. They can be used with catalysts, though their durability ·remains to be studied. Evaporative emissions are very low. Aldehyde emissions, however, can be four to eight times higher than for gasoline vehicles. Aldehydes, which are greenhouse gases, in turn lead to the formation of PAN, also a contributor to global warming. It appears though that aldehydes can be effectively reduced by catalysts. It is important to consider the overall environmental impact of the fuel cycle producing methanol or ethanol fuels. While natural gas-based alcohol fuels compare favourably with traditional liquid fuels, coal based fuels entail significant emissions at the synfuel plant. Countries which do not have sufficient quantities of nationally-produced surplus natural gas would have either to import natural gas or to turn to coal for the large-scale production of alternative fuels. With growing concern for CO_2 emissions, this option could be seen as trading off ozone pollution for greenhouse gas emissions.

While interest in alternative fuels (often derived from natural gas) is at the moment strong in the United States and parts of Europe, the use of LPG and the direct use of natural gas as an alternative transport fuel (as Compressed Natural Gas - CNG) is also attracting attention for environmental reasons. Considerable experience has been gained in countries where the use of CNG as a motor fuel has developed for a variety of local reasons, some of which are historical and others are related to a surplus of natural gas. There are some 400 000 vehicles operating on CNG in the world today; most of them are in Italy, where there are about 280 000 dual-fuelled motor vehicles. Canada is pushing forward with a substantial conversion programme, as is New Zealand, where about 100 000 vehicles can run on CNG (and another 50 000 on LPG). In terms of emissions, Otto cycle engines using CNG produce virtually no aldehydes and CO emissions, and unburnt fuels and PM are low. Data on NO_x emissions vary from lower than with diesel to about the same or even a little higher. However, with the universal dual-fuelling system most often used for vehicle CNG applications, the full potential of CNG as a high octane fuel cannot be realised, since the degree of compression is determined by the octane rating of the petrol. As in the case of natural gas-based alcohol fuels, CNG compares favourably with traditional liquid fuels. Emissions from the vehicle may be higher than for alcohol fuels. Taking a fuel cycle view of environmental impact, as up to 40% of the energy of natural gas is lost in the conversion of natural gas to methanol, overall emissions from CNG are in fact substantially lower, particularly for CO_2.

8.   Residential and Commercial End-Uses

When they exist, emissions standards for traditional pollutants (SO_2, NO_x, PM, etc.) for small combustion plants in most countries are such that control technologies are not required. The approach for controlling emissions from small plants is often to limit the sulphur content of fuel oil and coal. Denmark established ten years ago a mandatory maintenance scheme for small oil furnaces in the residential and commercial sector. There is a general trend towards controlling emissions from smaller combustion facilities in the residential sector. An EC Directive concerning PM emissions is being considered. In Germany, it has been shown that combustion plants ranging from a few kW power (single domestic heaters) to 10 MW (central heating plants for larger buildings) account for only 9% of total SO_2 and PM emissions, and 4% of total NO_x and VOC emissions. But depending on conditions prevailing in the region, the share in local emissions can be much larger and can in fact reach 50% in built-up areas due to a high concentration of sources and low chimney stacks. In the city of Dublin, severe smoke pollution is due mainly to the combustion of bituminous coal in domestic fires.

Air conditioning and refrigeration use CFC which have been identified as important gases both in terms of ozone depletion and of greenhouse effect. This is also true of foam used for thermal insulation. The Montreal Protocol on Substances that Deplete the Ozone Layer, signed in 1987 as a protocol to the Vienna Convention for the Protection of the Ozone Layer (1985), is an agreement which aims at reducing production and emissions of CFC. It was motivated primarily by the need to protect the earth's ozone layer. The possible effects of CFC on global climate were noted as an additional cause for concern. The Montreal Protocol entered into force in January 1989; it imposes a freeze on production and consumption of CFC at 1986 levels as from July 1989, followed by a 20 per cent cut in 1992 and a further 30 per cent in 1998. National approaches that are being developed to comply with the Protocol usually involve controlling CFC supply rather than demand, by regulating imports and imposing production limits on national manufacturers. This should encourage users to seek alternatives which are environmentally less damaging. Concern that these target reductions would not be sufficient to prevent the depletion of the ozone layer has already prompted several countries to adopt stricter reduction plans. This is the case of Sweden, the Netherlands and Germany.

9. Industrial End-Uses

As in the case of utility power plants, industrial combustion regulations distinguish between new and existing facilities [54]. There are usually additional distinctions between small and large facilities, as well as in some cases between industrial power plants and other industrial combustion facilities. For new plants, the environmental control of industrial power plants is uneven and depends to some extent on whether electricity generation is concentrated with electric utilities, or whether industry manufacturers are operating substantial electricity generation and/or heat production units, sometimes along with CHP (as is often the case in Germany and the United States). In Germany, control is the same as for utilities. In the United States, control depends on regional air quality as well as on state and national regulations for new plants. Emission control of small and industrial facilities in Japan is based on agreements with local authorities. The size distribution for combustion plants varies among regulatory systems. In the EC Directive for emission limitations from large combustion plants, for instance, if fuel oil is used, there are three categories; one for plants above 500 MWt, another ranging from 500 to 300 MWt, and one for plants below 300 MWt.

In countries where they exist, emission standards for the small plants (less than 50 or 100 MWt) are usually such that costly FGD and SCR technologies are not required. The approach for controlling emissions from small plants is often to limit the sulphur content of fuel oil and coal. A comparison of the various national approaches towards small plants is difficult. Small industrial boilers are numerous and of different types and differing fuel use in Member countries -- for example, there are 75 000 small boilers in the United Kingdom alone -- for which statistical information is thin. This illustrates the difficulties even for national authorities to obtain an overview of the environmental performance of these plants and of the feasibility of imposing emission limits as well as how they are affecting the operation of small industrial boilers and a variety of industrial processes.

As for other airborne emissions from industrial facilities, the problem of particulate emissions has been widely solved for large and medium combustion plants; national legislation has ensured the widespread use of highly efficient electrostatic precipitators. But there are very few regulations concerning the control of CO from industrial facilities, despite the existence, in many IEA countries, of ambient air quality standards for carbon monoxide.

The trend towards stricter emission limits is likely to focus on the existing stock of industrial combustion facilities, where the greatest potential exists for reducing emissions in the short term. This could lead to the use of industrial (sector-wide or industry-specific) agreements, as is already the case in some Member countries and notably Japan. It could also help develop new responses to stricter regulations such as changes in production technology as well as changes in operating facilities. Industry has just started responding to new regulations and it is still too early for an assessment of their effects. Concern that environmental legislation could inhibit the ability of national industry to compete on world markets is encouraging harmonization of regulation at an international level. This means that even more lenient national legislation will be upgraded regularly (particularly in EC-Europe). This process has its limits and more inventive measures are being considered. For instance, Sweden and Denmark are examining the cost effectiveness and feasibility of exporting subsidized "clean" coal technology to Poland. This approach has been used in the past, when the Federal Republic of Germany funded water pollution control equipment used in the Democratic Republic of Germany.

Finally, the need to further reduce levels of specific air pollutants could lead to the banning of certain fuels for industrial uses. This has occurred in the past, for instance, in the case of coal in urban areas in the United Kingdom. The persistence of excessive ozone levels has already prompted regional authorities in California to enforce standards that restrict the use of fuel oil and solid fuel in stationary combustion facilities. In the case of NO_x emissions, public authorities are likely to concentrate on sectors that are easier to regulate than transportation where the large fleet of privately owned vehicles is difficult to control. The ban on fuel oil that is currently being considered by the South Coast Air Quality Management District is a last resort measure that might well be taken up by the many authorities in industrial and urban areas faced with untractable ozone problems.

ANNEX 2: GLOSSARY OF TERMS AND ACRONYMS

Alcohol fuel	Fuel containing a minimum 85 per cent alcohol, such as methanol (CH_3OH) or ethanol (C_2H_5OH).
Aldehydes	Compounds produced by oxidation of alcohols, e.g., during combustion. Aldehydes are greenhouse gases. They lead to the formation of PAN, also a greenhouse gas.
Aromatic hydrocarbons	Compounds containing a benzene ring.
BACT	Best available control technology.
BAT	Best available technology.
BPM	Best practicable means.
Btu	British thermal unit.
CFC	Chlorofluorocarbons.
CH_4	Methane.
CHP	Combined heat and power.
CNG	Compressed natural gas.
CO_2	Carbon dioxide.
CO	Carbon monoxide.
DH	District heating.
ESP	Electro-static precipitator.
FBC	Fluidised bed combustion.
FGD	Flue gas desulphurisation.
Fly ash	Fine solid particles produced during oil or coal combustion.
HC emissions	Emissions of unburnt hydrocarbons.
High-level waste	Highly radioactive liquid which is separated during chemical reprocessing of irradiated nuclear fuel. It can also be solidified.
Hydrocarbons	Organic compounds consisting only of hydrogen and carbon.
IGCC	Integrated gasification combined cycle.
LNG	Liquefied natural gas (= methane).
LPG	Liquefied petroleum gas (= propane and butane).
NO_x	Oxides of nitrogen.
O_3	Ozone.
Oxygenate blends	Blends of traditional transport fuels, such as gasoline and oxygenated hydrocarbons, such as methanol.
PAH	Polycyclic aromatic hydrocarbons.
PAN	Peroxyacetylnitrate.

Photochemical oxidants	Gaseous pollutants -- formed by the action of sunlight on nitrogen oxides and hydrocarbons in air.
PM	Particulate matter.
PPP	Polluter Pays Principle.
Respirable particles	Particles of less than 5 microns diameter.
SCR	Selective catalytic reduction.
Scrubber	Air pollution control device that uses a liquid spray to remove pollutants from a gas stream.
SO$_x$	Sulphur oxides.
Synfuels	Fuels produced by a chemical synthesis process, such as those produced from the gasification or liquefaction of coal, or from the conversion of natural gas through methanol into gasoline.
Terpene	Unsaturated hydrocarbon found in oils and plant resins.
TPER	Total primary energy requirements.
TWC	Three-way catalyst.
VOC	Volatile organic compounds, including hydrocarbon vapour emissions. Non-methane VOC emissions are made up essentially of highly-volatile butane.

ANNEX 3: REFERENCES AND SOURCES

1.   International Energy Agency, *Emission Controls in Electricity Generation and Industry* (Paris: OECD, 1988).

2.   *OECD and the Environment* (Paris: OECD, 1986).

3.   World Commission on Environment and Development, *Our Common Future* (Oxford University Press: 1987).

4.   United Nations, *Air Pollution Across Boundaries* (New York: 1985).

5.   *OECD Environmental Data -- Compendium 1989* (Paris: OECD, 1989).

6.   The University of Chicago, *Environmental Trends Associated with the Fifth National Energy Policy Plan* (for U.S. Department of Energy, August 1986).

7.   D.J. Wuebbles, J. Edmonds, *A Primer on Greenhouse Gases* (for the United States Department of Energy, 1988).

8.   Environment Committee, *The State of the Environment* (Paris: OECD, 1985).

9.   Environmental Resources Ltd., *The Greenhouse Issue* (for the Commission of the European Communities, 1988).

10.   IEA Coal Research, *Carbon Dioxide -- Emissions and Effects* (London: OECD, June 1982).

11.   B. Bolin, B. Döös, J. Jäger and R. Warrick, *The Greenhouse Effect, Climatic Change, and Ecosystems* (for SCOPE-ICSU, Stockholm, 1986).

12.   United Nations, *Strategies, Technologies and Economics of Waste Water Management in ECE Countries* (New York: 1984).

13.   Electric Power Research Institute, *Western Regional Air Quality Studies -- Visibility and Air Quality Measurements: 1981-1982* (Palo Alto, California: January 1987).

14.   IEA Coal Research, *Solid Residues from Coal Use -- Disposal and Utilisation* (London: OECD, July 1984).

15.   IEA Coal Research, *Trace Elements from Coal Combustion: Emissions* (London: OECD, June 1987).

16.   United Nations Environment Programme and World Health Organisation, *Assessment of Urban Air Quality* (Geneva: 1988).